The Young Turks and the Ottoman Nationalities

The Young Turks and the Ottoman Nationalities

Armenians, Greeks, Albanians, Jews, and Arabs, 1908–1918

Feroz Ahmad

THE UNIVERSITY OF UTAH PRESS
Salt Lake City

The Defiance House Man colophon is a registered trademark of the University of Utah Press. It is based on a four-foot-tall Ancient Puebloan pictograph (late PIII) near Glen Canyon, Utah.

18 17 16   2 3 4 5

LIBRARY OF CONGRESS CATALOGING-IN-PUBLICATION DATA
Ahmad, Feroz.
  The Young Turks and the Ottoman nationalities : Armenians, Greeks, Albanians, Jews, and Arabs, 1908–1918 / Feroz Ahmad.
      p. cm.
  Includes bibliographical references and index.
  ISBN 978-1-60781-339-2 (pbk.) — ISBN 978-1-60781-338-5
  1. Turkey—Politics and government—1909-1918. 2. Ittihat ve Terakki Cemiyeti. 3. Turkey—History—Autonomy and independence movements. 4. Turkey—Ethnic relations—History—20th century. 5. Nationalism—Turkey—History—20th century. I. Title.
   DR584.5.A56 2014
   956.02—dc23
                       2013043811

COVER PHOTO: A scene from the election of 1908 in front of the election box in the Aya Triyada Church in Taksim. At the table sit the Greek Orthodox and Armenian Orthodox Patriarchs, alongside a Muslim Imam. Courtesy of Dr. Sacit Kutlu, collector and author.

Printed and bound by Sheridan Books, Inc., Ann Arbor, Michigan.

To the memory of friends who helped me to begin understanding Turkey:
Özcan Başkan, Sami Ferliel, Ali Alparslan, Ergun Balcı,
İzzet Ersöz, and Naim Turfan

Contents

Acknowledgments

I would like to thank a number of friends who read the entire manuscript or parts of it while it was in the process of being written, including Yaşar Geyikdağı, Emre Kayhan, David Waines, Leila Fawaz, and the two anonymous readers for the University of Utah Press. I apologize if I did not incorporate all the suggestions of my readers. Kathy Burford Lewis, my copyeditor, read the manuscript with diligence and improved the quality of the book. For that I am most grateful. I am responsible for any shortcomings that remain.

I also want to thank Professor Haluk Kabaalioğlu, who has encouraged and supported my research while I have been at Yeditepe University.

A Note on Sources

Whenever possible I have tried to use contemporary sources—newspapers, magazines, diplomatic reports—to avoid getting drawn into the politics of the subject. I have also relied on European-language sources, especially in English—the *Times*, *Near East*, and *Orient*, for example—so that curious readers might find such sources with ease in libraries. I have used Turkish sources when I could not find a source in a European language. Interested readers, however, will find Turkish sources in the bibliography. I have also tried not to burden the text with long and detailed notes.

1

Introduction

The Nineteenth-Century Background

Of all the intractable problems that the Young Turks inherited from the Hamidian regime after restoring the constitution in 1908, the "nationalities question" proved to be the most difficult to resolve. As a result of the worldwide impact of the French Revolution, by the beginning of the nineteenth century the Balkans were in the process of a radical transformation. Like national movements in Central and Eastern Europe, and even in far-away Spanish America, this process had been fertilized externally. In the words of L. S. Stavrianos, "The Age of Theocracy was giving way to a new Age of Nationalism—an age of secular ideas and leaders and aspirations."[1] In the Ottoman Empire the reform charters of 1839 and 1856, known collectively as the Tanzimat, transformed the role of the religious communities: the non-Muslim laity gained influence at the expense of the clergy. Ethnic and secular affiliations and the use of the vernacular began to subvert the universalist ideas of the church.[2]

The French Revolution of 1789 released the forces of nationalism throughout much of the world, which led to a process that would be later described as "decolonization." During the first half of the nineteenth century Spain was forced to surrender its empire in Latin America, and many of its colonies acquired their independence. A number of them celebrated the bicentennial of their independence during the summer of 2010. The American Revolution of 1776 against British rule was also part of the decolonization process, though the colonial rebels were white Europeans and not Native Americans. The great rebellion of 1857 in India is an example of a failed "proto-national" liberation movement.[3]

In this introduction we are concerned with the Ottoman case. The Ottomans also were forced to decolonize when confronted with emerging nationalism and national movements of their own subjects during and after the French Revolution. Though the Ottoman Empire is recognized as an empire, few writers discuss Ottoman imperialism. Only Max Kortepeter's monograph *Ottoman Imperialism during the Reformation* (1972) comes to mind as an example of a historian who does speak of Ottoman imperialism. The Ottomans practiced a premodern variety of imperialism, perhaps comparable to the Roman Empire, exploiting conquered territories for tribute rather than for raw materials or markets or places to invest capital, as later empires did. But like other empires the Ottomans were faced with the challenge of decolonization when subject peoples began to assume new identities.

The Ottoman ruling class, like other imperial rulers, naturally saw the entire process of decolonization as rebellion and betrayal by their subjects. Prior to the French Revolution Muslim and non-Muslims are thought to have lived in harmony, so why should they rebel? Christian and Jews were organized as *millet*s (religious communities) and were permitted to have their own religious identities, enjoying a great deal of cultural and social autonomy under their religious leaders. Such a system may even be described as one of "shared sovereignty," with the non-Muslim communities as junior partners. But the age of Enlightenment and later nationalism began to undermine the system of religious communities that had provided stability for centuries. As the religious communities were slowly transformed they began to find the imperial system oppressive. They acquired new identities, often described as national, and began their struggles for reform, autonomy, and even independence.

The first challenge to Ottoman imperialism came from the Serbs. The Ottomans had conquered the kingdom of Serbia at the end of the fourteenth century at the battles of Marica (1371) and Kosovo (1389). The occupation lasted until the nineteenth century. Due to local factors created by the disintegration of Ottoman administration in Serbia, Karageorge Petrovic led a rebellion that lasted from 1804 to 1813. The Serbs were not strong enough on their own to break the hold of imperial Ottoman rule. Therefore they sought help from a Great Power: in July 1807 Karageorge signed an alliance with Russia against the Ottomans, hoping to wage a war of independence. But he was let down by Tsar Alexander I, who signed the Treaty of Tilsit in 1807 with Napoleon Bonaparte and an armistice with the Sultan Selim III on August 24, 1807. Serbia became an autonomous principality in 1815, however, and later a kingdom ruled by the Obrenovich dynasty from 1882 to 1903.[4] Ottoman "nationalities" were to remain victims of Great Power diplomacy even after the fall of the Ottoman Empire.

Napoleon's defeat altered the diplomatic equation and Sultan Mahmud II (1808–39), fearing Russian support for the Serbian insurrection (which broke out again in 1815), issued an imperial decree in December, making concessions to Milosh Obrenovich. Soon after Serbia became an autonomous principality. Another decree in August 1830 recognized Milosh Obrenovich as a hereditary prince. Only the Treaty of Berlin (July 13, 1878) finally granted Serbia recognition as an independent state.

The Greek rebellion against Ottoman rule in 1821 also began under the sway of French revolutionary ideas, which were influential throughout the Balkans. The French also carried out propaganda to undermine Ottoman authority as they waged war. In 1797 Napoleon instructed his generals in the Ionian Isles to "flatter the inhabitants…and to speak of the Greece of Athens and of Sparta in the various proclamations which you will issue," thus reviving the Greeks' links with their past.[5]

The success of the insurrection was not inevitable. The Ottomans seemed to be on the verge of crushing the Greeks with the aid of the modern army of their viceroy, Mehmed Ali of Egypt. But Anglo-Russian intervention forestalled the Ottoman victory, and the Greeks achieved their independence in 1829. For the rest of the nineteenth century the goal of the Greek state was irredentist: to "redeem" peoples who belonged to the Orthodox Church and remained under Ottoman rule. That meant liberating Macedonia, Thrace, western Asia Minor, and other pockets of the Greek Orthodox population in the Ottoman Empire. Greece became an irredentist state par excellence obsessed with the *megali* idea of creating a greater Greece. Athens was the capital of the new Greek kingdom. But Istanbul, where the patriarchate was located, remained the center of the Greek Orthodox world. In 1870 the Sublime Porte, playing the classic imperialist game of divide and rule, permitted the creation of the Bulgarian Church independent of the authority of the Greek patriarch, thereby weakening Greek authority. But by doing so the Porte also succeeded in creating a Bulgarian "nationality," which began to struggle for its own independence and acquired it in October 1908.

Faced with the challenge of nationalism, Istanbul attempted to defuse the challenge by creating a new patriotic identity, focusing on the dynasty, that would replace the religious/sectarian one for all Ottomans. The Ottoman identity was to be the antidote to tribalism and sectarianism, though in the Ottoman case it was not territorial but dynastic and imperial. In January 1869 a law that may be described as the "nationality or citizenship law" (Tabiiyet Kanunu) was passed, stating that "all individuals born of an Ottoman father and an Ottoman mother, or only an Ottoman father, are Ottoman subjects."[6] The reformers wanted to promote the concept of Ottomanism (Osmanlılık): common Ottoman citizenship and loyalty to the dynasty, irrespective of religion or ethnicity. But the law did not meet with the success that the reformers had hoped for; it failed to transform subjects into citizens. The people had no common language to strengthen the common sense of citizenship that transcended the bond of the religious community (millet). Moreover, the concept of secular Ottoman citizenship never gained whole-hearted support among any of the communities, even the Muslims.

The very fact that the Ottoman Empire had no recognized citizenship until 1869 is significant. Citizenship, wrote Max Weber, ought to be based at least on a broad consensus regarding the society that citizens live in and the state they live under. They ought to have a common purpose. That was a fundamental problem in multiethnic and multireligious societies: how to create unity without denying multiplicity; how to continue effective pluralism in terms of cultural, linguistic, ethnic, religious, and other identities while constructing a common political allegiance to shared political principles.[7]

Though the Sublime Porte carried out reforms throughout the nineteenth century in order to deal with the problems of such a diverse empire, it continued to retreat. The Ottoman Empire was in a state of retreat rather than disintegration or decline because the nineteenth-century reforms had in fact made it more economically prosperous and modern. Perhaps it would be more correct to speak of "relative decline" when the empire is compared with the rising power of Western empires, which aggressively sought new lands to colonize and exploit. By the mid-nineteenth century European imperialism saw the Ottomans as an ideal case for partition. The non-Muslim communities, and later the Arabs, provided suitable clients for the Great Powers to manipulate.

The Young Ottoman and Young Turk movements of the late nineteenth and early twentieth century, rather than wanting to overthrow the system, were dedicated to saving the empire and the imperial state. They were imperialists who believed that the non-Muslims would become loyal Ottoman citizens and the empire would survive and flourish if the sultan's autocracy could be placed under constitutional restraint and the rights of citizenship could be guaranteed for all Ottomans regardless of religion or ethnicity. The first constitution was thus proclaimed in December 1876 and further reform promised.

But a peasant rebellion had broken out in the Balkans in 1875. Russia, with its own designs on the empire, supported the rebellion of its Orthodox co-religionists, declaring war on the Sublime Porte in March 1877. The defeated Ottomans were forced to make major concessions to Bulgaria in March 1878. The Treaty of San Stefano established a "greater Bulgaria" extending from the Black Sea to the Aegean. But thanks to the intervention of Great Britain and Germany, the Berlin Congress in June revoked some of these concessions. An autonomous Bulgaria was reduced in size and divided in two. The northern part was given political autonomy, while Eastern Rumelia in the south was given administrative autonomy under Sultan Abdülhamid II (1876–1909). Bulgaria succeeded in uniting with Eastern Rumelia through a bloodless coup in 1885, although Macedonia remained within the confines of the Ottoman Empire. But Serbia and Montenegro were recognized as sovereign states.

Under the 1876 constitution all Ottomans became equal in the eyes of the law, enjoying the same rights and obligations regardless of ethnicity or religion, though Islam remained the religion of the state. We can only speculate as to how the multireligious empire would have fared had the sultan continued to implement constitutional rule. But Abdülhamid, using the war with Russia as a pretext, dissolved parliament in February 1878 and shelved the constitution for the next thirty years.

The establishment of the 1876 constitution had raised the critical question of identity and loyalty. To what degree did the subjects of the empire identify with the imperial dynasty and proclaim their loyalty to it? Most non-Muslims continued to identify with their millets rather than with the dynasty. The Porte had passed the citizenship law of 1869 in order to prevent rich non-Muslims, usually merchants, in the empire from purchasing protégé status from foreign embassies and consulates in order to live under the regime of the capitulations. The 1869 law was based on territoriality like the French law of 1851, unlike the Prussian law based on ethnicity. But the law failed to transform subjects into citizens. They had no common language to strengthen the common sense of citizenship that might transcend the bond of their religious community. Until the 1908 revolution no attempt was made to introduce a common language. When the government tried to do so, neither the schools nor the teachers to teach Ottoman Turkish or Osmanlıca were available. Yet the proposal was enough to set off an antigovernment propaganda campaign against "Turkification."[8]

After 1876 discontent among both Muslims and Christians began to grow as a result of Abdülhamid's autocratic rule. The empire continued to retreat under Great Power pressure. The opposition argued that only by restoring the constitution, ending corruption, and introducing reform could the empire be saved. In 1889 Ottoman dissidents formed a secret organization in Paris, the Ottoman Committee of Union and Progress (CUP), with branches both inside and outside the empire. Their aim was to reform and save the empire from further retreat. More important from the point of view of the nationalities was the formation of the Armenian Revolutionary Federation (ARF: Dashnaksutiun) in 1890. In 1887 socialist Armenians had founded the Hunchak Society (The Bell) in Geneva. Both bodies were formed under the influence of revolutionary antitsarist ideological currents prevailing in Russia at the time.

The CUP was dedicated to undermining the Hamidian regime by restoring the 1876 constitution and reforming the empire so that it could function in the modern age. The goals of the nationalities, however, differed. Their leaders wanted radical reform on behalf of their communities but could no longer rely on the Great Powers. They saw that the Great Power consensus had become virtually impossible to achieve after the rise of the German Empire in 1871; thus foreign intervention on their behalf became virtually impossible. By the beginning of the twentieth century they had therefore decided to collaborate with the CUP against the sultan in the hope of reform. But the opposition—both Muslim and non-Muslim—could not agree on a joint program; they could agree only on restoring the 1876 constitution. The Young Turks were themselves divided. Those led by Ahmed Rıza wanted the union of all elements in the empire and then progress through reform. Prince Sabaheddin's faction, the Society for Personal Initiative and Decentralization (Tesebbüs-ü Sahsi ve Adem-i Merkeziyet Cemiyeti), in contrast, advocated decentralization and reform.[9] That was the policy that the majority of the non-Muslim nationalists supported. Armenian nationalist revolutionaries were themselves divided between those living under Russian rule and those in the Ottoman Empire as well as those in the diaspora in Europe. Writing in March 1908 from Van, the principal center of Armenian nationalism in the Ottoman Empire, the British vice consul described the workings of Armenian Revolutionary Federation before the constitutional revolution:

> The policy of the Society is determined by the Central Committees, the Eastern and Western, having equal powers. The headquarters of the Western Committee is in Switzerland, at Geneva,

and its duties are principally concerned with advertising the movement in Europe, and collecting money; they have a printing press. The Eastern Committee is at Tiflis... This Committee spreads the revolutionist propaganda in Russia, enrolls young Armenians for service if required, collects money, buys and steals arms and ammunition and passes them through to Turkey [the Ottoman Empire]. As it also has charge of the Russian revolutionary movement in the Caucasus, to which many of the terrorist atrocities and assassinations are due, it leaves the local Committee at Van a fairly free hand in Turkish [Ottoman] affairs...

In connection with the Eastern Committee, there are four local committees in Turkey, with their head-quarters at Van, Moush [Muş], Erzeroum [Erzurum], Trebizond [Trabzon]... Van is the most important revolutionary centre in Turkey... Formerly the Committee used to send bands of Russian "fedai" [volunteers] over into Turkey; they have now stopped this, and are devoting themselves almost entirely to propaganda, collecting depots of arms and ammunition, and trying to win over the Kurds and Young Turks... Their present policy is to lie quiet and do everything in their power to gain co-operation of the Moslems. This is shown by the numerous pamphlets which they are publishing at present nearly all of which are addressed to Moslems... They realize that without Moslem co-operation and support their cause is hopeless...

A few remarks about these "fedai" may interest your excellency... The ideas, on which they act, are as follows. They see that European intervention for the amelioration of the conditions of Armenia is out of the question. They see, moreover, that European powers, when they have anything which they wish to get out of the Sultan, effect their ends by what is practically terrorism, e.g., by the sending of a squadron of battle-ships to the Bosphorus. Thus they [the Dashnak] hope to attain their ends by a policy of terrorism, and the punishment of the instigators of organized oppression. In methods they are absolutely unscrupulous.

Their objects are, they say, to obtain a better government. They do not object to Turkish [Ottoman] rule as such, but are against the present system of bad government, and they are at present using every effort to induce the Young Turks and Kurds to join their movement.

During the time of the late Ali Bey they had some success in

their endeavour, but with this new Vali [governor] I believe that
the Turks have rather cooled.[10]

That is where matters stood when the Young Turks forced the sultan to restore the constitution in July 1908. The leaders of the various nationalities had come to believe that they could obtain concessions, and
even independence, from the Porte only if the Great Powers intervened
on their behalf. That was how Serbia had won its autonomy and Greece
its independence during the first half of the nineteenth century. But the
historical conjuncture had changed after German unification in 1871 and
the rise of German power. Thereafter the Great Powers of Europe found
it virtually impossible to achieve consensus when they wished to intervene in Ottoman affairs. With German support—the kaiser visited the
Ottoman Empire on two occasions, in 1889 and 1898—Abdülhamid no
longer felt threatened by Great Power intervention and was able to crush
nationalist movements. Thus the Ottomans crushed an insurrection in
Crete and defeated Greece in 1897 in the war that followed. As a result
Greek irredentism became dormant until the Balkan Wars of 1912–13.

Armenian nationalist and revolutionary movements were founded
precisely during this period of Great Power rivalry. But some nationalists continued to believe that Great Power intervention on behalf of their
goals was still possible. Theodor Herzl, the Zionist leader and author of
The Jewish State (1896), was convinced that the Zionist cause could be
achieved with the intervention of Europe. He recognized that the balance of power in Europe had changed: Berlin had become an influential
player. He therefore appealed both to Berlin and to London.

Some Armenian revolutionary factions remained convinced that they
could bring about foreign intervention by committing outrages against
the Sublime Porte that would provoke the Ottomans into carrying out
massacres against the Armenian community. Thus on September 30,
1895, Armenian revolutionaries (many of them foreign citizens) gathered
in the Kumkapı and Kadırga districts of Istanbul where the Armenians
lived and led a demonstration against the Porte. The army confronted
them at Sultanahmet Square, however, and the ensuing violence lasted
for three days. But no Great Power intervention took place.

The following year, on August 24, 1896, the Armenian Revolutionary
Federation carried out a more daring operation. Armed with homemade
bombs, they occupied the Anglo-French Ottoman bank and took hos-
tages before the police besieged the building. Even though the bank was

foreign owned and violence occurred, again the European powers did not intervene. But they did not permit the Ottoman government to arrest and punish the revolutionaries. Foreign ambassadors negotiated with the sultan, who was forced to accept the mediation of chief dragoman Maximof at the Russian embassy. As a result the revolutionaries were allowed to leave the bank and sail into the Sea of Marmara on the yacht of Sir Edward Vincent, the manager of the Ottoman Bank, before boarding a ship bound for Marseilles.[11] On July 21, 1905, Armenian revolutionaries, hoping to bring about "regime change" in collaboration with the Young Turk opposition, attempted to assassinate Sultan Abdülhamid in Yıldız Mosque, killing twenty-six and wounding fifty-six. The Armenian nationalists included someone called Kendiriyan and a Belgian sympathizer, Edward Jorris. Both men were tried and sentenced to death. But the Belgian ambassador intervened and demanded that their sentence be carried out in Belgium; the Porte was forced to acquit them both.[12] Thereafter revolutionary activities ceased for the moment, with no further attempts to bring about foreign intervention until after the constitutional revolution.

2

The Armenian Community, 1908–1914

The nationalities hoped that with the constitution restored and with parliamentary representation reform would lead to an amelioration of their situation throughout the empire. Photographs of the era show great rejoicing among the people as all religious communities celebrated the restoration of the constitution and freedom. But such optimism was not long lasting.

Sarkis Atamian draws a picture of the Armenian community in the constitutional period: it "was divided into three groups: The *Dashnak* [the Armenian Revolutionary Federation]—the counterpart of the CUP, representing the rising lower middle classes—was strong in Anatolia. They were the most powerful group in 1908. The Patriarchate represented the 'clerico-wealthy' Armenian community, the 'amira class,' which had cooperated with the Sultan and after the revolution feared losing its privileges. The Hunchakians were the Marxist faction with roots in Russian socialism. They were the most revolutionary but the least influential."[1] Citing contemporary Armenian newspapers, Atamian noted that the patriarch wanted the Dashnak to follow his lead. But the Dashnak, the more powerful body, which had class differences with the Armenian *haute bourgeoisie*, denounced them as money-worshippers and pseudo-patriots.[2] The Armenian bourgeoisie was an economic and social class that lacked a strong political organization. Under the millet system the patriarchate and the Armenian National Assembly shared sovereignty with the Sublime Porte, though as junior partners. That served the bourgeoisie's economic and political interests. After the revolution, however, such institutions began to lose their power and influence in the new constitutional state.

The Unionists, though still not in power, were nevertheless influential because they had the best political organization. Ahmed Cemal Bey, later Cemal Pasha, a ranking member of the CUP, wrote in his memoirs that the committee opened negotiations in August 1908 with the Bulgarians, Greeks, and Armenians as well as with Prince Sabaheddin's Decentralists.

The Unionists wanted to reach an agreement with all the other elements on how best to maintain the empire. The Bulgarians were represented by Sandinski and Cernopoyef; the Armenians by Malumyan and Sahirkiyan; the Ottoman Decentralists by Nihat Reşad.

The Dashnak agreed to support the constitution but demanded to be allowed to keep their revolutionary organization intact, only agreeing to make it public in order to operate as a political party. Presumably that agreement also applied to other nationalities. By these outward signs of cooperation, the Unionists wanted to give the CUP "the prestige of all revolutionary committees of the Ottoman nationalities, just as the Empire itself had come into being by the joint association of all these nationalities."[3]

As a result of these talks, the *Times* of London (September 14, 1908) wrote that the Van branch of the Armenian Revolutionary Federation (ARF) had announced that the Armenians had laid down their arms and were ready to make common cause with the Committee of Union and Progress. The CUP then sent Vehbi Bey, a General Staff officer, to discuss the situation with the Armenian leaders and draw up plans of common action.

Bulgaria's declaration of independence on October 5, 1908; Austria's annexation of Bosnia-Herzegovina the next day; and Crete's declaration of union with Greece had a detrimental effect on the political life of the empire, especially as preparations were being made for elections in November and December. Commenting on the progress of the elections, the *Times* (November 9, 1908) noted that some fifty deputies had been elected. Most of the Muslims from the European provinces and Anatolia were known to be nominees of the CUP; the Greeks appeared to be obtaining a fair share of the representation, while the Armenians, "owing to their wide dispersal in relatively small communities, are likely to be somewhat under-represented in the Chamber." In the province of Erzurum, which had a substantial Armenian population although the Muslim population constituted the majority, the electors chose three Muslims and two Armenians. Both were members of ARF: Serenghian (aka Varteks Serengulian) was a revolutionary who had been sentenced to death for militant activity but was saved by British intervention, while Karakin Pastirmaciyan (aka Armen Garo) had taken part in the memorable attack on the Ottoman Bank in 1896. The Unionists recognized the existence of all millet organizations and even negotiated with them about representation in parliament.

In conversation with Gerald Fitzmaurice, the British Embassy's chief dragoman, Monsignor Matteos Izmirlian, the newly elected Armenian patriarch, remarked that

> the changed conditions in Turkey implied that Armenians have ceased to exist as a separate national entity and were merged in the Ottoman whole, that consequently it was his duty to avoid discussing politics with foreigners... But he felt impelled to ask me to convey to Your Excellency in absolute confidence his views on the present situation in as far as concerned his people.
>
> He felt, he said, that the re-establishment of the Constitution was a most delicate experiment in view of the backward conditions of masses of the population, especially in Asia Minor, and the total lack of men and money as a result of thirty years of misgovernment and tyranny; that internal tranquility and the resultant confidence of foreigners in the new regime were essential to its success, and that any serious mishap would certainly be fraught with the most disastrous consequences, perhaps, the extermination of his people. He was therefore firmly convinced that the only safe course for Armenians, their only chance of pulling themselves together and making good the terrible losses during the old Palace régime, lay in working in loyal union with the Turks on the line of prudence and moderation and eschewing all extremist ideas in the way of autonomy etc.... He was counseling his flock in this sense and had let it be discreetly understood that he would resign the Patriarchate rather than countenance any advanced tendencies on the part of the Henchaq, Droshaq, or other Armenian societies...
>
> He said the Turkish Government and people were frankly and honestly disposed to treat the Armenians fairly and that he was using every endeavour to see that his people met them more than half way but that the abrogation of Article 61 of the Treaty of Berlin would certainly impair harmony now so happily existing among the two creeds.[4]

Elections in Istanbul showed the tensions that still existed between the Porte and the nationalities. For example, members of the Armenian community were satisfied with the way the elections were conducted and showed their pleasure by sending a deputation to the Porte. But the Greek community objected (see chapter 3). Representation in parliament was only one of the issues in contention between the Porte and the non-Muslim communities; military service was another. Until the restoration of the constitution, non-Muslims had been permitted to pay a tax that exempted them from military service. But under the constitution all Ottomans were liable to be called up.

After much discussion in the press and parliament, military service was opened to non-Muslims, which evoked an enthusiastic response from the Christian communities. The British military attaché, whose task it was to watch such developments, reported that 49 Greeks and 37 Armenians had signed up as volunteers at Bandırma alone. According to the *Times* (May 17, 1909) correspondent, minister of war Mahmud Şevket Pasha informed the leaders of the non-Muslim communities that twenty-five percent of the army would be composed of Christians. This was well received by the Christians, especially the Armenians, because it would provide them with a measure of protections that they had not enjoyed before. On November 1 an imperial *firman* (declaration) announced that non-Muslim troops would be attached to the sixteen battalions of the Istanbul Division.[5] On June 16, when the Military Service Exemption Tax Law was debated, Muslim and non-Muslim deputies were divided as to whether this tax should be applied to non-Muslims in lieu of military service. The non-Muslim deputies objected, and a number spoke against it. Mustafa Arif, a Muslim and a Unionist, joined the non-Muslim deputies and argued against the tax, claiming that it was a violation of the very concept of Ottomanism. By June 21 virtually all supporters of the CUP, led by Mehmed Talat Bey, came out in opposition to the tax. The idea of retaining an exemption tax was abandoned for the moment: universal military service was seen as the means of bringing all the communities under the umbrella of Ottomanism. On July 21, when Yorgaki Artas proposed that Christian troops be permitted to have their own chaplains, this proposal also was accepted. The debates showed that the non-Muslims in the assembly had a voice and were capable of leading the reformist bloc in the passage of legislation.[6]

E. J. Dillon, the journalist and author, also spoke to both the Greek and Armenian patriarchs (Joachim III and Matteos Izmirlian, respectively). Both agreed that they were willing to cooperate with the experiment. "But what we cannot and will not do is to sacrifice one iota of the ecclesiastical autonomy which we have enjoyed since Constantine XI died fighting on the walls over there." The Armenian patriarch said: "We demand a perpetuation of the privileges now enjoyed by the Armenian community, and a complete decentralization of the administration."[7]

The British ambassador, who maintained close contacts with the

Armenian leadership, noted: "The grant of the Constitution has greatly ameliorated their [the Armenians'] position, and thus altered the attitude of the well known revolutionary Tashnak Society...At the time the leaders of the Young Turk movement were still in exile...the chief of the Armenian revolutionaries imbibed the hope that, in return for any assistance they might render in attaining this end, they would obtain such a measure of decentralisation as would go far to re-establish one or two purely Armenian provinces."[8]

Such was the character of working relations between Muslims and Armenians in 1909. Some Armenians were so well integrated into Ottoman-Turkish society that they even joined Türk Derneği, a Turkish nationalist cultural association. The Armenian community, like the other communities in the empire, was not monolithic. It was divided between the educated minority that had participated in the "Armenian renaissance" of the mid-nineteenth century when the Armenian language was recovered from its purely theological roots and the Turcophone majority, between Istanbul Armenians belonging to the commercial bourgeoisie and the petty bourgeoisie and peasantry of the provinces. As late as January 1919, when establishing an Armenian state in Anatolia was a very real possibility, the American diplomat Lewis Heck wrote that according to Sir Adam Block, who knew and understood the Ottoman Empire intimately, the "Armenians were chiefly devoted to commerce and that, for example, the Armenians of Constantinople would not go to Armenia, nor would most of those had emigrated to other countries desire to go back to primitive conditions and real hardship."[9]

The outbreak of counterrevolution in Istanbul on April 13, 1909, and the incidents in Adana that followed in its wake undermined relations between Muslims and non-Muslims. The mutiny of the Istanbul garrison broke out two months after the fall of Kamil Pasha, the Liberal anti-Unionist, Anglophile grand *vezir*. Though the movement had a religious, reactionary coloring, it was in fact a liberal conspiracy designed to destroy the CUP. Despite its Islamic rhetoric and demand for the Sharia, the Greek political elite supported the reactionaries. Even the British Embassy and its dragoman Gerald Fitzmaurice, though not the government in London, supported the pro-British Liberals who hoped to bring about the fall of the Unionists.

The events in Adana had local reasons for the conflagration. But one of the aims of the Liberals was to bring about foreign intervention through a foreign naval landing. The town of Adana was located close to the port of Mersin, where marines could be landed in order to intervene. French ships were steaming toward the port during the violence. The Armenian journal *Trosag* in May 1909 wrote that "Armenian public opinion of the time related the Adana event with the mutiny in Istanbul. The beginning of the massacre on Thursday, April 1/14, was not an accidental coincidence. Naturally, Yildiz [the sultan] played an important role in the Adana massacre."[10]

After the mutiny, when the Third Army from Salonika had crushed the counterrevolution, the Porte took measures to repair the damaged relations with the Armenian community. In May the Senate approved the chamber's vote of 30,000 gold liras for the victims of Adana. Commenting on the assembly debates on the massacres, Ambassador Gerard Lowther noted that "while the deputies, without exception, deplored the massacres, their speeches expressed the views of the 'intellectuals' of Turkey, and everything tends to show that their feelings of 'brotherhood' for the non-Turkish people are not shared by the Moslem population."[11] On May 12 a large majority in parliament adopted a motion expressing regret for the recent events at Adana. The deputies proposed that the chamber address a proclamation to all the Anatolian provinces enjoining accord and fraternity on all elements of the population. The following day grand vezir Hüseyin Hilmi Pasha's memorandum was read, announcing the names of a special commission that the government was sending to inquire into the recent events at Adana. The chamber voted by a large majority to attach its own delegates to the government commission: Şefik Bey and Hagop Babikian (deputies for Karesi and Edirne, respectively) were elected by ballot. In his program, read on May 15, Hilmi Pasha noted that the troubles in Adana had been provoked by the same reactionary movement as in Istanbul. They had aroused great emotion and pain throughout the country and in the region of Maraş and Antakya (Antioch); the province of Aleppo had also suffered because of the troubles in Adana.[12]

The government was very serious about dealing with the counterrevolutionaries. Ahmed Cemal Bey (later Cemal Pasha)—a strict disciplinarian who was respected in the army and the CUP—was sent to Adana to restore confidence in the province among the Armenians and fear among the reactionaries. As a result security in the province improved. Dashnak representatives in the assembly reported that attacks on the Armenians had declined. A number of prominent figures from the old regime were exiled to Izmir and to the islands of the Aegean. They included Hamidian notables such as Rıza Pasha, ex-minister of war; Tahsin Pasha, first secretary to the sultan; Memduh Pasha, ex-minister of the interior; Reşid Pasha, prefect of Istanbul; Zülfülü İsmail Pasha, inspector of military schools; Ragıp Pasha, second chamberlain to Abdülhamid; Hasan Rami Pasha, ex-minister of the Marine; Ahmed Ratıb, ex-*vali* (governor) of the Hijaz; and Saadettin Pasha, ex-*commandant de place* of Istanbul. Such people would have welcomed the destruction of the CUP and the restoration of the sultan.[13]

In July a number of counterrevolutionaries were publicly executed in Istanbul, the first time Muslims were hanged for such activity. They included Derviş Vahdeti, the Nakshibandi sheikh from Cyprus and founder of the Muhammadan Union, who had edited *Volkan* and written inflammatory articles against the Unionists; general Mehmet Pasha; colonels Nuri Bey and İsmail Bey; lieutenant Yusuf Efendi; Yusuf Pasha, ex-commandant of a division at Erzurum; and a number of soldiers.[14]

Local notables were arrested in Adana, along with İhsan Fahri Bey, the owner of *İtidal*, a newspaper that is said to have instigated violence in the town. The investigating commission that had been sent to Adana was critical of the government's failure to prevent the massacres but admitted that the violence was designed to destroy the constitutional regime. In August interior minister Avlonyalı Ferid Pasha, who had connections with the palace, was forced to resign and was replaced by Mehmed Talat Bey, one of the most influential Unionists. Ferid Pasha's resignation was brought about by criticism in the Unionist press for trying to stifle the inquiry into the troubles in Adana.

Despite the bitterness and disappointment caused by these events, the Armenian Revolutionary Federation realized that the CUP was the best hope for the future of the Armenian community. It agreed to continue political cooperation and accepted that politicians like Gabriel Noradunghian, a conservative Armenian loyal to the old regime, ought to be replaced by those who were able to adapt themselves to the new order. Therefore Noradunghian resigned and Bedros Halaciyan, an Armenian intellectual considered sympathetic to the new order, was appointed in his place.[15]

The *Times* (September 23, 1909) wrote that "the agreement concluded between the CUP and the Dashnaksutian, to the effect, among other things, that there should always be an Armenian in the cabinet, may legitimately be regarded as a sign that the leaders of the new regime want to work in friendly cooperation with the Armenians." Through the columns of *Azardamard*, the ARF's Western Bureau decided to support the minority, progressive wing of the CUP led by people like Talat Bey and Mehmed Cavid. They recognized the threat posed by the Young Turk Liberals and conservatives to bring down the constitutional regime and introduce other regressive measures.[16] In 1911 the Dashnak was still ready to defend the constitutional regime.

But another issue affected relations between the Porte and the Dashnak: the land question. In the late nineteenth century Kurdish tribes had seized the land of Armenian peasants. The Hamidian régime had done nothing to rectify the situation, forcing many Armenian peasants to flee to the northern Caucasus in Russia. After the revolution the Dashnak gave the land issue priority in relations with both the CUP and the Sublime Porte. It proposed "resolving the land issue by having the government pay financial compensation for disputed lands which were returned to rightful owners."[17] While the Porte was willing to consider Armenian proposals, other forces were at work in the eastern provinces, undermining the efforts of Istanbul. For example, Vice-Consul Matthews reported from Erzurum that Feizi Efendi (Pirincizade Feyzi Bey), "the local Kurdish deputy [and notable], who made a tour during the summer months in the north of the district ... told the Kurds that they should not give way to despair, promised that so long as they did nothing flagrant the Government would close its eyes to the oppression of the Christians, and assured them that Sultan Reshad [who succeeded Abdülhamid in April 1909] was as much their father as Abdul Hamid had been."[18] Thus not even Unionist like the Pirincizades could be relied on to give their support to the constitutional order or government policy if their local interests were threatened. The Istanbul press devoted a great deal of attention to the land question and the grievances of the Armenian peasantry in the region. "The question of the restoration of lands seized during the Armenian troubles [during the 1890s] by Kurdish Beys and Agas has been discussed ... The Minister of the Interior may be trusted to do his utmost on behalf of the Armenians, who have deserved well of the new regime."[19]

The daily *Sabah* (June 15, 1911) warned of the dangers of the situation in eastern Anatolia, particularly in Bitlis, due to the passivity of the government in response to the land usurpation by Kurdish chiefs. The newspaper called for the government to settle the land question as the only way to restore peace in the region. Kaligian notes that the Porte had been settling Circassian immigrants on land that had belonged to Armenians since Hamidian times and that this policy was continued after the revolution. The aim of such settlement was to secure the borders with Persia and Russia.[20]

In June 1911 the Unionists decided to send a delegation led by Cavid Bey to Anatolia to celebrate the third anniversary of the constitution. He was a prominent liberal Unionist deputy belonging to the Talat faction who had been elected from cosmopolitan Salonika and enjoyed good relations with the Armenian leaders. The delegation was to go to Samsun, Trabzon, Erzincan, Erzurum, Van, Bitlis, Diyarbakır, Urfa, Birecik, Aleppo, and Damascus and, if time permitted, to Egypt. Cavid was accompanied by Ömer Naci (another influential Unionist), Ahmed Şerif, and Mustafa Necip. Ahmed Şerif was the correspondent who had toured Anatolia after the revolution and written a description of his tours, first serialized in the daily *Tanin* and then published as *Anadolu'da Tanin*. Mustafa Necip was a Unionist who would be killed during the attack on the Sublime Porte in January 1913, the coup that would bring the CUP back to power.

When the Porte began to take measures to restore land seized by the Kurdish aghas and beys, they organized fresh attacks on Armenian villages in the Muş and Bitlis region, an area in which the Porte's authority was too weak to protect its citizens. The local correspondent of the *Near East* reported that some of the attackers "are said to have been agents of the infamous Musa Bey, one of Abdul-Hamid's vilest provincial tyrants."[21]

The outbreak of war with Italy in September 1911 aggravated the political situation throughout the empire. Muslims and non-Muslims watched with great interest the founding of the principal opposition liberal party, Hürriyet ve İtilaf Fırkası (Freedom and Accord Party), also known as the Liberal Union (Entente Libérale). Fresh elections were held after a Unionist measure had been defeated in the chamber, and the assembly was dissolved in January 1912. The patriarch-led Armenian community, already estranged from the CUP, gave its support to the Liberal Union. Other communities—Bulgarian, Arab, and Albanian—that sought greater autonomy or independence also turned against the CUP. The Unionists realized that if the Armenian community voted against them en masse they would face difficulty in controlling the new parliament. The committee therefore sent a delegation of pro-Unionist Armenian deputies to the patriarch, promising concessions and declaring that grand vezir Mehmed Said Pasha had agreed to institute a program of reform. They asked the patriarch to issue a circular calling upon his flock to support the CUP. Patriarch Hovannes Arşaruni (also appears as

Arscharduni), following the example of the Greek patriarch, Joachim III, gave an ambiguous reply: "We are neither Unionists nor Liberals. We shall always be on the side of the Government that will do justice to all, respect our legitimate rights, and make an end to misdeeds in Armenia." The two patriarchs were on good terms and were collaborating at the political level. Count Nicholas Vassilievich Charykov, Russia's ambassador at the Porte, visited the Armenian patriarch; his "attitude towards the Armenians recently has been extremely cordial." The patriarch took the opportunity to make an appeal on behalf of Armenians, intellectuals, and commercial classes who had been arrested by the tsarist regime.[22]

The following week the "Armenian Letter" of January 26 reported that the Armenian council had met a day earlier to discuss the coming elections and the choice of Armenian deputies. While the patriarch would not openly take part in the campaign, he decided to form a campaign committee that would prepare a list of candidates. The committee was made up of Armenian notables, the president of the Armenian National Assembly, and representatives of the three parties—the Dashnak, the Constitutional Democrats or Cadets, and the Hunchaks. The *Near East*'s correspondent wrote: "I learn on good authority that the Armenians will vote with the CUP, provided the Committee guarantee the land and the school question."[23]

In the same "Armenian Letter" a correspondent from Bitlis reported that some twenty-five villages that he had visited kept night patrols for fear of the Kurds:

> I have learned that the Government have instructed the Armenians in Moush [Muş] to buy arms for protection against the Kurds. In my opinion, this does not augur well for the peace of the country. Neither the Kurds nor the Armenians should be allowed to carry arms. A well-organized gendarmerie and a force of sincere, honest, and liberal officials will suffice to create normal conditions in the Armenian provinces. The arrest of Mousa Bey, the Sheikh of Khizam, and a few other ringleaders is earnestly desired by all friends of constitutional Turkey.

But Istanbul was extremely weak in the Anatolian provinces. The government lacked the authority to enforce disarmament, arrest the troublemakers, and maintain law and order. Allowing the Armenian community of Muş to arm itself was the only way to provide protection. Such was the dilemma of a weak state.

The tribal chiefs, not to be intimidated, responded with a counter-measure of their own. In Van province the Kurdish tribes formed "a kind of confederation, the purpose of which is said to be a general conspiracy against the Government." That caused great concern in the local administration—and no doubt in Istanbul too. People feared a Kurdish uprising at a time when the Russian army was on the border.[24]

The patriarch continued to receive letters in which Armenians in the east complained of fresh Kurdish raids. The government could do nothing to protect the communities, and the special commission appointed to visit the region had failed to leave even after two months of temporizing. The *Near East*'s correspondent reported how Musa Bey, who had terrorized the Muş region for twenty years, had returned to the town in triumph accompanied by his horsemen. He had been pardoned and honored by the local government even though Celal Bey, the former interior minister, had ordered his arrest. Another Kurdish chieftain, Kör Hüseyin Pasha of Arcis in Van province, was again playing a prominent role in the region. Under the Hamidian régime Hüseyin Pasha had been a general in the Hamidiye, the Kurdish tribal force organized by the sultan in order to co-opt the chiefs and their tribes. No one had dared to oppose him when he had terrorized the population and seized lands.

After the constitution had been restored and Armenian refugees returned to Anatolia from the Russian Caucasus, the lands that Hüseyin Pasha had seized were returned to their rightful owners. He had escaped to Iran and was said to be planning a Kurdish rebellion against the Porte. On his return to Van, Hüseyin Pasha was received by the vali, acting independently of Istanbul. The patriarch was told that the organizer of massacres was active again and that he had begun to confiscate villages.[25]

Abdülhamid had supported the feudal tribal order in Anatolia in order to bolster his own power. But under the constitutional regime the tribal sheikhs and notables possessed a different kind of power: electoral power. As the example of the Pirincizades showed, they controlled vote banks in their provinces, won elections, and sent their protégés as deputies to Istanbul. The deputies from eastern Anatolia were elected by the likes of Hüseyin Pasha and local notables, whose interests the deputies naturally supported. Under these conditions the Ottoman state was just too weak to establish law and order.

In February 1912 the Porte announced that Ürgüplü Hayri Efendi (minister for religious foundations), accompanied by Gabriel Noradunghian, would lead a commission to the eastern provinces. The principal duties of the commission were to examine all the issues of the dispute between Kurds and Armenians regarding land ownership. In his "Armenian Letter" of February 9, 1912, the *Near East*'s correspondent wrote that the Young Turk government had come to the conclusion that the integrity of the empire depended upon the solidarity of all peoples and was serious about the decision to carry out reforms in Armenia as well as in Albania and Macedonia.

Hayri Efendi, who was later appointed Şeyhülislam, visited the patriarch and assured him that he would do his utmost to secure justice for all Armenians, who had suffered at the hands of certain notorious malefactors for so many years. He added that he was well acquainted with the issue, which only needed time to be settled. Hayri Efendi had had to postpone his visit until spring because of bad weather.

The *Near East* also reported Cavid Bey's speech at the Unionist club at Nuri Osmaniye, where the former minister spoke with great enthusiasm about the Armenian community. He assured his audience (made up mostly of Turks and Muslims) that the rights of the Armenians would be acknowledged and that Turkish voters must assure the election of Armenian deputies in the coming election. The correspondent thought that this was an election ploy, "yet I believe that this is a way a body of public opinion will be formed which will help in the future to eliminate the Armenian question, by guaranteeing safety of life and property in the eastern provinces."[26]

In the 1912 general elections it seemed as though the Greek vote was going to the Liberals (see chapter 6). The Armenian vote was divided, with the Istanbul bourgeoisie voting Liberal while the Dashnak, after considerable discussion, supported the CUP. The Jewish community adhered to the principle of "Union and Progress." In the Balkans, however, the Internal Organization of Macedonia (IMRO) was unwilling to compromise. On March 18 Şükrü Bey, general-secretary of the Interior Ministry, and Abdülkerim, inspector of public instruction, arrived in Sofia. They asked representatives of the Internal Organization about the kind of reforms that would satisfy them and under what conditions they would put a stop to their revolutionary activity. Members of the organization refused to negotiate and said that they would continue revolutionary activity until they had attained their object—autonomy through international European intervention. The Macedonian Committee sent a delegation led by Professors Miletich and Georgov of Sofia to St. Petersburg to agitate in favor of European intervention. The delegates then proceeded to London and the other capitals of Europe.[27]

Hacı Adil's mission to the Balkans returned to Istanbul on May 29, 1912, empty handed, after a tour lasting three and a half months.[28] His objective had been to win the Greek and Bulgarian vote by making concessions to both sides. He offered a number of concessions: to admit Bulgarian bishops as representatives of the commission on the district administrative councils in accordance with the law of the vilayets; to end torture and the use of the bastinado; to institute prompt trials and exemplary punishment of Muslims guilty of murdering Christians; and to restore Bulgarian monasteries handed over to the Serbs in the past. In the end, when it seemed as though negotiations were not achieving the desired results, the CUP decided to resort to coercion and intimidation in the election campaign in order to guarantee favorable results. The Unionists won by fair means and foul. The 1912 election came to be known as the "big stick election."[29]

An event that dramatically affected Unionist-Armenian relations was Russia's decision to recall Ambassador Charykov in March 1912. He was replaced by M. N. Giers, an appointment indicating a radical change in Russia's policy toward both the Armenian and Greek communities. Charykov and his first secretary and dragoman, André Mandelstam, had enjoyed good relations with the Unionists, especially with the Talat faction that included the journalist Hüseyin Cahid and Mehmed Cavid. Russian policy toward the Porte changed from conciliation to tension. Giers preferred to establish cordial relations with the Armenian patriarch rather than with the Unionists or the Dashnak. Later in the month reports that Russian forces had been increased on the Caucasus border created alarm in Istanbul.[30] Ambassador Giers arrived in Istanbul on April 13, 1912. Andrew D. Kalmykov, who had served in his embassy, later remembered that "Giers was imbued with the idea of Russia's might and full of contempt for Turkey which, according to the then prevailing notion, was soon to be divided into zones of influence or parceled among the Great Powers."[31]

The manipulation of the Armenians (and paradoxically some Kurdish tribes) became an instrument of Russian policy for furthering Russian power and diminishing the power of European rivals. Existing relations between the Armenian patriarchate and the Russian Embassy became more intimate. Soon after his arrival Giers visited the patriarch's residence in the Kumkapı district of Istanbul in order to pay homage to him. In May 1912 Foreign minister Sergei Sazanov made a speech in which he referred to the social and cultural needs of the Eastern Christians in Turkey and the necessity of the new regime to take the aspirations of these communities into account. The Unionists were naturally alarmed by the implication of Sazanov's words.[32]

Encouraged by Russian support, the leader of the Christian communities—Armenian, Greek, and Bulgarian—decided to form a Mixed Committee to prepare a scheme of joint action for the maintenance of their
rights. Some felt that the Unionists "have decided to hamper the social
[and economic] progress of the Christians in order to give the Turks [and
Muslims] a chance to get on an equal footing." This policy began to be
described as "Turkification" after the Porte attempted to establish its authority over the millet system, bringing millet schools under the jurisdic-
tion of the Education Ministry. The *Near East* also reported on a meeting
between the Greek and Armenian patriarchs to discuss the attack on their
privileges by the constitutional regime. They expressed the view that the
government intended "to deprive the Patriarchs of their ancient privileges
and introduce legislation making them mere State officials, appointed
or dismissed by Imperial *irade* or decree. The Armenian Patriarch's comment, 'They must know that we are not Sheikhs-ul-Islam,' foreshadowed
greater resistance on his part. 'And if the Armenians resist, what will the
Greeks and Exarchist Bulgars not do?'" asked the correspondent.[33]

The signing of an anti-Ottoman treaty between Serbia and Bulgaria
in March 1912 suggested that the Balkan states were preparing to further
their claims against the Porte by force. The treaty stipulated: "The two
parties guaranteed their political independence and territorial integrity
against an attack by any other state"; they "agreed to oppose with all their
forces any attempt on the part of any Great Power to annex, occupy or
attempt to take possession, even temporarily, of any part of the Balkans
under Turkish suzerainty, if one of them considered such action contrary
to their interests; and peace was to be made in common." Later a secret
military convention was drawn up and became an integral part of the
treaty. The treaty was to remain secret and would enter into force at once
under certain circumstances. In May Bulgaria and Greece reached a similar accord, but without boundary delimitation. They agreed on united
action in case of war with the Ottomans. When Montenegro joined the
alliance, the states were ready for war.[34]

The military coup d'état and the fall of the CUP marked by Said Pasha's resignation on July 17, 1912, delighted the nationalities (see chapters
2 and 4). Ahmed Muhtar Pasha appointed the Armenian liberal Gabriel Noradunghian as his foreign minister. Murat Koptaş, the biogra-
pher of Krikor Zohrab Efendi, an important Armenian intellectual and
political figure, wrote that "there was great happiness amongst Hnchag
[Hunchak] supporters with the fall of the CUP and the emergence of
a Liberal government." The Dashnak organ *Troshag* (July–August 1912,

177) wrote: "The anti-İttahadist government came on the scene with the slogan of decentralization and the real equality of the nations. There are a lot of stupids—even in our national [Dashnak] circles—who believed them, and applauded the fall of İttihad... The miserable slogan [was] 'the İttihad had fallen, it is necessary to overthrow its Armenian partner [the Dashnak].'"[35]

The Liberal anti-Unionist government could not stop the lawlessness in eastern Anatolia. Reports kept coming in from Beyazit, Van, and Bitlis about the murder of Armenian peasants, the abduction of women, and the burning of villages by the followers of Kurdish chiefs like Mir Mahe, Sheikh Hüseyin, and "other brigands." The notorious Musa Bey of Bitlis is even said to have threatened the bishop. The Porte responded to such reports by dismissing the governors of Bitlis and Van and ordering the military commander to arrest the guilty Kurds within forty-eight hours. Ali Pasha, a Circassian general, was dispatched to Bitlis to undertake the task.[36] Istanbul then allocated 20,000 gold liras to each of the five Armenian vilayets, 100,000 liras in all, to enable them to bring about a settlement of the land question. In February the Porte had already decided to open a credit of 100,000 liras for the settlement of land disputes. Armenians wrongfully dispossessed were to be reinstated, while Kurdish squatters were to be given compensation. The new valis of Bitlis and Erzurum were to be given additional powers to introduce reform.[37]

In its editorial the *Near East* noted: "In view of its difficulties elsewhere [the Balkans] the Porte must be anxious to avoid complications with the Armenians; but, as may be gathered from conditions in the Eastern provinces, the *Central Government is virtually powerless to impose its authority upon some of its more unruly subjects* [emphasis added]."[38] In this climate of Ottoman weakness, the Balkan states ordered general mobilization. They could see what difficulties the Porte was facing in the war with Italy. The "Servian Minister in Sofia, for instance, warned the Turkish chargé that the surrender of Tripoli would teach others how easy it was to make a meal of Turkey."[39]

The mobilization for war also shows how citizenship and the capitulations worked in the late Ottoman Empire. While the Greek Ottomans were loyal to Athens (see chapter 3), the Armenians were divided over the war in the Balkans. The Istanbul bourgeoisie (the amira class), made up of bankers and merchants and led by the patriarch, supported the Ottoman cause in the hope of retaining their privileges when the Ottomans won. The Armenian Revolutionary Federation was divided. Those in Anatolia supported the Ottomans; those in Thrace followed the lead of Antranig

Pasha, the Armenian revolutionary, and fought alongside the Bulgarian army. The Ottoman army already had eight thousand Armenians, however, and more were enlisting during mobilization. Fifteen chaplains had been appointed "to provide for the spiritual needs of Armenian troops."[40]

The *Near East*, which supported the patriarch's leadership, had written how the Armenians had supported the Ottomans. But Diana Agabeg Apcar, an Armenian nationalist, wrote from Yokohama, Japan, and refuted the *Near East* correspondent's claim. Her letter "Armenians and the War," dated December 15, 1912, is worth quoting extensively:

> Your correspondent writes: "During the present Balkan War the Armenians have given proof of their sincere attachment to the Constitutional régime by both pecuniary contributions and personal sacrifices by enlisting in the Ottoman army."
>
> What may be the feeling in Constantinople among a certain number of clique [*sic*] of Armenians towards the Turks of the Constitutional régime I am not prepared to assert, but according to all the news that has reached us regularly during the last three years, or rather, since the horrible massacres of Cilicia in April 1909, the Armenians who unhappily are subject to Turkish rule have tried every available and possible means to escape enlistment in the Turkish army, large numbers leaving the country in order to escape Turkish military service. As far as we have been given to know through information coming from authentic sources the Armenians who get enrolled in the Turkish army belong to the hapless families who were so mercilessly plundered in 1909 ... that they have not the money to pay the military exoneration tax, and these ... are hounded into the Turkish ranks.
>
> On the other hand, information comes to us that about 60,000 Armenian volunteers enlisted in the Bulgarian army, and it is now common knowledge that the Christians in the Turkish army have held back in fighting against the enemies of the Turks, large numbers (as the telegraphic dispatches and European war correspondents inform us) have surrendered to the Balkan and Greek armies.
>
> It is not many months ago that the Armenian Patriarch of Constantinople resigned his office as a protest against Turkish atrocities in Armenia, and appealed to the Armenian Catholicos, whose seat is in Russian Armenia, to take over the protection of Armenians subject to Turkish dominance. News comes to us that

the Armenians in the Caucasus have called upon the Catholicos
to appeal to the Russian government to occupy that portion of
our country which is under Turkish domination. This is a development which we Armenians are willing to accept, because we
recognize that there are degrees of hell, and if there is no escape
for our unfortunate people from the lowest depths of hell (which
is the Turkish hell) except by Russian occupation, then let us have
Russian occupation.

. . . The feeling of Armenians abroad towards the Turk is one
of loathing and hatred—bitter, burning, undying hatred—and we
pray daily and hourly for the day when the Turks shall be driven
out of our country. The Balkan States and Greece have been fighting to drive the Turks out of Europe. We Armenians want the
Turk driven out of Armenia.

There may be, as I have already admitted, a clique of Armenians in Constantinople who support the Turkish Government.
If there are any such, we regard them as traitors to their own race;
but a clique does not comprise a nation or a people.[41]

In a letter dated January 27 an Istanbul Armenian protested to the
editor of the *Near East* about the Apcar letter. He claimed:

Miss Apcar is too far distant from the important centers of Armenian communities to know what is taking place among them, and
she will be sorry to hear that her letter is likely to injure just the
very cause that she means to defend.

Miss Apcar and other Indian Armenians would do well
to work in this direction and to say nothing ill-natured against
Turks, Kurds, and Turkish Armenians.[42]

Generally speaking both individual Ottomans and the press were dis-
appointed by the behavior of Christian troops in the army. Hasan Cemal,
an Ottoman officer who kept a diary of the war, wrote on December 29,
1912, that

we treated all soldiers equally in our battalion, and because we
did not say a bad word about their *milliyet* (nationality) and religion, we had great confidence in the Christians. We thought that
they also had affection for us. Today these ideas had unfortunate
results . . .

This morning, the Greek we most liked and trusted in our company, and a Greek and Armenian from another company deserted to the enemy... He said he could understand why a Bulgar [in the Ottoman army] might want to go over to the Bulgarian army; he said that he himself would desert if he were a Bulgarian in the Ottoman army. But he could not understand how an Ottoman Greek [*Rum*] could go over to the Bulgars after "The Greeks have heard what the Bulgars did to their villages and to their girls. They knew about the religious and ethnic hatred that existed amongst them..."

As for the Armenians...! We made no distinction between them and Muslim soldiers. There were plenty of Armenian sergeants and corporals. The freedom that was shown to Armenians, the affection and closeness shown to them was not shown to Muslims.

The desertion of Armenians affected us more because of the affection we had towards them. We looked upon them with genuine trust and affection. *Now we trust only the Greeks and Armenians of Anatolia* [emphasis added]. We have confidence in their goodwill and trust, and that they will remain true to the bread they have eaten. These people, that is to say the Armenians and Greeks of Anatolia, were sorry about the desertions of their coreligionists. They were ashamed and cursed them.[43]

Armenian revolutionaries saw in the rout of the Ottoman armies the impending disintegration of the empire and the opportunity to make gains for their own cause. On October 14, 1912, Mikael Varantian wrote a report to Simon Zavarian from Geneva, noting that the "Armenians were dispersed on different sides" in the war.

The young ARF members in the Balkans were enthusiastically forming battalions and going to fight against the Ottomans.

The Armenian Revolutionary Federation saw that the Ottomans were being soundly beaten and expected that there would soon be a peace conference at which the Europeans would divide the spoils of war. This would provide an opportunity to obtain the essential reforms needed to guarantee security and a livelihood to the Armenian population of Eastern Anatolia.[44]

Russia also saw the Ottoman collapse as imminent and made preparations to obtain its share of the spoils in the partition of the empire. Reports of Russian troops being concentrated on the Ottoman-Armenian frontier were confirmed by dispatches received from Batum, Kars, and Erivan. That gave rise to speculation that Russia would claim territorial compensation in Anatolia in the final settlement of the Eastern Question. It had long been Russia's ambition to push its Caucasian frontier westward to include the strongly fortified town of Erzurum. The Russian vice-consul at Van wrote to Ambassador Giers: "We must not allow Britain to oversee the realization of reforms in Kurdistan and Turkish Armenia which lie in the sphere of our political influence. A Russian protectorate for Turkish Armenians is a must; this gives the possibility for the Russian government to have a permanent influence in Turkey. This is one way to penetrate by peaceful means."[45]

Within weeks of declaring war the Bulgarians had advanced to the very outskirts of Istanbul and were finally halted at the Çatalca lines. Neither the Ottomans nor the European powers had expected such an outcome. At the outbreak of war Baron Eugene Beyens, the Belgian ambassador at Berlin, wrote that undersecretary of state Arthur Zimmermann was not alarmed by the situation in Turkey. "When Montenegro gave the signal for hostilities, Baron Beyens found the Turkish Ambassador beaming with satisfaction. His expectation of victory was shared by the German statesman, Kiderlen-Wachter, who was stupefied by the triumph of 'an army of peasants' at Kirk Kilisse. The [German] Foreign Minister, however, believed that the Turks would recover, and 'being a very bad Christian,' as he remarked with a smile, he ardently hoped they would win."[46]

When war broke out even Great Britain expected an Ottoman victory. Sir Edward Grey declared in parliament: "Whatever the outcome might be of those hostilities, in no case would the powers permit any alternation in the *status quo*."[47] But following the Ottoman collapse, Britain reneged on its declaration and called for an Ottoman Empire restricted to Asia. That is what the Agha Khan, the Anglophile leader of Indian Muslims, proposed: "the withdrawal of Turkey to her Asiatic provinces, as Britain had no territorial ambitions over there. Britain, he said, wanted a strong and powerful country in the region in order to prevent rivals established on the road to India."[48]

The defeats restricted the Ottomans virtually to their "Asiatic provinces" and had a dramatic demographic impact. A quarter of a million

Muslims from the Balkans poured into Istanbul before the retreating Ottoman armies that succeeded in halting the Bulgarian offensive at Çatalca. The arrival of the refugees created tension with the Christian population, leading to the forced migration of Christians to Greece. The Armenian population also felt threatened. Michael Llewellyn Smith estimated that more than 100,00 Muslims fled through Eastern Thrace before the advance of the Bulgarian army in 1912; some 10,000 left Macedonia in the same year; nearly 50,000 left Western (Bulgarian) Thrace in 1913 under the terms of the Turco-Bulgarian Treaty; and after this more that 100,000 Muslims evacuated Macedonia. The upheaval of Muslim communities in Europe led to reprisals against the Anatolian Christians. "One motive was desire for revenge. There was also the practical motive that for every Christian family expelled it was possible to settle a Muslim refugee family in the empty accommodation."[49]

By the Treaty of London of May 1913 the Ottoman Empire was restricted to Anatolia, except for a sliver of land in Europe. Therefore Anatolia became vital for the empire, though it was also territory contested by both Greece and Armenian nationalists. The setbacks in the Balkans created such a menacing situation in eastern Anatolia that on November 16 the Şeyhülislam, the highest religious authority in the empire, issued a proclamation to the provinces of Anatolia and Arabia calling upon people to show tolerance toward the non-Muslims and to treat them on terms of absolute equality, "as enjoined by the Sharia." They were also told that the perpetrators of the slightest incidents would be held responsible before God and would be punished by the government.[50]

Because of the breakdown of law and order and the sense of insecurity in the provinces, many Armenians began to emigrate to the Caucasus and America. The Dashnak tried to stop the flow of emigration, but to no avail. By 1912 a substantial Armenian community already existed in America: about 70,000 Armenians, mostly located in New York, Providence, Boston, and Worcester. The *Near East* correspondent wrote: "during the last ten years 28,916 Armenians have emigrated from Turkey to the United States, the majority having left since the constitution; and apparently the exodus is increasing... [and] almost every immigrant sends money to his relatives in this country."[51]

When cooperation with the CUP broke down in early February 1913 the Dashnak members decided to purchase arms for self-defense. They began raising funds: "most of the party's work in the first half of 1913 was arms related... They appealed to the Patriarchate to help them raise money but they held out little hope of success. It was also an opportune moment to buy arms in the Balkans because they were so cheap. The U.S. Central Committee also collected money to buy arms for specific villages from expatriates from those villages. Military preparations were foremost in Dashnak activities."[52]

The Dashnak instructed its members not to depend on wealthy merchants for funds for self-defense. The well-to-do made too many excuses not to give, but members were told that they should not threaten violence against rich Armenians. If the wealthy refused to donate, the Dashnak should approach the general population. The Armenian bourgeoisie in the Caucasus and Istanbul feared revolution and therefore refused to contribute. The Egyptian-Armenian politician Baghos Nubar Pasha, who was engaged in negotiations with the powers, argued that collecting arms might damage his diplomatic position. "But if negotiations failed," he said, "I will put all my skills in the revolutionary effort." He was concerned that "distributing arms could lead to a premature uprising."[53]

The crushing defeats of the Balkan Wars ushered in a period of self-doubt, demoralization, and introspection among the Unionists. In March the Dashnak noted that the CUP had tried to strengthen its political position by appealing to Liberal opponents and had even invited Prince Sabaheddin to join the cabinet. The CUP then approached the Armenian Revolutionary Federation to resume cooperation. But the Dashnak refused.[54] The Unionists were so demoralized that they abandoned their idea of "union and progress" in favor of decentralization. On March 28, 1913, the new law for the administration of vilayets was officially promulgated, subject to sanction by the assembly. The scheme for decentralization granted provincial councils the right to decide matters of local interest, while provincial budgets were separated and the powers and duties of local officials were enlarged and defined. The power of governors was increased: they became the highest executive officials. The general provincial councils were to be elected by second-degree electors (the local notables) rather than appointed by Istanbul.[55]

In April 1913 the Porte decided to send a commission led by Mustafa Hayri Bey and two Armenian judicial functionaries to investigate the lawlessness in Anatolia. In November Talat expressed his intention to visit the provinces himself. The government was convinced of the necessity of taking serious measures to remedy the present state of affairs.[56] The Porte was forced to reconsider the Armenian question because the situation in Anatolia had become critical as a result of the Balkan Wars. The "Kurds are boiling over." The Kurdish chiefs in the Bitlis, Van, and

Diyarbakır regions had become more defiant, possibly with Russia's encouragement. The Armenian revolutionaries in Van also believed that the Kurdish attacks were encouraged and organized by Russia, although they had limited evidence.[57] As Vice-Consul Molyneux-Seel observed:

> The Turkish authorities are so thoroughly alive to the danger of a Russian armed intervention that I am convinced that they will never allow, much less incite, a massacre of Armenians by the Kurds. The danger of the Kurds on their own initiative creating disorders, such movements being directed more against the Turkish Government than against the Christian inhabitants, does exist. No wonder the Porte had allowed the Armenians to not only purchase arms but also provided large quantities of arms to the Kurds.[58]

The local authorities simply lacked the strength to control the tribes. Istanbul tried to calm the situation by appointing the former governor of Kosovo as the strongman who could restore the Porte's authority. The real problem was that he lacked sufficient troops to enforce such authority.

In this critical period the patriarch also began to put pressure on the Porte. In May he threatened to resign. A deputation of the Armenian National Council visited grand vezir Mahmud Şevket Pasha and complained about the crimes committed against Armenians, the lack of promised reforms, and the Porte's attitude toward the patriarchate. Şevket Pasha responded by stating that war had prevented reforms but that they were now his government's priority. The patriarch declared that he no longer trusted the Porte to carry out the reforms and insisted on European supervision of the reform process that the Porte proposed to introduce.[59]

European direct intervention came in June 1913 when Ambassador Giers proposed to the ambassadors of the Great Powers that the grievances of the Armenians in eastern Anatolia be met by placing the "Armenian provinces" under a Christian governor and that local Christians and Muslims be given an equal share in the administration. The land question still remained the most important issue between the Kurdish tribes and Armenian peasants, however, and therefore for the Dashnak.[60]

Even with the promise of European intervention the patriarch was pessimistic. He wondered whether European inspectors would be given any real power to carry out reform. If reforms failed to be implemented, he feared that extremist Dashnak and Hunchak, described as anarchists, would turn to violence and revolution. Meanwhile Unionists were afraid of foreign intrigue in Anatolia. The committee circles spoke of Russian *agents-provocateurs*, though *Tanin* referred "with unexpected freedom to the fact that German workmen and others employed on the Baghdad Railway were the principal promoters of massacre rumours in Cilicia." Some Unionists had concluded that no question of foreign intrigue would arise if eastern Anatolia was decently governed. "Who ever heard of foreign intrigue in Wales, in Brittany, or French-speaking Switzerland?"[61]

The German initiative was a response to Russia's activity in the Caucasus and was intended to deter that. Therefore a German-Italian naval demonstration took place off Mersin, allegedly to prevent a massacre. But the *Near East's* "Constantinople correspondent" reported on May 16: "It is quite possible that the Armenians are overstating their case, and that things are not as bad as they are said to be." The appearance of the *Göeben* and some other European warships seems "to have caused memories of Kiao-Chau in China to rise in Turkish minds, and to have given the impression that the Germans are making the first step towards establishment of a sphere of influence in the region between the Taurus and the Euphrates, the 'vitals' of their railway system. The idea certainly prevails among foreigners that the Germans did not go to Mersina merely to show their desire of protecting the Armenians."[62]

In June Vice-Consul Molyneux-Seel reported that Kurds had attacked the Armenian village of Karagündüz, but

> were repulsed by the villagers. Gendarmes were sent but they only confiscated the Armenians' arms. That led to protests before the governor's office in Van and he ordered the arms returned and for Government rifles to be sent them in addition…One hundred and fifty government rifles have been sent to be distributed among the village in the Shattakh district. Rifles are also being sent to Armenian villages in other districts where thought necessary. Certain Rayah Kurds [settled peasants] have also been promised arms.[63]

While Vice-Consul Molyneux-Seel approved of the government's measures, he did not believe that they could be a permanent solution to the situation:

The suppression of the Kurds by spasmodic punitive expeditions, the forcible restitution of lands by the Kurds to the Armenians, the arming of the Armenian population by the Tashnakists, the policing of the entire country by detachments of gendarmes or soldiers, none of these will bring about permanent good relations between Kurds and Armenians, since the evil remains untouched. The source of the evil is the maintenance of feudal conditions among the Kurds and the influence exercised by the religious sheikhs. Let the Turks abolish the...Hamidie regiments; let them emancipate the Kurds from their beys and aghas, allowing each Kurd family to own its own lands and cattle; let them break the influence of the sheikhs and replace it by the authority of the Government..., let them accentuate the conditions which in the course of events will bring about the settlement of nomadic tribes; let them educate as well as instruct the Kurds and govern them with firmness and justice, and...there will no longer be an Armenian question.[64]

The vice-consul was correct about the need for breaking the feudal power of the tribal chiefs, for land reform, and for distributing tribal lands to the peasantry. But the Porte lacked the power and the authority to do so. In July a Severekli Pashazade Mehmed Fikri wrote that "the land question is the most vital problem between Kurds and Armenians. But Armenians wish to condemn to inaction the active members of the Kurdish nation and to work only for their own betterment. Why does not the Patriarch approve of the principle of indemnity? Is his sole aim to see the Kurds oppressed? If an incident is reported between...a Kurd and an Armenian, it is always the Kurd who is blamed...If a Kurd or an Armenian is a brigand, that does not imply all the Kurds and all Armenians are brigands."[65]

In July 1913 the *Near East* analyzed the Armenian question, noting that the Adana massacres of April 1909 may have dimmed the hopes of the Armenian leaders after the proclamation of the constitution. Yet the journal admitted that the CUP did act on behalf of the Armenians after the Adana massacres. The gendarmerie in the Armenian provinces was strengthened, and some of those guilty of rape and murder were hanged. The government also promised to disarm the Kurds and to settle the agrarian question. But during those years Istanbul was also forced to concentrate its attention on Arabia and Albania and neglected Anatolia. The army was being used in Albania, Syria, and Yemen, so the Kurdish tribes were not disarmed, only the settled Armenians and Kurds. That made the situation of law and order worse as the settled population—Armenian, Kurdish, and Turkish—became the prey of the armed tribes. The tribes resented the claims of restitution of the lands that they had seized during the troubles of 1894 and 1896.

War in the Balkans had aggravated the situation in Anatolia even more, because many Armenians joined the army. The villages were left defenseless against tribal raids. "The Government could not even protect the salt works belonging to the Public Debt administration near Van against local Kurds." The Armenians felt more insecure, while the land question could not be settled due to lack of funds. The patriarch protested, but the Porte could do little. "Some Armenian leaders are beginning to wonder whether loyalty to the Turks is a very remunerative virtue...Finally, the Armenians, though they realize that the position of their kin in Russian Asia is infinitely superior to their own, still cherish the belief that the formation of an Armenian 'nation' possessing religious and educational independence is more feasible under the aegis of the Porte than under the sovereignty of the Tsar or Kaiser." The Armenian leaders did not trust Germany, and Russia attracted only a certain number of Armenians. "[T]he leaders of the Dashnaktzutiun, who intrigued with the Nihilists in the past, are not altogether certain that a Russian occupation would altogether fit in with their programme or prove conducive to the longevity of their organization. They have it always in their power to provoke a Russian movement on Van or Erzeroum, but they realize that such a movement might result in anything but the formation of an Armenian 'Eastern Roumelia.'"[66]

Having lost faith in the Porte and the CUP, Armenian leaders demanded foreign control of any reform to be carried out. The *Near East* reached a prophetic conclusion: "But...if Europe fails to take any steps to enforce Article 61 of the Treaty of Berlin this year, trouble—and very serious trouble—is to be anticipated from the Armenian revolutionaries...If they [the Unionists] fail or refuse to adopt radical measures of reform...the Armenians must be forced willy-nilly to turn to Russia for assistance...In that case German and Russian interests may clash so formidably as to bring Armageddon on an unimaginative world."[67]

The *Near East* agreed that it was doubtful whether a "Government of angels" could do much for the Armenians if it found itself in the position of the Porte. It also noted "the unpleasant fact" that the Armenians formed about 35 or 40 percent of the population of the so-called six "Armenian Vilayets" of eastern Anatolia. They were mostly disarmed. If their leaders contemplated any sort of action, that would provoke an anti-Armenian movement among the armed Muslim population or arouse the suspicions of the Istanbul government.[68]

The Unionists hoped to defuse the tense situation by sending a commission led by an English officer, Captain Wyndham Henry Deedes, to examine the demands of the Armenian population. Another English officer, a Colonel Hawker, who had organized the gendarmerie of Aydın province after the revolution and had a reputation for honesty and fairness, was placed at the head of the gendarmeries of Erzurum, Trabzon, and Van.[69]

Judging by Cemal Pasha's conversation with Sir Henry Wilson, director of military operations, the Unionists wanted Britain to loan more officers like Alfred Milner to supervise the reforms in Anatolia. But Cemal said that he understood that "England was afraid of offending Russia [and asked]: 'What business was it of Russia? He would prefer to go to hell on his own rather than to paradise under the tutelage of Russia…A strong Turkey in Asia would be good for England.'" He wanted the assistance of England, of "men who could administer, execute, and command. The Turks could not change their military teachers [the Germans], but in all else, in finance, administration, navy, they wished to be under British guidance." Wilson, the soldier, was at a loss as to how to answer.[70]

Count Leon Ostrorog, having lived for many years in the Ottoman Empire, had intimate knowledge of its political and social life. He confirmed Cemal's desire to acquire the services of Lord Milner to resolve Armenian grievances. He wrote that the Ottomans, "aware that the Armenian Question had absolutely to be settled by means straight and effective," wanted the task of Armenian reform to be done under British control. But "diplomatic considerations alone prevented the scheme from being carried out. The Porte wanted Lord Milner to undertake the matter in hand; he was to be given full powers to reform and administer Anatolia."[71]

The Armenian Revolutionary Federation's World Congress met in Erzurum in August 1913 and discussed relations with the CUP. The discussions seem to have been inconclusive, though the leaders of the Armenian community decided on October 30 to fight the 1914 election as a group.[72] In November Unionist and Dashnak delegates discussed the situation. The Unionists agreed to meet Armenian demands if the Dashnak would "join them to oppose foreign control [without] European guarantee of the reforms." The members of the Armenian bureau refused to give such a guarantee, declaring that "they did not believe that there could be any real reform without European guarantees."[73] The Dashnak, seeing that the Porte was unable to deal with the tribal violence against the Armenians, decided to change tactics and respond in kind, as in the province of Van. Kurdish beys and aghas who oppressed Armenians would be intimidated and terrorized in turn and lands that they seized would be taken back by force. The Kurds, rather than the Armenians, would have to protest to the government and ask for assistance. An earlier World Congress had sanctioned such revolutionary activities.[74]

On November 19, 1913, *Tanin* reported that the Armenian patriarch had presented a note to the Justice Ministry, requesting proportional representation in the 1914 elections. The patriarch claimed that the 2 million Armenians ought to be represented by about twenty deputies in parliament. In fact not even half that number of seats were held by the Armenians. The Porte replied that it was not competent to deal with such claims, which would require amending the constitution. It promised to safeguard the interests of the non-Muslim communities and pointed out that matters touching on the rights of the Ottomans were not in the competence of the patriarch.

The CUP's Central Committee met on November 23 to discuss the Armenian question and decided:

1. To oppose European control of the proposed administrative reform in the eastern provinces of Anatolia;
2. To offer the Armenians eighteen to twenty seats in the next parliament provided that the seats were occupied by candidates supported by Armenian parties and had the CUP's approval. This offer satisfied the patriarch's earlier complaint.[75]

Tanin complained that the Armenians were making a grave error by wanting to give deputies who represented the Ottoman nation (millet) the quality of religious/ethnic representatives. In this way the Armenians would always remain a minority without the strength to achieve their demands. After much bargaining the differences between the CUP and the Armenian parties on the question of parliamentary representation had been settled by February 1914. The Armenians agreed to sixteen seats.[76]

In Vice-Consul Smith's opinion Armenian demands were not just political. He thought that the aspirations of the majority of Armenians of Van were economic rather than political, viewing the Armenians as "above all" a commercial people. He wrote that if the Porte constructed roads, placed a few motor boats on Lake Van, and hurried the construction of a railway, the country would then become "prosperous" and "the so-called Armenian question at least with regard to this vilayet, would to a great extent cease to exist with the advent of increased trade and prosperity."[77] Anticipating the need for roads in eastern Anatolia, the assembly passed a bill for the construction of roads from Diyarbakır to Bitlis; Erzurum to Keghi and Harput; and Erzurum to Rize as well as roads in the region of Saray and Thrace.[78]

Vice-Consul Smith reported that the Armenians in Van were better armed than the Kurds by 1914. They had obtained a number of modern rifles as well as the few old Martinis that the Sublime Porte distributed to each village. The villagers had obtained arms because of the general lack of security, which had resulted in the loss of life at the hands of "certain Kurdish brigands." The Dashnak had made the most of its opportunity, its policy being for the Armenians to hold their own against the Muslims should the necessity arise. "Also, the selling of arms in Van is a very profitable trade—a rifle or pistol being sold for nearly three times its real value—and this makes arming the villagers a not unattractive business for Dasnakist leaders who have taken it up."[79]

By 1914 Armenian nationalists seem to have arrived at a consensus on achieving reform in the eastern provinces. The Istanbul journal *Orient* (April 1912) published an article on Baghos Nubar Pasha's interview In *Le Réveil* (Beirut) regarding reform in the Ottoman Empire. He was the principal leader and spokesman for the Armenian cause around the world.

Nubar Pasha noted how the six Great Powers had reached consensus on the need for reform. But it was from Russia that "I found the most active assistance and the most direct." That was because Russia was most directly interested in seeing the Armenian problems solved at last. "For you know that this Power has in its Caucasian provinces two millions of Armenian subjects, who are at one heart with their Ottoman brothers. So it was Russia that took the initiative in the pourparlers negotiations with the Porte." Nubar Pasha emphasized that Armenian demands were based on international rights and on article 61 of the Berlin Treaty. The Great Powers were unanimous in recognizing the need for reform in Armenia. That was because they recognized that reforms were necessary for the peace of Europe. "The Powers are in fact agreed as to the future of

Turkey and their policy was based on the recognition of the 'absolute integrity of Asiatic Turkey.'"[80]

The reforms in Armenia, Nubar Pasha said, would be "purely and exclusively administrative" so as to maintain the fiction of Ottoman territorial integrity. The reforms would consist of the Porte choosing two European inspectors-general from second-class powers from a list of candidates nominated by the Great Powers. These inspectors-general would have extensive powers that would allow them to undertake the necessary reforms. Armenia had also been divided in a new way. Formerly it consisted of six provinces; now it was seven, with the addition of Trabzon:

1. Each inspector-general would head one division, consisting of three and four provinces, respectively.
2. A special gendarmerie would be organized whose personnel would be half Christian and half Muslim.
3. In the council of three vilayets, half of the members would be Christian, half Muslim; in the other four, representation would be proportional, based on the census. The use of the Armenian language would be allowed in public documents.
4. Taxes for public education would be divided proportionally between the communities.

The inspectors-general would preside over a commission that would regulate the agrarian question and "restore for a compensation the lands seized from the Armenians."[81]

The Unionists, who had rejected the idea of European control in November 1913, accepted Great Power proposals of reform in the eastern provinces in February 1914. The scheme adopted was virtually the same one that Nubar Pasha had spelled out in his interview, though the province of Trabzon was not included. The provinces of eastern Anatolia would form two zones, with an inspector-general for each chosen from among the minor states of Europe. The inspectors-general would supervise civil, judicial, and gendarmerie administrations in the zones and call in the army when the gendarmerie was insufficient to enforce measures. They would have the power to dismiss incompetent officials and to appoint their replacements.[82] Some critics in the Dashnak found the plan "unsatisfactory and far from the party's original plans." They only accepted it as "an initial step," presumably hoping to achieve independence later on.[83]

Nubar Pasha was right: under these reforms Ottoman sovereignty would be a fiction. Later the journalist Ahmed Emin (Yalman), witness to the era, observed that such reform under foreign supervision always meant "in the phraseology of the Eastern Question, a preliminary to amputation. The fiction of the maintenance of Turkish sovereign rights was, in every case, offered merely as an anaesthetic."[84] In February a Russo-Ottoman agreement was signed. Russia was given the authority to supervise the reforms that provided for the appointment of foreign inspectors-general as well as for the elected assemblies of representatives of the Christian and Muslim communities. André Mandelstam, the influential first dragoman of the Russian embassy, had drawn up the reform document.[85]

Before any reform could be implemented, a Kurdish rebellion led by Sheikh Molla Selim (aka Caliph Molla Selim), a powerful chieftain of Hizan, broke out in the Bitlis region on April 2, 1914. He was opposed to the projected scheme of reform; instead he called for the restoration of the Sharia, according to which he wanted to reform the world. The town of Bitlis was threatened, but the tribal forces were driven out of the town by armed Armenian resistance and Ottoman troops while Sheikh Selim took refuge in the Russian consulate. But 150 people were killed and the Armenian church was damaged before troops from Van and Muş arrived to restore order.

Tanin feared that this rebellion might lead to foreign intervention and the loss of these provinces. The pro-Unionist daily therefore called for decisive action by the government. An Armenian newspaper congratulated the government on its policy and wrote: "For us Armenians there is another fact still more significant and satisfactory, and that is that the Government has complete confidence in the Armenians. In fact, arms were distributed to the Armenians of Bitlis that they might defend the city against the reactionaries."[86]

As in the past, nothing revealed the weakness of the Unionist state more than its failure to protect the Armenians of Bitlis and its decision to arm them so that they could defend themselves against the onslaughts of the Kurdish tribes supported by Russia. For the Unionists it was a candid confession that their imperial state was too weak to defend its subjects and thereby perform the principal function of a modern state: to protect its citizens from tribal aggression.

For the moment the Kurdish tribes in the region had been subdued. A delegation of Kurds from the Siirt region, led by the newly elected Kurdish deputy Sheikh Nasreddin Efendi, came to the Sublime Porte and to the Unionist headquarters in Nuruosmaniye. He made a demonstration of loyalty to the caliphate and denounced the behavior of the

Kurds of Bitlis.[87] If the aim of the delegation was to appease the Unionists
and obtain amnesty for the rebels, it was an abject failure. The missionary
Mary D. Uline wrote from Bitlis that in May eleven Kurds found guilty
of taking a prominent part in the uprising had been hanged and their
bodies displayed in the city. Said Ali, one of the eleven, had been captured on April 13. He was said to have inherited a fortune and vast lands
from his father, Sheikh Celaleddin, who had fought in the Russo-Turkish
war of 1877–78. Said Ali had been forty years old and owned thousands
of gold liras besides six houses, 3,200 goats and sheep, 200 mules, and 100
horses:

> He lived in a great stone house, which with its surroundings
> formed a ziaret [*ziyaret*], a kind of shrine frequented by many trav-
> elers. He lived in splendor in the midst of mirrored walls, carved
> ceilings, rugs, and antiques. He had only four wives, not many for
> a man of his position, but he kept 200 servants … He was a bold
> chief whose power caused people to fear and tremble. He was a
> master robber who filled his coffers with gold and silver …
>
> Among other Kurdish victims was Shehabeddin, a sheikh
> whom the Kurds honored and worshipped. His very presence
> filled the atmosphere with a kind of sacredness, they said. They
> considered him so holy that they bowed and knelt before him … It
> was Shehabeddin whom the Kurds were to have made their king
> after "Turkistan" and "Haiastan" had been destroyed and the
> whole country had become Kurdistan.[88]

The remaining Kurds who were hanged were Mehmet Şirin (a brother
of Shehabeddin), Agha Khalil, Hoca Heiro, Hoca Babir, Ali Agha (a
former servant of Sultan Abdülhamid), Abdülmecid (a noted robber),
Gindi Agha, and Hurshid Agha. Molla Selim took refuge in the Russian
Consulate but was captured with his companion Hakik bin Hamo and
hanged after the Ottomans entered the war in November 1914. His last
words according to an official dispatch were: "The Russians will wreak
vengeance on you for me."[89]

In April the Porte appointed Louis Constant Westenenk and a Major Hoff as inspectors-general of the eastern provinces. Westenenk, a
Dutchman, was in his mid-forties but unfamiliar with Anatolia and the
Armenian question in the Ottoman Empire, having had years of military
experience in the Dutch East Indies. On April 30 Westenenk and Hoff,

a Norwegian, met the revolutionaries Armen Garo and Dr. Zavriev in Paris. The two Armenian revolutionaries briefed him on the problems in eastern Anatolian and "stressed the need for the inspectors to work with the Armenian Revolutionary Federation and the Church if they were to be effective in improving the conditions for the Armenians."[90]

Westenenk and Hoff arrived in Istanbul in early May to negotiate their contracts and receive their instructions from the Porte.[91] During the negotiations Westenenk refused to sign unless he was given authority sufficient to "be able to govern the country." The negotiations included meetings with interior minister Talat Bey and Count Leon Ostrorog, the chief Ottoman negotiator, "a Pole whom the Armenian revolutionaries had warned Westenenk was *plus turc que les Turcs.*" They would leave Istanbul after their powers had been settled and the bill for reform in the eastern provinces had been passed by parliament, which was to meet on May 14.[92]

Westenenk and Major Hoff returned to Europe after signing their contracts in order to interview candidates for their staffs. They returned to Istanbul during the first week of July and concluded negotiations with Talat in early August. Meanwhile, on July 13 the chamber voted 40,000 Turkish gold pounds for the salaries and expenses of the two inspectors-general and their staffs.[93] As Westenenk was preparing to leave for Anatolia, Istanbul heard the news of mobilization in Europe. Talat asked Westenenk to postpone his departure; Hoff had already left and was inspecting his provinces. Talat recalled Hoff, and "there the Armenian reform movement died," as Kaligian writes. The two men returned to Istanbul and waited; in late September they decided to return to Europe.[94]

3

The Ottoman Greeks, 1908–1914

Unlike the Armenian community, the Ottoman Greek community—called by the Ottomans "Rumlar" (Romans) in contrast to the Greeks of the kingdom, who were called "Yunan"—did not have a flourishing national movement. They had been part of the Eastern Roman Empire until they were conquered by the Ottomans in 1453. After the creation of the Kingdom of Greece in 1830 they depended on Athens to "redeem" them: Greece became an irredentist state. Meanwhile the Ottoman Greek millet simply wanted the church and the community to retain whatever privileges they had acquired as part of the millet system, in which they had shared sovereignty with the Sublime Porte. In order to protect their privileges, the Greek community under the leadership of their patriarch provided the most determined opposition to the constitutional regime. But Athens continued to strive to bring about union (*enosis*) with the Greek-inhabited regions ruled by Istanbul.

After the constitution was restored in July 1908, the Ottoman Greek community, like all the other communities, responded favorably in the hope that a liberal regime would carry out reform while not attempting to alter the status quo that guaranteed the traditional rights of the patriarch. But tensions increased after Bulgaria's declaration of independence (October 5), Austria's annexation of Bosnia-Herzegovina (October 6), and Crete's declaration of union with Greece (October 6).

The community led by the patriarch intended to pursue its interests through its deputies in parliament. When elections were held in Istanbul in November the Greeks complained of irregularities when they did not win the representation that they had expected. They demonstrated outside the Sublime Porte, the office of the grand vezir, protesting against irregularities and demanding that the elections be annulled. Before the election the authorities had demanded that the Greek community produce candidates and voters with proper Ottoman identity papers. But the Greeks had failed to do so. The government's precaution was to prevent Hellenic subjects, thousands of whom lived in the cities like Izmir and Istanbul, from voting.[1] In the nineteenth century thousands of Greeks, citizens of the Greek kingdom, had migrated to the Ottoman Empire, where they found better economic opportunities. They remained Greek citizens and could not be differentiated from the Ottoman Greeks. This was also a major problem that the Ottomans had to deal when it came to their non-Muslim subjects who had become protégés or "clients" of a Great Power by purchasing foreign citizenship from embassies.

The Greeks also raised objections when the law on military service came under discussion and military obligation was to be imposed on all Ottomans. The Greeks claimed that they wanted to be commanded by Greek officers if they had to perform military service. The Ottoman army at that time had no Greek officers, so that condition was impossible to meet. Therefore the Greek community wanted a postponement of this obligation until Greek officers became available. They also wanted Greek regiments to be separate from Muslim ones. The Porte refused to accept such arguments and claimed that all Ottomans must share the responsibilities of the state as well as its privileges.[2] But by 1910 Ottoman Greeks had begun to join the army along with other non-Muslims.

As early as April 1909 the Ottoman Greek elite hoped that the anti-Unionist counterrevolution in the capital would bring the Liberal decentralists led by Prince Sabaheddin to power. The Greek-language press in the capital as well as the Greek Political Association, founded largely by Greek deputies in the Ottoman assembly, both praised the rebellious soldiers of the Istanbul garrison who were bent on overthrowing the constitutional regime. *Neologos* wrote: "The Army [the soldiers of the Istanbul garrison who had mutinied] has won a great prize for patriotism and April 13, 1909. That date henceforth ought to be marked with no less splendor than July 24, 1908 [when the constitution was restored]. The Army was inspired yesterday by its love for the country and by no other sentiment." But the counterrevolution was crushed by the army from the Balkans. The Greek community had to continue biding its time. The soldiers in Athens, unsure of what the revolutions in Istanbul would mean for Greek ambitions in Macedonia, carried out their own revolt.[3]

Alexis Alexandris, the historian of the Ottoman Greek community of Istanbul, wrote that "by the 1910s Ottoman Greek self-assertion had become one of the most visible aspects of life in the empire. With their overwhelming emphasis on Hellenic studies, Ottoman-Greek schools overlooked the ideas of liberal Ottoman modernizers who envisaged a multiracial and cohesive Pan-Ottoman state."[4] Thus when the anti-CUP Liberal Union (Hürriyet ve İtilaf Fırkası) was founded in 1911, the party was received enthusiastically by the Greeks and other communities seeking autonomy or even liberation. That increased tensions with the Unionists, and the Porte expelled four prominent Greek journalists for promoting the disunion of peoples. Their real offense, wrote the *Times*, was to conduct propaganda on behalf of the opposition.[5]

Even after the 1908 election a tacit alliance had developed in parliament between the Liberals and most of the Greek deputies, twenty-six of whom were elected in 1908. Following the example of other minority communities, sixteen Greek deputies formed a "Greek party" (the Greek Political Association) during the 1909–10 parliamentary session.[6] They voted collectively on all issues and supported the opposition. The remaining ten deputies, who were either Unionists or independents, refused to take part in such a grouping. But the anti-Unionist alliance culminated with the electoral pact of 1911, when conservatives and liberal Turks, Arabs, Albanians, Armenians, and Greeks harnessed their energies to defeat the government in the election of 1912. In return for their support the newly formed Liberal Union (Entente Libérale, or the Freedom and Accord Party) promised to make important concessions to the Greeks. They promised to restore the traditional privileges of the patriarchate and decentralize the provinces in the empire.

Responding to these concessions that the Liberals were promising, the Unionists also sought an agreement with the Greek community. This desire to accommodate the communities first became apparent during the Turco-Italian War that broke out in September 1911. In response to the coordinated demand of the non-Muslims, the government officially recognized the privileges of the religious heads. In fact, through a government order of November 4, 1911, "the status of the non-Muslim millets was restored to what it had been before the revolution of 1908."[7]

The Unionists went even further to placate the Greeks in order to form an electoral agreement with the patriarchate. According to Paul Karolidis Efendi, the deputy for Izmir, the Unionists promised to increase Greek representation to forty-five and to appoint senator Aristeidis Georgantzoglou to the Ministry of Justice, "an unprecedented step in Ottoman history." In return the Unionists wanted the patriarch's support in the forthcoming elections. Under pressure from the Greek party, the patriarch "remained politically aloof"; Greek unresponsiveness to Unionist proposals backfired after the abysmal performance of the Liberals in the 1912 elections.[8]

The flight of Cretan Muslims to Izmir, where they formed a large community of refugees, increased tension between Greeks and Muslims. They "are a factor today which has to be seriously reckoned with. They have seldom failed to take a very prominent part in boycotts and in all labour questions." Cretan Muslims arrived "in a rather destitute condition. The presence of these refugees is giving rise to strong feeling, especially as they are spreading many, probably coloured, reports of the oppression which compelled their hurried departure from the island." The arrival of these refugees in western Anatolia was one of the factors responsible for the growth of anti-Greek sentiment.[9]

The leaders of the non-Muslim communities did not remain passive when they saw their interests under threat. In July the Greek and Armenian patriarchs and the Bulgarian exarch decided to act together against the proposed law to enroll Christians up to the age of forty-five in the army. This action deserved attention, noted the *Times* (July 12, 1912) "not only as a symptom of the widening gap between Christians and Muslim elements in the Empire, but also as an indication of the growing tendency of the Christian races to unite in defence of their common interest." The Porte backed down and allowed Christians "to redeem themselves of this duty by a payment" of fifty liras, to be raised to sixty liras.[10]

Even before the first Balkan war with Greece broke out in October, the question of Ottoman citizenship came up again when the Greek consulate in Izmir began to conscript Greeks residing in the empire into the Hellenic army. The *Near East*'s correspondent in Izmir wrote: "At the moment of writing—9 October 1912—war has not been declared with Greece, it was announced that evening that Greek subjects are enrolling as fast as possible at their Consulate for service in the Greek army...A Greek ship, seized and then released by the Turks, was chartered by the Greek Consul to take conscripts." The British Khedival Company's ship *Osmanieh* arrived with Greek conscripts from Istanbul en route to Greece.[11]

The outbreak of war in October 1912 aggravated the situation in Anatolia and dramatically increased tensions and violence. The government could do little to control the situation as Muslim refugees fled from the Balkans, bent on revenge and determined to seize Greek property in compensation for property that they had left behind. As a result of Ottoman defeats, 250,000 Muslims from the Balkans poured into Istanbul ahead of the retreating Ottoman armies. Their arrival created tension with the local Greeks, leading to forced Christian migration.

> More than 100,000 Muslims fled through Eastern Thrace before the advance of the Bulgarian army in 1912; some 10,000 left Macedonia in the same year; nearly 50,000 left Western [Bulgarian] Thrace in 1913 under the terms of the Turco-Bulgarian Treaty; and after this more that 100,000 Muslims evacuated Macedonia. The upheaval of Muslim communities in Europe led to reprisals on the Anatolian Christians. One motive was desire for revenge. There was also the practical motive that for every Christian family expelled it was possible to settle a Muslim refugee family in the empty accommodation.[12]

Ottoman losses in the Balkans were huge. The empire shrank from 169,845 to 28,282 km, losing 83 percent of its territory in Europe. Most of its Muslim population was left behind, though many fled to Anatolia. The empire "lost two-thirds of her European population." According to the Carnegie Commission, which later studied the impact of the wars in the Balkans, the Ottoman Empire was left with 83 percent of its territory, having lost 69 percent of its population in the European provinces.[13] To gain some perspective, Muslims were the majority community in the Ottoman Balkans before the war began, according to Justin McCarthy; they "were the largest single religious community."[14]

If the Ottoman Empire shrank as a result of war, the Greek kingdom expanded. By the Treaty of London (May 30, 1913) Greece acquired the major part of Ottoman Macedonia (including Kavalla), southern Epirus (including Janina), numerous Aegean islands, and the long-sought prize of Crete. Its territory increased by about 68 percent and its population from about 2.7 to 4.4 million, "in the latter respect gaining parity with Bulgaria...It became...a state important enough to figure positively in the calculation of the major powers."[15] After all the gains that his kingdom had made, King Constantine of Greece now had his eye on gaining Istanbul. A letter that C. F. Dixon-Johnson received from an Englishman residing in Greece reported "great talk of a third war and marching on Constantinople. King Constantine, not satisfied with calling himself 'Smiter of the Bulgars,' has assumed the title, Constantine the Twelfth in order to hold himself forth as the direct successor of that Constantine who lost the Byzantine throne."[16]

The Muslims in Anatolia strengthened the anti-Greek boycott, at the same time encouraging Muslim commerce. The purpose of the boycott was to discourage Muslims from buying from Greek traders and to support Muslim trade, thereby creating a Muslim-Turkish merchant class. Children's journals even tried to indoctrinate the young about the boycott by using lullabies.[17] The Greeks in western Anatolia continued to be persecuted in reprisal for the persecution of Muslims in Macedonia. Aubrey Herbert even raised a question about that issue in the House of Commons.[18]

Because of the territories that Greece had acquired in the war, especially the Aegean islands, friction between Istanbul and Athens became a major factor in the relations with the local Greeks. After the Treaty of London (May 30, 1913) the Istanbul press was up in arms against the cession of Sakız (Khios) and Midilli (Mitylene) to Greece. These islands, commanding the Dardanelles, were considered to be of vital importance for the defense of Istanbul and the empire. The press argued that western Anatolia would now be insecure. In his letter dated October 9, 1913, Dixon-Johnson agreed: "The possession of Chios, Mitylene, and the islands commanding the Dardanelles is of vital importance to the maintenance of the Turkish Empire. Without these islands the position of Turkey would be analogous to that of Great Britain with the Sicily Islands and the Isle of Wight in the hands of, say, Germany."[19] Ankara used the same strategic argument after the beginning of the Cyprus crisis in the 1950s. Dixon-Johnson was right: Sakız and Midilli provided a naval base in case of war and isolated Izmir. Limni (Lemnos) was of greater strategic value, with its natural land-locked harbor and dominant position that effectively commanded the Dardanelles.

Haris Vamvakas (aka Dr. Charles Vamvacas), formerly a deputy in the Ottoman parliament, responded to Dixon-Johnson's allegation and defended Greece, denying arguments regarding Greek *irredenta* in Asia Minor. He had been elected deputy for Serfice in Albania in the by-election of December 19, 1909, and served in the Ottoman assembly until the outbreak of the Balkan Wars. Using language less picturesque than Yorgi Boşo Efendi (George Bousios), who had said that "he was as Ottoman as the Anglo-French Ottoman Bank was Ottoman," Haris Vamvakas said that he felt more Greek than Ottoman. That was the position of virtually all the peoples in the empire, even Muslims, who also would have identified with their religion and the region or *memleket* (the country) that they hailed form. Only the few who belonged to the ruling elite—Muslim,

Greek, Armenian, Albanian, Jewish, or Arab—had adopted an Ottoman identity. In 1919 Haris Vamvakas wrote an article titled "Constantinople and the Straits," describing himself as a "recognised authority on Moslem law."[20] The two identities—Ottoman and Greek—were not mutually exclusive: Ottoman identity was dynastic and cultural, while Greek identity was essentially religious. Vamvakas would have known Ottoman Turkish and been culturally at home in Istanbul.

With Greek control over the islands so close to the mainland, the Unionists feared that the Greeks could easily land troops in the region of the Dardanelles on the western coast of Anatolia. Consequently the Porte armed not only the Muslim peasantry but also the Ottoman Jews of the region, who were considered totally loyal.[21] The Unionists' fear was not farfetched, for the Entente powers used the Greek islands to launch the Gallipoli campaign in 1915.

The friction over the islands led to a Greek-Ottoman naval race, further damaging the Muslim-Greek relationship. Captain Hüseyin Rauf Bey (who adopted the surname Orbay in 1934), who commanded the *Hamidiye* during the Balkan Wars, was sent to Rome and London in October 1913. His mission was to buy warships and engage foreign naval officers in order to strengthen the navy. A naval agreement with Britain was signed on October 29, 1912. Admiral Arthur Limpus, whose mission since March 1912 had been to reorganize the Ottoman navy, claimed that the agreement "may well be considered not only as the day of the renaissance of the Turkish navy...but more important still, a really vital nucleus for the building of up a large industry in Turkey."[22]

Despite the tensions with Athens, in Istanbul negotiations between the Unionists and the patriarch regarding Greek representation in the 1914 parliament continued. The Unionists approved the candidacy of Paul Karolidis and Emmanuel Emanualidis Efendi. But the patriarch, following the demands of the Armenian leaders, demanded three Greek deputies for Istanbul and proposed d'Eleco Pangiris Bey and d'Orphanidi Efendi as his candidates. He also demanded proportional representation.[23] If the elites of each millet in the empire chose their own representatives, *Tanin* commented the next day, the state would become a confederation. It would be necessary to have separate chambers for the Armenian, Greek, Turkish, and Arab elements, with different constitutions for each one.[24]

Despite war in the Balkans and the departure of Hellenic Greeks from western Anatolia, the presence of Greeks from the kingdom remained significant. The *Near East* correspondent reported in July:

There are still close on 1,500,000 Hellenes living under Ottoman rule. They hold Smyrna strongly, and are well established in the Aivali [Ayvalık] district, in parts of the Brusa [Bursa] vilayet, in Karamania [Karaman], and the Dardanelles district. Their numbers are increasing; they make money and save it, and are efficient as cultivators as their Ottoman rivals, and far more efficient as traders and fishermen; and, with the improvement of communications, they spread like patches of oil, following the new railways and making for all the important centers.[25]

Hilmi Uran, who became *kaymakam* (deputy governor) of Çesme (a town on the Aegean coast) in May 1914, felt that he had come to a foreign land. "The dominant language was Greek (*Rumca*); the Turks all knew Greek and spoke Greek with the Greeks. It was not possible to act in a different manner because the Greeks [probably Hellenic] did not know a word of Turkish and did not feel the need to learn." In Çesme the "Turks were crushed under the economic pressure of the Greeks who owned the wealth and property and controlled the commerce and industry. In the population of 45,000 the Greeks constituted 40,000 and the Turks were a minority."[26]

Though the 1914 parliament had no Liberal opposition as in 1912, the Unionists were still forced to negotiate with the Greek, Armenian, and Arab leaders. A few of the deputies elected in the 1914 were non-Unionists. Avoiding the mistakes of 1912, the CUP did not coerce the opposition and even permitted Independents to be elected. The election was completed in February 1914, and parliament met in March.

In early 1914 the Greek chargé d'affaires in Istanbul called the attention of his government to the grave repercussions of the policy of ridding the Asia Minor littoral of its Greek inhabitants. He wrote that this policy seemed to be directed by the fear that the Greek population might prevent quick mobilization of the Ottoman army and hinder speedy movement in the event of a new war. The persecution was also in retaliation for the uprooting of Muslim communities in Macedonia, Western Thrace, and the Balkans and actions of Turkish migrants resettled on Greek lands.[27]

Tanin (January 24, 1914) complained that the Great Powers had favored Athens on the question of the islands despite their geographical location so close to the mainland and the permanent danger that they posed to Anatolia. The tension between Athens and Istanbul held the Greek population hostage during the negotiations. The formation of the Fleet Committee (Donanma Cemiyeti) with the goal of collecting money for the dreadnoughts being constructed in Britain now involved and politicized ordinary people, introducing populism into the Ottoman-Greek equation. The government temporized, hoping to reach an agreement with Athens if a reasonable settlement was offered. But the boycott continued at the popular level, and a press campaign of "Turkey for the Turks" was forcing Greeks to leave Anatolia. "The authorities deny that there is any actual [official] boycott, and aver that they are simply trying to waken their own countrymen to carry on the business of the country instead of allowing it to remain in the hands of the Greeks. There are comparatively few Turks in business, and it is pointed out that considerable support is given to Greeks by Greece who have made all their money in Turkey."[28]

At the local level the boycott was becoming violent. Consul-General Barnham reported from Izmir that in small towns such as Manisa and in villages where the "ubiquitous Greek petty trader" was to be found the boycott had become violent: those entering non-Muslims shops were beaten. The position of the Greeks and Armenians in many districts had become untenable. "This boycott is the direct result of the Committee of Union and Progress influence, and Committee emissaries are everywhere instigating the People."[29]

While this was the situation in Anatolia, Muslims in the territories lost during the Balkan Wars were also being persecuted. The London branch of the All-India Muslim League, founded in 1908, protested their persecution and the destruction of Ottoman/Muslim monuments in territory conquered by the Balkan states. The Muslim League asked the British government to intervene to prevent further destruction. Meanwhile the Porte presented a note to the Great Powers declaring that 163,000 Muslims had fled from Greek tyranny and had sought refuge in the Ottoman Empire.

The *Near East*, reporting on the situation of Muslims in the Balkans, noted that the Greek government in Macedonia was unable to prevent the Greek peasantry from inflicting similar treatment on the poorer Muslims of certain districts and was itself expelling Bulgarophile Slavs with minimum consideration for their rights. The Bulgars were doing the same to the Greeks near Xanthi. A huge emigration was taking place, "amounting to something like 90,000 souls, from Servian territory; and the Bulgars in Eastern Thrace have been sent packing by the Turks." All the governments were engaged in what is today described as ethnic cleansing. According to Ambassador Hans von Wangenheim, Russian Ambassador

Giers had "declared that not the Greeks, but rather the Turkish peasants of Macedonia were victims of oppression at the moment."[30]

The Porte's note claimed that measures were being taken to protect local Greeks from the anger of the masses while the threat of war between Istanbul and Athens was in the air. In April the Porte proposed exchanging populations in the Anatolian littoral for Muslims in Macedonia. A commission convened in Istanbul to discuss this matter and met from May to December 1914. War was averted with the diplomatic intervention of the Great Powers. On June 28, 1914—the day of the assassination at Sarajevo—Greek prime minister Eleftherios Venizelos accepted the idea of the population exchange, but implementation was prevented by the outbreak of war in Europe.[31]

Despite diplomatic progress, tensions with the Greek community continued. The patriarch protested against the ill-treatment of Ottoman Greeks, while the Ottoman press reported on the persecution of Muslims. A minor crisis arose when the patriarch sent a note to the minister of justice, complaining about the boycott and other grievances. The minister found the language in the note disrespectful and offensive and returned it unanswered, asking the patriarch to alter its offensive wording. That angered the patriarch, and some of his flock even wanted him to break off relations with the Porte. But the patriarch refused, arguing that the rupture would not improve the temper of the Turks or the situation of the Greek community. Finally grand vezir Mahmud Şevket Pasha intervened, explaining that the minister had no desire to be offensive. The patriarch in turn withdrew the objectionable expressions, and the situation returned to normal.[32]

The Greek minister in Istanbul complained to the British ambassador about continuing persecutions, and Sir Louis Mallet raised the question with the interior minister. Talat assured him that "he had given the strongest orders for the cessation of Greek emigration, and had personally visited many of the Greek villages to reassure the inhabitants."[33] Andrew Kalmykov, the Russian consul in Izmir, wrote that Greeks were being expelled from the villages along the coast and from the interior, but few were being killed. No systematic killing of Armenians was occurring either, though the persecution of the Greeks proceeded relentlessly.[34]

The patriarch made further representation to the Porte concerning the situation of the Greek population in Thrace. The Porte gave assurances that measures would be taken to protect his flock. Meanwhile Greek delegates were sent to the region to persuade people not to emigrate en masse. The church is thought to have lost 50 percent of its population in the empire as a result of the Balkan Wars.[35] Athens's protests against the expulsion of members of Izmir's Greek colony proved effective: the Porte issued an order permitting the return of those affected. The Unionists were doing their best to be conciliatory and reduce tensions with Greece.[36] But the patriarch kept up the pressure and even threatened to leave for Russia: "His Holiness Kavakopoulos Germanos V (1913–1918) hinted that if Greek grievances were not remedied he may find that the presence of the Oecumenical Patriarch at Constantinople lacks justification. In that case the Patriarch might conceivably repair to Mount Athos but more probably he would retire to Russia, the Head of the Orthodox world."[37]

Some Unionists believed that the departure of the patriarch might actually be good for the empire. Others argued that his departure could have serious consequences, however, because the patriarch kept the community in line and prevented pro-Athens, Hellenic agitators from assuming the leadership. Unlike Athens, the patriarch was not interested in decolonizing the Ottoman Empire and redeeming its Greek population: he "kept alive the wish to restore the Byzantine Empire." The patriarch and his supporters were "encouraged by the decline of the Islamic Ottoman state" and hoped to achieve "a Greek/Christian take-over of the empire," reviving "a long cherished dream."[38] For its part the Porte was apprehensive that the patriarch's departure would undermine the friendly relationship that was developing between Istanbul and St. Petersburg. Tsarist Russia, after all, was a religious country, and the patriarch's treatment would only inflame opinion there.

The *Near East*'s Istanbul correspondent noted that that the main object of the Porte "affecting these transfers of population is a military one." After the loss of territory Ottoman Thrace was regarded as a "great frontier fortress, which should be held as far as possible by Moslems." The policy of the army was to encourage the Turks and to discourage the Greeks inhabiting all regions near the main roads, railways, and principal bridges. "Over 60,000 Greeks are said to have left Thrace, replaced by Muslims coming the other way."[39]

In the prevailing anti-Greek atmosphere the Unionists celebrated the conquest of Constantinople for the first time on May 29, 1914. On Ambassador Wangenheim's advice the capital's municipality "let the day pass in relative quiet." Not to be outdone, Istanbul's Greek community celebrated the birthday of King Constantine in early June. "The Greeks permitted themselves a noisy parade that included a salute to the German embassy." Meanwhile the patriarch continued to exert pressure on the Porte and on June 10 "closed down every school in Constantinople, as well as a number of churches." Two days later Athens presented a note to the Porte—which some interpreted as an ultimatum—protesting against the persecution of Greeks in the Ayvalık and Edremit regions. The note demanded the restoration of property and compensation for the victims of persecution.[40]

The Porte denied Greek allegations, though it accepted that certain "regrettable incidents" had occurred. These were "due to the incoming of thousands upon thousands of persons who, forced to quit territories occupied by the Balkan states, have come to settle in Turkey." The Porte in turn complained about the persecution of Turks in Macedonia. In his tours of western Anatolia interior minister Talat, accompanied by delegates of foreign embassies, found that Greek claims of persecution were fabrications. The Porte asked for reciprocity in Macedonia. Meanwhile the Greek patriarch had closed all churches and schools to protest the talk of war.[41]

When parliament opened in May the 1914 chamber consisted of some 240 deputies: about 200 Muslims, about 20 Greeks, 20 Armenians, and 3 Jews. It included fewer Greeks than before because the patriarch had refused to participate in the elections unless the Greek community was assured of a certain proportion of the representation. The CUP refused to give such an assurance. There was some saber rattling in the sultan's speech from the throne when he spoke of the events of 1912–13 and the courage of the army, the anti-Ottoman London Protocol, and the need to regain the Aegean islands through negotiations with Greece. He also spoke of the need for military reform, a strong navy, and more foreign experts in the administration.[42]

On his election as president of the chamber the speech of Halil Bey (Menteşe) was more bellicose and irredentist. He glorified the army and the nation (millet) and told parliament to remember Salonika, "the cradle of liberty," as well as Manastır, Kosovo, Üsküdar (Albania), Yanya, and Rumelia. Future generations must be brought up to remember that these places had to be rescued from their conquerors.[43]

Throughout June the Istanbul press talked of the danger of war with Greece. It issued the warning that the Dardanelles would have to be closed because Greece would blockade the Straits, injure trade, bring about European intervention, and be given guarantees for the possession of the islands. The islands, wrote the press, not the refugees, posed the real problem. Athens was using the refugees as a pretext to heighten tension. If the islands were ceded to Greece, the Porte might as well cede the province of Aydın. Greece would be able to make trouble through Ottoman

Greeks who worked for its interests. Greece wanted to act before Istanbul acquired the two dreadnoughts from Britain and was manipulating the refugee question. Again the press repeated that 250,000 Muslims had fled to the empire and that the Ottomans were the aggrieved party, yet Athens continued to make out that it was the victim.[44]

Dispatches from the German embassy reported that the new grand vezir, Said Halim Pasha (Şevket Pasha had been assassinated on June 11, 1913), called for an international conference to discuss Greek and Ottoman claims in Albania and the Aegean Islands. To prepare for such a meeting he wanted to send a mixed commission into Macedonia and Izmir to investigate the atrocity stories and to fix responsibility. "Rumania and France immediately expressed their interest, together with their assurances that Turkey had behaved toward Greece in good faith." Mehmed Talat arrived in Izmir on June 16 to investigate, returning to Istanbul in early July. In his conversation with Ambassador Henry Morgenthau, Talat was "very frank" about the expulsion of Greeks. Morgenthau wrote that he "seems determined to have Greeks of the countryside expelled, not the cities; he said the Greeks here pay taxes to Greek Government collected by Metropolitan."[45]

On Talat's return the *Near East* described the situation in Izmir as dangerous because the press there was said to have inflamed religious tensions, leading to the expulsion of Greeks by local petty officials, local Unionists, and Muslim refugees. Because of Turco-Greek differences over the Aegean Islands the populations of both communities had suffered. According to the *Near East*'s Izmir correspondent, the treatment of the Greeks had become a political and economic issue dividing the CUP. Talat Bey was strongly opposed to the chauvinistic policy supported by war minister Enver Pasha, minister of the Marine Cemal Pasha, and the vali of Izmir, Rahmi Bey. Talat went to the province of Aydın to put an end to the persecution, arriving on June 16, 1914, and spending about three weeks there. His arrival had also put an end to the anti-Greek press campaign.[46]

The *Near East* correspondent also examined the "Results of the Greek Emigration" for the local economy. Some 130,000 Greeks had emigrated from Anatolia and Thrace. Business had suffered. The emigration also affected harvesting the crops owing to the shortage of labor. The regions of Balıkesir and Trabzon had also suffered as a result of the anti-Greek campaign. Apart from emigration, rain had done much damage to agriculture in parts of Anatolia.

Negotiations between the Porte and the patriarch eased tensions. The patriarch agreed to reopen Greek schools and churches. He was swayed less by the interests of Athens than by the local Greeks, who had criticized him. The Russians are also said to have urged the patriarch to regard the Greco-Ottoman question purely from the church's point of view and "to abstain from demonstrations which can only injure the best interests of the most ancient branch of the Orthodox Church, the Mother Church of Eastern Christianity."[47]

When the patriarch appealed to Russia in July to protect his flock and sent missions to autocephalous Orthodox churches, the Istanbul press was most indignant. It asked rhetorically how Russia would react if the mufti of thirty million Muslims in Russia appealed to the caliph or if the Irish appealed to the pope. Turkey had permitted a commission of inquiry made up of dragomans of the foreign embassies to look into the condition of Greeks in Anatolia—let Greece do the same in Macedonia.[48]

Given the crisis in Europe, by July the Unionists had other concerns and therefore tried to restore stability in the region by putting an end to the boycott. The Porte issued a communiqué to the provincial authorities instructing them to end the boycott and "to prevent by force everything that has caused serious discord to arise between the various elements of the Ottoman nation." Those suspected of "preaching a boycott propaganda, publishing or circulating false news, tending to arouse ill-feeling between different races... will be tried by court-martial and severely punished if found guilty."[49]

The Ottoman state was so weak that (though the provincial administration had been ordered to desist from the boycott) local Muslims disregarded the order and continued to enforce a severe boycott and to intimidate local Greeks.[50] Even in western Anatolia Istanbul's writ did not carry much weight. How reliable the account of the "Occasional Correspondent" was is not clear. But we know that the while the CUP controlled the situation in the capital, it did not do so in the provinces. If the situation was serious in western Anatolia, where banditry had become a major problem (especially after the Balkan Wars when disbanded soldiers became outlaws), the situation was worse in the east. There the tribal chiefs were virtually autonomous and out of control. Moreover, even local Unionists did not obey instructions from the Central Committee in Istanbul and acted according to their self-interest. That had been true since 1908 and remained true until 1918. Before discussing the situation of the Armenians and the Greeks as it developed after the "July crisis," the position of the Albanians, Ottoman Jews, and Arab elites has to be considered.

4

The Albanians

In the Ottoman Empire the Albanians did not constitute a millet. They were divided by tribal and religious affiliations (Muslim, Greek Orthodox, and Roman Catholic) and therefore belonged to the religious communities. They could even boast of the fact that they had become Ottoman before the people of Istanbul and much of Anatolia, having been conquered in 1389. The Albanians had played a prominent role throughout Ottoman history. Before Ottoman conquests Latin Catholics lived to the north of the Shkumbi River and Greek Orthodox to the south. After the conquest Istanbul was hostile to the Catholic north because it was allied to the papacy and the West, while the Orthodox Church was part of the Greek millet system, with its patriarch residing in Istanbul, and was part of the Ottoman administrative structure. This situation deteriorated after 1774 and the Treaty of Küçük Kaynarcı, which permitted Russia to intervene on behalf of the Orthodox.[1]

The Tanzimat reforms (1839–76) had an impact in the province of Albania. The reforms marked "the transition from the administrative system of *millets*, which divided the population according to religion, to a new uncertain reality, where the main criteria of self-identification became linguistic and cultural."[2] Around 1848–49 the Porte decided to apply the new regulations to Albania and began to impose direct taxes and compulsory military service. The nobles and the general public alike resented these measures. That led to a general uprising and turmoil throughout the region.[3]

Developments among other national groups in the Balkans also had an impact on the Albanians. Interest in the Albanian language grew after the formation of the Albanian League (the League of Prizren) in 1878, formed as a protest against the cession of territory to Montenegro and Greece by the Treaty of Berlin. That marked the beginning of a growing national sentiment and an awareness of Ottoman weakness. The league took advantage of the situation and called for greater autonomy, the opening of more schools, and the use of the Albanian language with its own script. In 1879 the Society for Albanian Publication was set up in Istanbul and the "Constantinople Alphabet" became widely used.[4]

At first the Sublime Porte encouraged Albanian nationalism as a counterforce against Greek and Slavic expansion in the Balkans. But soon both the league and the society were suppressed. The Porte, like any imperial power, then used the religion card of "divide and rule" and exploited the gulf between Muslim and Christian Albanians. The Albanian language was banned, and schools were closed down. The Greek patriarch backed this policy, while British and American missionaries opposed it because the Foreign and British Bible Societies supported the new language. Austria-Hungary also supported Albanian nationalism as a counterbalance against the Slavs.

In October 1896 Albanian nationalists petitioned the Great Powers. They asked for the establishment of schools in which the official Ottoman language would be taught alongside Albanian and requested that government officials in Albania know the Albanian language.[5]

Although adjutant-major Ahmed Niyazi (1873–1913), one of the heroes of the constitutional revolution, was Albanian, he probably thought of himself as primarily Ottoman. Some Albanians were also ardent supporters of Sultan Abdülhamid, mostly irregulars known as *bashi-bozouks*. When Şemsi Pasha, sent from Istanbul to crush the rebellion in Manastır, was assassinated by a constitutionalist, the British consul reported that "there was great excitement in the town, especially as the probable action of the late General's own men, a body of some 30 Albanians armed with Mausers and apparently dressed as soldiers, but I am assured, not belonging to the army. There are, of course, good reasons to fear that this band of Bashi-Bozouks might wish to avenge their master."[6] Albanian soldiers, along with Arabs, were also part of Abdülhamid's palace guard. After the revolution of 1908, when the government wanted to replace them with troops from Anatolia loyal to the new regime, the sultan's loyalists drove them out. Troops from Macedonia had to be sent in to subdue the Albanians and Arabs, and Albanian troops were sent to Kosovo.[7]

The constitutional revolution gave an impetus to the Albanian movement. "During the first ten months of the revolution, sixty-six Albanian cultural and political clubs were formed for the defence of Albanian rights. Apart from this nationalist element, there were also 'traditionalists' who demanded that their privileges from the days of Abdülhamid be maintained."[8] Most Albanians disliked centralization and the modernization of the administration because this meant that they would have to pay taxes and be liable for military service like all Ottomans, while also surrendering their arms.

The announcement of a census was seen as a threat to Albanian privileges and a prelude to obligatory military service. When the governor ordered in June 1909 that a record book of property be kept to serve as a basis for taxation, that led to rebellion. The central government in Istanbul began to institute a policy of repression. The rebels responded by forming a union to oppose the Young Turk regime, which they believed was bent on suppressing "their age-old rights and traditions."[9]

The aims of the constitutional revolution were still unknown, but the Albanians believed that they would "enjoy the same rights as the other peoples of the Turkish [Ottoman] empire." One of these rights was the use of a national language. Meetings were held between November 14 and 22, 1909, to decide which alphabet to adopt. They decided to use the "Constantinople alphabet." This decision "contributed to making Moslems and Christians more conscious of their common patrimony."[10] This decision went against the CUP's aim to unify the empire. Using Islam as the vehicle, Istanbul began an extensive propaganda campaign in favor of the Ottoman script.

On July 23, 1909, the CUP organized an Ottoman-Albanian Constitutional Commission (Osmanlı Arnavut Meşrutiyet Komisyonu), which held its congress in Dibir/Debra. The congress decided that while Albanian would be taught in schools, the use of the alphabet would be a matter of choice.[11] As İbrahim Hakkı Pasha told an Albanian deputy: "The government considers the desire to adopt Latin characters as the first step to be detached from Turkey... The government must do everything, and will do everything, to prevent the adoption of the Latin alphabet."[12]

In the Albanian province the opposition to centralization soon became even more militant. In early April 1909 a revolt broke out in the İpek region, forcing Istanbul to declare martial law. The local population not only supported the demand for the Albanian language but also opposed the "octroi" tax levied on goods brought into Albanian towns. Negotiations led to a temporary suspension of hostilities. İsmail Kemal, the Albanian deputy for Vlora and a spokesman for Albanian autonomy, defended the rebels and their cause in the chamber, arguing that they were not reactionaries. But he pointed out that they did not appreciate a constitution because the new regime had brought no benefits to the province.[13] On April 26 a party of Albanian deputies visited the grand vezir and urged the government to dispatch a special mission with a view to ending the fighting. But Kamil Pasha declined, declaring that such an act would be seen as a sign of weakness.[14] By the end of April what had seemed like a minor skirmish had developed into a full-fledged rebellion.

On May 31 the Democratic Club, an Albanian political body in Manastır, was closed down and some of its members were arrested. The club was denounced as a reactionary organization for supporting the rebels. The CUP grew apprehensive about the growing popularity of this body in Macedonia and its criticism of the regime's policies. This group made no secret of its opposition to the government and the CUP's monopoly of power.[15] In November 1908 an Albanian National Congress, representing Muslims, Catholics, and Orthodox, met in Manastır. Discontent in Albania continued throughout 1909 and into 1910, leading to rebellions in 1910 and 1911. When the CUP's annual congress met in Salonika in October 1910 Albanian delegates were conspicuous by their absence.[16] That was a reflection of the ongoing troubles. The *Times* (April 25, 1911) reported calls for Austrian intervention in Albania. The Austrian Catholic organs, the *Vaterland* and the *Reichspost*, continued to urge Austro-Hungarian intervention, direct or by proxy, on behalf of the Catholic Malissori also in revolt. Initially the Porte had been fighting Muslim Albanians. But the religious factor had been introduced with the threat of foreign intervention, especially if Şevket Turgut Pasha carried out his threat of burning Catholic villages unless they surrendered.

Şevket Turgut Pasha did not burn down Catholic villages, no foreign intervention occurred, and the struggle continued. But the Ottomans suffered reverses even more severe than in the insurrection in Yemen. The political position of the CUP weakened, while the Liberal opposition became stronger. As a result the Porte backed down and made important concessions, granting permission to use the Latin alphabet in Albania. Martial law was also abolished.[17]

In June Sultan Reşad, accompanied by his two sons, the grand vezir, and the ministers of the interior and the Marine, began a tour of Macedonia. His purpose was to conciliate the Muslim population and end the revolt. He arrived at Salonika on June 7, Üsküb on June 11, and Priştina and Kosovo on June 16. The sultan attended the Friday Selamlık prayer service on the plain of Kosovo. They celebrated the Ottoman victory of 1389 over the Serbs by the tomb of Sultan Murad I, praying with an estimated 100,000 Albanian clansmen. The sultan announced an amnesty for all the insurgents of the past year's rebellion. The rebels were now divided on the basis of religion. The next day in İşkodra Şevket Turgut Pasha followed suit and announced an amnesty for all insurgents who surrendered in the next ten days, promising to reconstruct all houses that had been destroyed or damaged during military operations. The Albanians were also promised that there would be no interference with their customs and institutions. Having made these concessions Sultan Reşad returned to Istanbul on June 24 via Manastır and Salonika.[18] The religious ceremonies during the tour, especially the one at Kosovo, were designed to reawaken Islamic sentiment, because "Ottoman patriotism was on the wane in Albanian hearts."[19] Slobodan Milosevich would do something similar in 1989 in order to stir up Serbian national sentiment.

The Ottoman press described the sultan's tour as an unqualified success and claimed that the prestige the CUP had lost since the revolution had been restored. The committee played a prominent role in all functions and receptions and made the greatest effort throughout the tour to present the sultan as a potent factor in the empire. Its intention was to give a lie to the assertion being generally made against the committee that its policy was aimed at debasing the authority of the sultan and caliph.

But all was not well. Wilfred Scawen Blunt, a keen observer of Ottoman affairs, noted in his diary (June 11, 1911): "There is more trouble brewing in Albania, the Catholic Mirdots having joined the rebellion, and the Austrian Govt. having issued a warning of a moderating kind to Turkey." But Blunt noted that Austria's warning need not be taken seriously, given Germany's growing support for Turkey.[20] Once again the Ottomans feared foreign intervention on behalf of Albanian Catholics, protected by Vienna. The anticipation of European intervention made the Albanian insurgents more extreme in the belief that outside help was around the corner if only they kept up the pressure. The Ottomans, however, fearing intervention, continued to make concessions to the insurgents.

At the beginning of July 1911 the Porte offered reparations for damages inflicted by the army, allowed some of the Malissori to retain their arms, and offered concessions on military service, education, and taxation. The insurgents regarded the concessions as a trap and refused to disarm or submit without adequate international guarantees.[21]

In turn the Albanian nationalists made seven demands:

1. A promise that their religion, customs, and traditions would be guaranteed.
2. The recognition of their national existence, free elections, and the

right to found and maintain schools in which their own language would be taught under their own religious chiefs.

3. The reorganization of the administration of the province.
4. The nomination of Albanians to the higher administration and judicial posts.
5. The appointment of an inspector-general for the application of reforms.
6. The use of Albanian as an official language.
7. Special revenues and financial control of their province.[22]

On June 23 the Albanians gave a memorandum to the Porte that had been approved by a meeting held in Gerçe, Montenegro, under the leadership of İsmail Kemal and Luigi Garakugi. They again demanded provincial autonomy and a guarantee by the Great Powers. The Porte rejected these demands but made more concessions in August 1911. As a result a compromise agreement was signed. For the moment an uneasy truce had been established. The Albanians were allowed to retain their arms in the villages but not in towns and bazaars. They could use their language, and the Latin alphabet could be taught in schools. Districts that had suffered from the rebellion were given a tax remission for two years. The Porte provided funds for rebuilding.

Hacı Adil, a prominent Unionist leader and member of parliament, was sent to Macedonia with two foreign experts, R. W. Graves and Lieutenant-Colonel Foulol, both well versed in Macedonian affairs. They were accompanied by a Turkish staff of officials who were also familiar with the region. Hacı Adil's powers were those of a plenipotentiary: the cabinet—including the War Minister—had delegated all power to him, allowing him to implement all remedial measures on the spot. He had also been invested with the power to dismiss or suspend the higher provincial officials, hitherto only done by imperial decree. Hacı Adil's program included the reorganization of the gendarmerie, the improvement of communications and the construction of schools, the granting of concessions to Albanian tribes, and the settlement of the land question. The tour was planned to last for three months because Hacı Adil himself wanted to supervise and inspect the progress of work that he had authorized.

Albanian Muslims, long part of the Muslim millet, also copied the non-Muslim nationalities and began to make demands and seek support from Europe for their aspirations. The ambitious İsmail Kemal, representing the Muslims, presented a memorandum in May to the consuls of the Great Powers and to the Porte. It demanded that the boundaries of Albania be established; that the Albanian flag be recognized by the Porte; that an Albanian notable be appointed governor of the province; that Albanian officials replace Turkish-speaking officials; that Albanian be adopted as the official language of the province; and that these reforms be guaranteed by the Great Powers. The memorandum added that Albania would henceforth refuse to pay taxes or furnish fresh troops for the army; before the 1908 revolution the Albanians had been exempted from both obligations. Sultan Abdülhamid had permitted the Albanians to carry arms, so the tribes naturally resented disarmament being enforced by the constitutional regime. The Albanian notables claimed that the new regime was trying to undermine their traditional rights.[23]

The Albanians took advantage of the state of turbulent politics in Istanbul and the weakness of the Ottoman state. The war with Italy threw political life into even greater turmoil. Responding to the mutiny in the Manastır garrison in which twelve officers and sixty-three soldiers had deserted, claiming that the government was selling out the country, on July 1 the assembly passed a bill forbidding officers to take part in politics.[24] But that did not prevent the anti-CUP movement from continuing to grow.

The increasing hostility between the Unionists and Liberals had found an echo in Albanian politics as well. In his report of June 29, 1912, Vice-Consul Peckham reported from Üsküb that pro-Liberal and anti-CUP Albanians had issued a manifesto, which declared: "The whole civilized world, and particularly the Ottoman world, knows the service rendered by the Albanians for the establishment of the Ottoman Constitution. The Albanians are, and always will be, firmly attached to the Caliphate and the Ottoman Fatherland with a fidelity which nothing can shake. If they have raised the flag of revolt it is not simply in the interests of Albania, but to save the Fatherland." The Albanians had taken up arms, the manifesto claimed, because the Young Turk government's "accursed and execrable policy" would lead sooner or later to an invasion of the empire. A "few ignorant upstarts" were sending the great Ottoman Empire "along the road to ruin with the speed of lightning." The notables understood that they could do nothing to correct the situation and therefore found it necessary to act in accordance with local needs.[25]

To prepare the ground for military intervention, on July 14 officers and civilians from the Djakova Municipality sent an anti-CUP telegram to the sultan, declaring:

The incapable persons who have composed the Cabinet during the past four years have driven the Empire to the verge of liquidation. The clique recently used the power of the government to dissolve parliament in order to form a new Chamber that permits it to take uncontrolled possession of the country. You, as Khalif, must observe the march of the Empire towards catastrophe. You have the power immediately to dissolve parliament and command the re-election of Deputies in accordance with the desire of the population. If you continue to remain inactive and indifferent to our demands, while there is yet time to apply a remedy, the day is not far distant when you will see Albania, plunged into bloodshed, pass under the protection of another state.[26]

The rebellion led to military intervention. The Said Pasha cabinet was forced to resign on July 17, 1912, marking the eclipse of the CUP. In his memoirs Cemal Pasha wrote that the activities of the Halaskar Zabitan Grubu, the "Group of Savior Officers" who brought down the government, had promoted such anarchy in the army that the troops in Albania, Izmir, and Çanakkale were in a state of revolt.[27] The new Liberal, anti-Unionist cabinet led by Gazi Ahmed Muhtar Pasha, a nonpolitical general popular with the army, faced difficult choices: to end the war with Italy, which was leading to financial ruin; pacify the Albanians; remedy sedition in the army in Macedonia; replenish the treasury; and take diplomatic measures against the Balkan states whose activities were beginning to cause anxiety.

The Ahmed Muhtar Pasha cabinet took measures to appease the Albanians and end their rebellion. Negotiations began on August 3. Priştineli Hasan Bey, representing the Albanians, demanded a program of reform similar to the one that had been drawn up in June 1911. The program included the inauguration of a special system for the administration of justice in the province as well as eleven other points. The military service of Albanians was not to be affected in time of peace in the European provinces. The demands also included the nomination of capable, honest, and experienced functionaries who spoke Albanian; the creation of agricultural schools in Yanina, Manastır, Scutari, and Kosovo similar to the one existing in Salonika; more schools devoted to science and religion; the teaching of several languages in schools; the construction of roads and railways; absolute liberty to set up private schools; the reorganization of *nahiyes* (administrative subdivisions of a province);

the impeachment of İbrahim Hakkı Pasha and Said Pasha; a general amnesty; and the restitution of arms to Albanians. The Porte accepted ten of the twelve demands, rejecting only impeaching the former grand vezirs and restoring arms to the Albanians.[28] But now that the Unionists had been overthrown and the Liberals were in power they were in no mood to meet all Albanian demands, and negotiations broke down.

Despite the concessions the Albanians launched another rebellion, determined to win even more from the Porte. But the Porte responded by sending in the army, which captured the town of Üsküb on August 12. Fearing the Balkan alliance of Greece, Montenegro, Serbia, and Bulgaria, the Albanians and the Porte agreed to compromise and limited themselves to the concessions that had already been made. With the outbreak of war in the Balkans on October 8 and the rout of Ottoman armies that followed, however, the Albanians took unilateral action. On November 28, 1912, an assembly of Albanian notables proclaimed the independence and neutrality of Albania. After constituting a provisional government, they hoisted the Albanian flag, nominating İsmail Kemal as their president. The Austrians supported the creation of Albania in orders to prevent the Serbs from acquiring a port on the Adriatic.[29] These decisions were made during the battle at the Çatalca lines when Istanbul was in danger of falling to the Bulgarian army. The battle began on November 17, 1912, but the Ottoman army held its ground and continued to hold the lines until April 16, 1913. Meanwhile the Serbs had captured Priştine (October 22), Üsküb (October 26), and Manastır (November 18).

During negotiations at the London conference in March–April 1913 to settle the Balkan crisis, the ambassadors of the Great Powers are said to have offered autonomy for Albania under Ottoman sovereignty. But grand vezir Mahmud Şevket Pasha categorically declined the offer, declaring that five hundred years of such sovereignty had merely involved his country in frequent, expensive, and disastrous campaigns.[30] The London conference went on to create an independent Albania stretching from Montenegro to Greece, marking the emergence of a new state and nationality. The Porte recognized the fait accompli and decided to make the best of a bad situation.

After the Balkan Wars Istanbul also required an ally in the region in order to forestall the ambitions of Serbia, Bulgaria, and Greece. A strong Albania could serve such a purpose admirably, especially if led by a Muslim head of state. The Porte proposed Ahmed İzzet Pasha, an Albanian general who had served as Ottoman minister of war. To popularize the idea an Ottoman delegation of Albanian origin was sent to Albania in July 1913. İsmail Kemal even signed a secret agreement with Istanbul for a joint attack on Serbia and Greece. When this agreement was discovered, he was forced to resign on January 22, 1914.[31]

The political situation in the new Albania remained unstable. The French had predicted that the new state was not viable and had opposed its formation, along with Russia. France and Russia wanted to split Albania between Greece and Serbia; but Vienna, supported by Berlin, opposed that and got its way. Thus Vienna became the de facto protector of Albania.[32] There was tension and conflict between the feudal pro-Ottoman north dominated by Muslim chiefs and the more advanced south, where Muslims and Christians lived together. The south talked of expropriating the landlords and executing land reform. Esad Pasha, at the head of northern forces, captured the town of Elbasan from southern troops. Amid this confusion İsmail Kemal intrigued with Istanbul to bring in a Muslim prince to replace the prince of Wied, the Great Powers' candidate. Greek bands remained active in Lower Albania, though the Greek army had evacuated the region.

Although the province of Albania had been lost to the Ottoman Empire, for the moment the Unionists could not simply forget it. For one thing, Albanian refugees who had fled Greek and Serbian occupation were settled in Anatolia, a community that came into existence and continues to exist to this day. When Halil Bey was elected speaker, he made his inaugural speech in parliament on May 19, 1914, and asked Ottomans to remember Salonika, "the cradle of liberty," as well as Manastır, Kosovo, and Üsküdar in Albania, Yanya, and all of Rumelia. Future generations, he said, must be brought up to remember that these places had to be rescued from their conquerors.[33] But this region had been lost, and no Ottoman government ever made a claim to it again.

Albania had become a European concern. Vienna had succeeded in having the prince of Wied appointed the head of state. But the new state was unstable. At the end of June 1914 the prince was forced to flee to Vienna to find troops to restore him to his recently acquired throne.

5

The Greeks and Armenians, 1914–1918

Throughout June and July 1914 Greek-Ottoman tensions continued over persecutions in western Anatolia and Macedonia as well as over the islands. The result was an acrimonious naval race. The "Letter from Athens" of July 1 reported that the Greek government had received formal authorization from the United States to purchase the *Idaho* and the *Mississippi*. These two ships were expected to assure Greek supremacy in the Aegean until the *Osman* and *Reşadiye*, being delivered by Britain, were added to the Ottoman fleet. The letter also reported that the exchange of populations was being discussed between Athens and Istanbul. A week later the situation had improved from the very "critical situation a fortnight ago." The Porte proposal for a mixed commission for the exchange of properties in Macedonia and Asia Minor had been accepted, and "everything points to a more peaceful future."[1]

The Porte's principal concern during the world crisis was to join one of the two blocs in order to end its diplomatic isolation. After negotiation with Britain, France, Germany, and Russia, the signing of the secret treaty with Berlin on August 2 ended the Porte's nightmare. With the outbreak of war in Europe, the Young Turks, like the other powers, also suffered from a "short-war illusion" and were determined to stay out of the war, as was Athens.[2] But the Ottoman-German alliance added another weapon to Germany's arsenal: propaganda.

The Triple Entente—Britain, France, and Russia—ruled over substantial populations of Muslims in their colonies. Berlin, with Istanbul's help, intended to exploit pan-Islamic propaganda in Persia, India, and North Africa as well as Central Asia, where pan-Turkism could also be exploited. Russia, however, had acquired a reputation as the "prison of nationalities."[3] The German General Staff naturally wanted to adopt the strategy of mobilizing nationalities against the tsarist regime. Berlin encouraged rebellions among the border peoples. Poland was chosen as the first target for revolution. Berlin also encouraged rebellion among the Finns, Russian Jews, and minorities in the Caucasus. Even Vienna expected the return of exiled revolutionaries from Russia who would then be used to further Allied aims. Germany, for example, supported Ukrainian nationalists, who were sent to Istanbul to organize their movement closer to home.

Russia suspected the loyalty of the Georgians, Ukrainians, and Armenians, owing to their highly developed sense of nationalism and socialist ideas; the entire region had been deeply affected by the revolution of 1905. Russia had been hostile to Armenian nationalists and other revolutionary groups. But the policy began to change in 1911 due to the need for Armenian support in a possible Russo-Ottoman clash.[4] It was therefore natural for Berlin to want to exploit Armenian nationalism in 1914 to subvert the Russian war effort.

Once the possibility of a short war no longer existed, "every warring State sought to enlist the help of disaffected peoples." Germany's military attaché in Washington, Franz von Papen, spoke to Sir Roger Casement, a British diplomat and Irish nationalist, about achieving independence with German help: "Casement suggested...the setting up of an Irish brigade that would fight alongside Germany."[5] On November 28, 1914, Casement wrote a letter to Eoin Macneil, an Irish nationalist in Dublin, which was intercepted by Britain's secret service, the MI5. Casement wrote: "The enemy [the British] are hiding the truth. The Germans will surely, under God, defeat both Russia and France and compel a peace that will leave Germany stronger than ever... India and Egypt will probably both be in arms." He concluded: "We may win everything by this war if we are true to Germany. And if we do not win today we ensure international recognition of Irish nationality and hand an uplifted cause for our sons."[6]

Most Unionists were opposed to the idea of exploiting nationalism because such a policy was likely to boomerang on their own empire. They were even reluctant to use the weapons of pan-Islam or jihad in their multireligious empire and had refrained from using these weapons against the Italians and the Balkan coalition. But being junior partners, if not clients, and totally dependent on Berlin, they were forced to go along with the German strategy. Initially they resisted the temptation, as an episode in September 1914 illustrates.

While the Unionists were still neutral, and not yet totally under German control, in September 1914 Berlin brought a delegation of Indian nationalist revolutionaries recruited from students in Europe and North America. Germany's goal was to use this group to instigate revolution

in British India, where a confident national movement had emerged by
1914. The delegation, made up of Hindus, Muslims, and Sikhs, was totally
secular and nationalist. While the Unionists were willing to support the
delegation, they insisted that its propaganda be pan-Islamic and not nationalist. They had their way: the Indian delegation agreed to use only Islamic propaganda. But Har Dayal, the leader of the delegation, disagreed,
resigned, and returned to Berlin.[7]

Berlin was the first to use the propaganda weapon against the Entente
in neutral America. At the beginning of the war the tsarist regime carried
out a wholesale deportation of Jews from the western war zone, the Pale
of Settlement, which included Russian Poland, Lithuania, Belorussia,
most of Ukraine, Crimea, and Bessarabia. The expulsions "en masse assumed such proportions that they were said to overshadow the Spanish
exodus. By December 1915 the figure reached 2,700,000 and five months
later 3,300,000."[8] Russia's persecution aroused bitter anti-Russian hostility among the Jews throughout the world, especially in America. Russia's
action and the hostility that was generated led to France and England
having to bear the odium for their allies' behavior. As Russia's allies "they
were reproached for tolerating the persecutions of the Jews and labeled as
Russia's indirect accomplices."[9]

Britain, embarrassed by Germany's anti-Entente propaganda in
America, enlisted Arnold Toynbee to counter the effects of German propaganda. The propaganda was thought to be dangerous in neutral America, where it would have a detrimental impact on its substantial Jewish
population. Toynbee wrote:

> In Whitehall it was recognized that some counter-measures must
> be taken quickly by H.M.G., and opportunely, H.M.G. was pre-
> sented by the enemy with counter-propaganda ammunition. At
> the very time when the Russians had been committing barbari-
> ties against the Jews, the Turks had been committing considerable
> worse barbarities against their Armenians. If the Russian barbar-
> ities were telling against Britain and France, would not Turkish
> barbarities tell against Germany and Austria-Hungary? The line of
> reasoning in Whitehall lay behind H.M.G.'s application to produce
> a Blue Book in what the Turks had been doing to the Armenians.[10]

In fact, there had been no Ottoman persecution or violence against
Armenians since the counterrevolutionary violence of April 1909. The

perpetrators of that violence had been severely punished: some Muslims were even hanged. In 1914 the Porte had even armed and protected the Armenians of Bitlis against an attack by Kurdish tribes instigated by Russia (see chapter 2).

Despite Toynbee's efforts and Lord Bryce's reputation in Washington, Toynbee notes that the Blue Book, published in 1916, did not have the same effect as German propaganda did in America. Toynbee concluded: "So, as far as World Jewry was concerned, H.M.G.'s Armenian Blue Book was predestined to fall flat; the Armenians in the United States were still not a sufficiently strong electoral bloc or lobby to have great influence on US policy."[11] Britain's propaganda may not have had the desired effect, but it led to a diplomatic incident: the Ottoman ambassador was declared persona non grata and asked to leave the United States. The ambassador was Ahmed Rüstem Bey (aka Alfred de Bilinski), a Polish convert to Islam who had only assumed his duties in June 1914. He has defended his country and spoken openly about the persecution of the black population in America, causing an uproar in the State Department and the press.[12]

While these events were taking place in Europe and America, the Armenian Revolutionary Federation held its Eighth World Congress in Erzurum in August. Before completing its agenda the congress adjourned because of the outbreak of war. But a committee of nine was formed to complete its work. While this committee was meeting, Dr. Bahaeddin Şakir and Ömer Naci arrived in Erzurum as the representatives of the Unionist government. They met for three days with Rosdom, Agnouni, and Vramian, three Armenian revolutionaries. The CUP representatives wanted to know what the Dashnak position would be concerning the two possible developments that they foresaw. The first was the invasion of the Ottoman Empire by Russia. The second was an Ottoman advance or Ottoman support for a Caucasian rebellion against Russia. The Dashnak revolutionaries responded that in the first case the party would obviously defend the sovereignty of the Ottoman Empire, including its territory and its constitutional laws. That is said to have made the CUP representatives very happy, especially Şakir. Concerning the second case, the Armenian revolutionaries stated that they could not answer without more information, noting that it was only serendipitous that the two parties were even discussing the issue.[13]

After lengthy discussion the two Unionists disclosed that the government had decided to take advantage of what they hoped would be the

German defeat of France and Russia to take care of their own unfinished business. First, they would come to an accord with Bulgaria to restore Turkish-inhabited lands to Macedonia and then make Macedonia independent of Serbia. Second, they wanted to come to an understanding with Greece to recover some of the Aegean islands. Third, they wanted to cancel the Capitulations. Furthermore, should the Russians be completely defeated, they would advance into the Caucasus to conquer them or incite a revolution there.

> According to Shakir and Naci, the Georgians and Tatars in the Caucasus were already preparing for a rebellion against Russian rule. They thought that the position of the Armenians would be vital to their success. They were convinced that the Dashnak had the power and the ability to persuade the Russian Armenians to remain loyal to the Russian government until a critical juncture at which point they would shift their allegiance to the Turks. The Unionists assured the Dashnak that the Porte had no interest in occupying the Caucasus; it merely wanted to pull the region out of Russia's orbit and then give it autonomy. The extent of autonomy would depend on the extent of the "dedication and service" to the Ottoman Empire each of these peoples of the region displayed. Finally, they stated that "Germany was committed to helping the Ottomans execute the entire plan."[14]

The ARF representatives replied that they lacked the authority to make a commitment, especially as the World Congress had adjourned prematurely. Only the bodies responsible for the Caucasus could make such a commitment. But in any case Russian Armenians no longer had the same enthusiasm for Ottoman constitutional rule that they had from 1908 to 1910. The errors that the Sublime Porte and the CUP had made concerning Ottoman Armenians gave Russian Armenians no confidence that support for the Ottomans would improve conditions for their compatriots across the border. The Russian government had been using that lack of confidence to win the support of its own Armenian population. The Ottoman government's stance toward Armenian reform also was not encouraging. Before promising autonomy to the Armenians in the Caucasus, the Porte should help Ottoman Armenians. The ARF representatives concluded that Turkey should hurry to implement policies that would win over the Armenians just as the Russians were doing toward the Poles.

The two Unionists, Şakir and Naci, insisted that they be told what the Armenian Revolutionary Federation wanted. The ARF representatives answered that Istanbul was fully aware of ARF demands and that "those in power knew better what they could and could not give the Armenians, especially during wartime." The Unionist delegates promised to convey the ARF responses to Istanbul by telegram. But "in spite of their assurances to the contrary, Vramian believed that the Turks considered them Russian sympathizers. This came from their misunderstanding of conditions and what the real issues were as well as their political savvy."[15]

Even before war broke out St. Petersburg had stepped up its activities among the Armenians in eastern Anatolia. Russian consulates had been opened at Diyarbakır, Sıvas, Harput, and Mosul, while the consulate at Van had been raised to the rank of a consulate-general. That may have influenced Dashnak policy.[16] As for the situation in "Russian Armenia," the *Near East* reported that a great Armenian demonstration in Tabriz on behalf of an Entente victory occurred on August 16, 1914. "Bishop Melik-Tangian held a special service where prayers were offered in front of the Russian Consul-General, the British and French Consuls, as well as Russian troops stationed in the town...After the service the crowd marched to the consulates of the Entente Powers."[17]

Vahan Papazyan, deputy for Van in the 1908 and 1912 parliament, gave a similar account of a conversation with Ömer Naci in September 1914. His article was published in Russian in *Birzhevyya Vedomosti* on May 16/29, 1916, and was later adapted by B. Bareilles and published in France in 1917.[18] Published in 1916 and 1917 while war was raging and propaganda was crucial, Papazyan's article gave his interpretation of the conversation. He noted that before the war relations with the Sublime Porte had been cordial. But the Turks knew that in case of war with Russia the Armenians would side with the Russians. In the Papazyan-Naci conversation Naci said that "Turkey's duty as a nation and a State" demanded that it should take an active part in the present war and that this was only possible on the condition that all the nationalities living in Turkish territory would join. It was not enough that the Armenian people should remain loyal or neutral.

What we require is that the Armenians should form volunteer bands and send them against Russia. We require your men as well as your material and moral support. The Turkish nation and the Ottoman Government will not forget your services, but it is necessary that the initiative should come from you. After the war the nationalities of the Caucasus will receive a federal constitution. The Turkish Armenians will be able to emigrate to the Caucasus and combine with their Russian brothers there. The Muhammadan population of the Caucasus will emigrate to Asia Minor, and in this way your ancient dreams will be realized.

I and my companions answered that the Armenian people would not fight against Russia, but they would remain loyally, remain neutral until the end.

Naci "went off to Mush and Ezuroum, but he met with the same opposition from the Armenians... Life was almost normal until January [1915], and it was only after the battle of Sarykamysh that the authorities began to requisition supplies from the Armenians, to disarm the local population and the gendarmes... This continued until April 1915."[19]

Papazyan gave three fundamental reasons for Turkish action:

1. They were convinced that the Armenians of Asia Minor would sooner or later receive freedom and become the vanguard of European civilization among the surrounding Muslim masses. They could be dealt with in wartime.

2. The Armenians were a serious threat as a fifth column.

3. The Armenians did not agree with the internal policies of the Young Turks.[20]

Members of the Armenian bureau met and discussed the situation. They were convinced that the Ottomans would ally with the Germans but were also convinced that they were inviting destruction by doing so. They had two opposing viewpoints as to what would be the result of the beginning of hostilities between the Russians and Ottomans. "The minority opinion was that the Russian army would strike a 'lightning blow' and easily advance into Ottoman territory. In that case, Caucasian Armenian volunteer units would have to be ready to act as an advance guard to protect the Armenian population centers from Turkish and Kurdish retaliation. Thus, the Armenians would have to negotiate with the Russian government and get their agreement on Armenian political demands before the war started."[21]

It is worth noting that the position of Ottoman Armenians was not monolithic. Armenian revolutionaries differed sharply from the community led by the patriarch, who remained loyal to Istanbul. When the

Ottomans began to mobilize in August, the patriarch, Zavene Efendi, appealed to Enver Pasha to postpone the call-up of four employees of his office so that the working of the patriarchate would not suffer. Enver Pasha agreed in order to show his goodwill toward the community. But the law did not permit the war minister to grant this privilege, so he paid the exoneration tax for these four officials from his own pocket, "as asked by our Armenian brothers."[22] The patriarch's flock in Istanbul and Izmir was not composed of nationalists or revolutionaries. That explains Istanbul's desire to retain their loyalty and Enver's gesture. Patriarch Zavene Efendi went further to show his loyalty when he delivered his sermon on Sunday, November 15, at the Armenian Church at Beşiktaş. He enjoined his flock to do its duty during the war and to serve the throne faithfully.[23]

From this meeting between the Dashnak and the Unionist delegation, Richard Hovanissian concluded that "[t]he Armenian [Dashnak] reply, considered prudent by some, has been judged by others as contributory to the subsequent national cataclysm. The dissatisfied Turkish mission departed from Erzerum without having achieved its objective." He then quoted Gotthard Jåschke's article "Der Turanismus der Jungtürken: Zur osmanischen Aussenpolitik im Weltkriege" to support his conclusion. Jåschke had written that "an unconditional positive response from the leaders at Erzerum would have altered the tragic fate of the Armenians of the Ottoman Empire. Turkish publications during the World War referred to the Armenian decision at Erzerum as proof of disloyalty."[24] Jåschke cited circulars that the Porte distributed on November 12, 1914, *after* Istanbul was at war: "Enver's expectations were great. His Pan-Turanian views [called] for the destruction of Russia, expansion of the natural frontiers, and unification with all Turkic peoples in the Moslem world's struggle for the liberation from the infidel oppressors."[25]

Ottoman wartime publications would have seen the actions of the Armenian revolutionaries as "proof of disloyalty." The Ottomans were an imperial power determined to defend the empire and were unlikely to recognize the actions of any nationalist movement to fight for its rights as legitimate. Even when the Turkish national movement was waging its war of liberation (1919–22) against both the invading Greek army and supporters of the sultan, Istanbul denounced the nationalists as traitors and enemies of the Ottoman dynasty. A *fetva* (declaration issued by the Şeyhulislam) denounced them as bandits and declared that it was legitimate to kill them.[26] Historians today, however, ought not to have any difficulty in being objective in considering the struggles of nationalities to decolonize the Ottoman Empire.

In August the Unionist delegation had discussed theoretical questions with the Armenian revolutionaries, months before Istanbul entered the war, asking: if the Ottomans had to fight against Russia, what would be the response of the Dashnak? In August the Porte had no intention of becoming a belligerent. The prognosis everywhere was a short war that would be over by the end of 1914 or by the spring of 1915. The Unionists expected to maintain armed neutrality in the hope that they would have Berlin's support when peace was negotiated.

Armenian revolutionaries in turn expected an Entente-Russian victory in a short war that would unite the two Armenias, Russian and Ottoman. Ottoman Dashnaks proved to be right in anticipating an Entente victory—though only after a long, destructive war—even after Russia's defeat in 1917–18. Thus their decision not to fight against Russia or subvert the Russian war effort was a rational one. Russia's Armenians were too integrated into the tsarist system to consider rebellion against the tsar; they even had generals fighting in his army.

Ottoman diplomats in Paris noted that Armenian nationalists in the French capital were supporting the Entente war effort. They had collected the statements issued by the Hunchak Social Democrat Committee and sent them to Istanbul. Such statements claimed to represent the Armenian nation, which had been deprived of its rights and had been struggling for over a quarter of a century to obtain the liberation of Armenians in Turkey. It was now willing to wage war against Ottoman tyranny.

> In this gigantic struggle where the existence of nations is at stake, the Hintchak Committee, as well as the entire Armenian nation, was willing to join their forces, moral and material, and waving the sword of revolution in their hands, enter the world war.
>
> As comrades in arms of the Triple Entente and part of Russia they will cooperate with the Allies, making full use of all political and revolutionary means they possess, for final victory in Armenia, Cilicia, the Caucasus, and Azerbaijan.
>
> It is only by these means that the Armenians...may represent the nation at the Congress to be held on the morrow of war.
>
> Let it obtain its political freedom; let it show to the world that it has the right to live, and finally let it obtain, through the consent of the Triple Entente, the independence granted to their fatherland for which it has shed its blood.[27]

Hunchak (Paris, 1914), organ of the Armenian Hunchak Committee, issued a proclamation "To the French People":

> At the beginning of hostilities some fifty of our small Armenian colony have hastened to join the Foreign Legion as volunteers, thus giving plain proof of their deep sympathy for France, France which always defends the oppressed people, and showing their gratitude which imposes on us the duty of uniting around her.
>
> Our interests are mixed with those of Russia. The proclamation made by His Majesty Nicholas II...is a brilliant homage paid to our secular loyalty to the Tsar of all Great Russia and King of Armenia. (signed) Turabian Aram for the committee of the Organisation of Armenian volunteers.[28]

As noted above, the Armenians in the Russian Caucasus had also demonstrated on behalf of an Entente victory.

When the Ottomans entered the war in November, their relationship with Berlin changed. The Germans, already in control of the army, the navy, and Ottoman finances, strengthened the relationship in December by establishing the Ottoman-German Friendship Society (Osmanlı-Alman Cemiyet Dostanesi) in Berlin.[29] Militarily the Ottoman war effort had already become totally dependent on strategy devised in Berlin. Thus the Ottomans were told to open a front in the Caucasus in order to draw the Russians away from the Austrian front. To do so Enver Pasha arrived in Erzurum on December 6, accompanied by General Bronsart von Schellendorf, his chief of staff. He took command of the Third Army to lead the operation against the Russians in the Sarıkamış campaign. Hüsameddin Ertürk, a staff officer with Enver, claimed in his memoirs that Enver was reluctant to fight at Sarıkamış until he was told by military intelligence (probably briefed by the Liman von Sanders mission) that Berlin might end the war and sign a separate peace with Russia and sacrifice the Ottoman Empire. Enver then saw the need for immediate action and came to Erzurum with his staff officers. That is why he took command of the Sarıkamış campaign.[30]

This was the first time that the Ottoman army came face to face with Armenian volunteers fighting alongside the Russians. The *Near East* reported:

> The Third Armenian Volunteer Regiment, about 2,000 strong, under the revolutionary, Hamazasp...[fought] hand-to-hand

and the Armenians wrought havoc among the Turkish ranks
with their hand grenades…The [Ottoman] enemy, who were
exhausted, were simply mown down in large numbers, and
the remainder, seeing their hopeless position, surrendered *en
masse*…The Russian General commanding congratulated the
volunteers on the bravery they had displayed in holding the pass
pending the arrival of reinforcements…

The Fourth Armenian Volunteer Regiment, under Keri, dis-
tinguished itself in this terrible battle at Sarikamish. They blew
up several Turkish trenches by means of hand grenades, and their
cavalry charges were so effective that the Armenian commander
Keri, was decorated with the Cross of St. George.[31]

Some months later Ambassador Morgenthau confirmed the *Near
East*'s report, noting that shortly "after Turkey entered the war, Enver
went to the Caucasus and took command of the army. As you know he
was defeated by the Russians and the losses of the Turks were enormous.
This was greatly due to the assistance rendered to the Russians by the Armenian volunteers who also caused the failure of the Turkish expedition
in Azerbaijan."[32]

The memoirs of Rafael de Nogales, the Venezuelan officer who served
in the Ottoman army during the war, are generally unfavorable to the Ottomans. He wrote that after hostilities had begun "Garo Pasdermichian,
deputy for Erzurum," went over to the Russians with almost all the Armenian troops and officers of the Third Army. After the Ottoman defeat
he returned, "burning hamlets and mercilessly putting to the knife all of
the peaceful Mussulman villagers that fell into their hands. These bloody
excesses have as their necessary corollary the immediate disarmament by
the Ottoman authorities of the gendarmes and other Armenian soldiers
who still remained in the army…and the utilization of their labor in
the construction of highways and in carrying provisions back and forth
across the mountains."[33]

On January 20, 1915, *Orient* published a communiqué issued by the
Ottoman Committee of Information. Quoting the Russian press, it
claimed that the Armenians in general were furnishing all sorts of help to
the Russian armies and especially to the army of operations in the Caucasus. Not content with enlisting as volunteers in the Russian regiments,
they were organizing independent regiments and were providing for all
the expenses for these troops.

Despite the defeat and reports from the Russian press, the Ottoman response to the Armenian population in general remained friendly. The communiqué continued: "Our Armenian compatriots established in Turkey have always been noted for their faithfulness and for their attachment to the Ottoman Empire; and they occupy a remarkable position among all the Ottoman elements who rival one another in their zeal and the devotion to the emancipation of the common fatherland, and this has been demonstrated by palpable proofs. So the publication of the Russian newspapers, reproduced in the British press, which seems to portray all the Armenians, without distinction of country or citizenship, as friends of Russia, has no other motive than to raise doubts in the minds of Mohammedans in regard to the Armenian compatriots in Turkey."[34]

It was not only the defeat at the battle of Sarıkamış and the support that the Armenian revolutionaries gave to the Russians that dramatically altered the Unionists' relationship with the Armenians in Anatolia. It was also changed by Britain's decision to launch the Dardanelles campaign in January 1915. The heavy bombardment at Gallipoli in February created great excitement in the capital; preparations were made to move to Anatolia. When finance minister Cavid Bey went to pay his respects to the sultan before leaving for Berlin, the sultan was most anxious about the bombardment at Gallipoli, especially the possibility of abandoning the capital. In March the Anglo-French fleet continued its attack at Gallipoli. The *Near East*'s correspondent in Athens learned from private sources that the Germans were planning to leave Istanbul before the arrival of the Allied fleet, which was expected daily. Izmir was expected to surrender as soon as the fleet arrived at Istanbul.[35] So confident was Admiral Sackville Hamilton Carden of success that on March 2 he "signaled that he hoped to be before Istanbul in fourteen days unless the storms returned. The Allies were jubilant and grain prices from Russia fell sharply."[36]

A day later Ambassador Morgenthau sent a telegram reporting that "Gov[ernmen]t has compelled Constantinople banks, Public Debt and Tobacco Régie to send their gold to Konia, Eskishehir and Adrianople." He also reported that measures were being taken to fortify Istanbul against possible invasion, and guns were being placed on the islands so as to protect the approaches to the city.[37] On March 5/6 came the news (via Berlin) of the utter precariousness of Turkey's defenses. "Constantinople seemed bound to fall." The Turkish government was so apprehensive that the Allies would force the Dardanelles and take the capital that it had two trains in readiness: one for Konya in Asia Minor and the other for Edirne in Thrace. The Germans let it be known that if the Porte was obliged to leave Istanbul, they would go to Edirne to keep open the Turkish connections with Germany. The Unionists preferred Konya so that they could keep their hold upon the Asiatic provinces.[38]

Tanin, the unofficial mouthpiece of the CUP, reflected Unionist thinking when it wrote that the bombardment at the Dardanelles was not a military act but a political maneuver designed to bring Greece into the war. The Greeks wanted to realize their dream of restoring the Byzantine Empire.[39] Winston Churchill, in turn, was hoping for "an uprising of the Greek and Armenian minorities and a Moslem movement against the Young Turks."[40] Henry Morgenthau was perhaps not far off the mark when he wrote later that "the whole Ottoman state...when the Allied fleet abandoned the attack [on March 18, 1915], was on the brink of dissolution. All over Turkey ambitious chieftains had arisen...who were looking for the opportunity to seize their part of the inheritance."[41]

On March 18, however, the Anglo-French fleet entered the Straits. Three of its ships struck mines and sank, forcing the armada to retreat. After the failure of naval attacks the Entente fleet never returned to resume the naval offensive. In London the War Council decided that the army could best capture the Dardanelles, marking a new phase in the Gallipoli campaign. The Unionists expected an offensive by land and prepared accordingly.[42] Meanwhile Ambassador Morgenthau reported trouble between Ottoman troops and Armenians at Zeytun: "Serious friction has occurred between Turkish troops and Armenian deserters at...[Zeytun] but government claims there is no fear of trouble spreading to surrounding districts. Reports of troubles with Armenians in Bitlis districts also have been received. Colleagues and myself have urged upon the Sublime Porte extreme importance of taking strong preventive measures."[43]

At this point Ottoman authorities began to take actions against Armenian troops. The American consul in Baghdad wrote that all the arms had been taken from the Armenian soldiers in the Baghdad army because of a report that Armenian soldiers in Ottoman Armenia had deserted to the Russians. "All the Armenians here are now very much worried. The soldiers from whom the arms have been taken are made to work on a small railroad...and are reported to be being treated badly."[44]

All such activity was the prelude to the Armenian rebellion at Van that began on April 13, 1915. The Armenian revolutionaries in Van, convinced that Russian victory was assured after Sarıkamış, believed that the time had come to launch their own rebellion. On March 17 a force of 2,500 Armenians captured Van and proclaimed a provisional government. The proclamation of a provisional independent government led the Ottoman government to take measures against the Armenian civil population all over Anatolia while Russian troops advanced to occupy positions west of Muş. Later in June the Armenian Revolutionary Federation handed the town over to the Russian army.[45]

In early May news was received in Tiflis that Van had been occupied by Russian troops under General Oganesov (aka Ohanesian), an Armenian general in command of the Russian Army in the Caucasus. Six Armenian volunteer regiments commanded by Antranig Pasha had assisted him. Antranig was the famous Armenian revolutionary hero who had fought alongside the Bulgarian army during the Balkan Wars and had been given the rank of general by Tsar Ferdinand of Bulgaria. Some 40,000 to 50,000 Armenians in Van fought and defended the city for twenty-nine days. On the thirtieth day the Russian Army arrived from the north, and Armenian volunteers from the east relieved the town. Minister Sazanov, in a speech in the Duma, made mention of the month-long defense of Van by Armenians and of the valuable service that the Armenian volunteer regiments (*droojina*) rendered to the Russian Army.

After the siege Armenian committees began to restore Van, rebuilding houses and cultivating the fields. Hospitals were opened in the province. "Before closing this letter I must add that since the occupation of Van and the vilayet of Van by the Russian troops the number of Armenian volunteers has been increased six to eightfold, and perhaps more, because nearly all the young men able to bear arms have since been armed, and have enlisted in the volunteer fighting lines. Besides, a good number of the refugees who were in the [Russian] Caucasus have returned to Van, are armed, and have entered the volunteer lines."[46]

Ottoman Armenian support for Russia was naturally described as disloyalty and treason by the Ottoman imperial state. Some writers continue to do so even today. Such accusations of treason and betrayal are lodged by imperial powers against nationalists struggling for their independence and self-determination. The British accused Indian nationalist Subash Chandra Bose and his Indian National Army of treason during World War II. He had escaped from house arrest in India and organized Indian prisoners of war captured by the Japanese in southeast Asia and fought against the British army in Burma. In both India and the Ottoman

Empire it was a case of nationalists fighting to liberate their land. That is
how the imperialists interpret the action of other nationalist movements,
but that is not how historians today ought to interpret such struggles.

On another front in the south, Armenians in the highlands of Zeytun
had been in open rebellion against the Ottomans virtually since the beginning of the war. Entrenched in inaccessible mountains, they had refused to
answer the call to mobilize. In time Armenian deserters from the Ottoman
army joined the rebels; Greek and Muslims deserters were taking to banditry. Thousands of Armenians from the plains swelled the ranks of the
rebels. By March 1915 the *Novoe Vremya* of St. Petersburg estimated their
number to be about 20,000 and increasing. "Sometime in February British
and French warships landed contingents of blue jackets at Alexandretta
and Mersina and destroyed the railway lines in those parts."[47]

The Temporary Relocation Law (Geçici Tehcir Kanunu) was passed
by the cabinet under these extraordinary conditions on April 27. But the
law did not mention Armenians by name because it was to be applied to
Greeks in the western Anatolian war zone as well. The law was to end
when these conditions no longer applied.[48]

In the summer of 1915 King Constantine, the pro-German king of
Greece, protested to Berlin about the relocation of Ottoman Greeks
from the coast of western Anatolia and sought Berlin's help to protect the
community. The kaiser replied that the Ottoman Greeks were "obsessed
by a unique determination to betray Turkey to her enemies." Greek diplomatic dispatches from Vienna and Berlin expressed the futility of Greek
démarches to Germany "and *confidential memoranda from Constantinople stated that the Ottoman authorities proceeded with the deportations only
after the German High Command had given its consent...* German activities now went as far as direct involvement in the economic boycott." In
1915 the German-controlled Palastina Bank circulated a memorandum
recommending the rupture of all commercial relations with the Greeks.[49]

In 1918, after the Ottomans had signed the armistice and the war was
over, Greek deputies in the Ottoman parliament were free to accuse Liman von Sanders of the Ayvalık relocations and massacre. They presented
a memorandum to the chamber "naming Liman von Sanders as the in-
stigator of the Aivali massacre."[50] We do not have similar documentary
evidence for Germany's role in the Armenian deportations. But we may
assume that Liman von Sanders, alarmed by the activities of the Armenian revolutionaries in Anatolia, would have asked the Porte to take similar action.

Though Armenian nationalist activity in Anatolia was a factor in the Porte's passing the relocation law, the more immediate cause was the Entente landing at the Dardanelles on April 25 with the aim of breaking through the Straits and occupying the capital. The struggle for the Dardanelles lasted until December 1915. The Entente withdrew in early January. The fear of the fall of the capital and the occupation of western Anatolia forced the Germans and Ottomans to rethink their entire strategy for fighting on the Ottoman front. The Unionists did not intend to surrender if forced to abandon the capital. Instead they decided to move into the interior and establish their headquarters in Ankara or Konya in order to continue the war. The German military mission was to move to Edirne and continue waging the war from there.

Neither the Armenian population nor the Greek population of Istanbul was relocated, because neither was considered revolutionary or nationalist. The Armenian amira were bankers and merchants and did not consider moving to an Armenian state in eastern Anatolia when there was a strong possibility of establishing such a state there after the war. The Istanbul Greeks also had no desire to move to Greece and were allowed to remain in the city when the transfer of population was negotiated at Lausanne in 1923. The Armenians of Anatolia and the Greeks on Ayvalık, in contrast, were considered a potential fifth column in the path of the retreating Ottoman army.

James Barton, a witness to the era, wrote that the Armenians in Istanbul were "for the most part unmolested." There the Porte compiled a "register of Armenian inhabitants, singling out those who were immigrants from the provinces from those actually born in the city, and a considerable number of Armenian people in the former class were deported about the middle of August 1915. Apart from this, there were few deportations from Constantinople and almost none from Adrianople."[51]

The implementation of the relocation law caused tremendous suffering to the Armenian community of Anatolia. Much depended on the officials and local notables who implemented the law, because the Armenian relocation was seen by some as a way of enriching themselves by seizing property that Armenians were forced to abandon. A few honest officials stood up to the demands of the local committee that ordered the deportations. One in particular was immortalized in an Armenian memoir: Mutassarrıf Faik Ali, the governor of Kütahya. The author of the memoir wrote that around the date of the passage of the relocation law he and a group of thirteen others were sent into exile from Adapazarı.

When they reached the town of Kütahya, Faik Ali Bey refused to deport the Armenians of his town despite pressure from local Unionists, who seemed to want to use the occasion to seize the property of those being deported. Local Unionists complained to Talat Bey in Istanbul. Minister Talat wrote to Ali Faik and ordered him to comply with the law. But the governor refused and offered to resign if Talat persisted in pressing to have his order fulfilled. Talat backed down. The Armenians of Kütahya were not deported.[52]

This incident shows the weakness of the Ottoman state. Talat Bey is often described as one of the triumvirate who ruled the empire throughout the war. The other two were Enver Pasha and Cemal Pasha. But Talat was unable to impose his will on the governor of a provincial town. Another incident shows that even Enver Pasha was unable to impose his order on local provincial Unionists. This was the case of Captain Sarkis Torosyan. Like other Armenians in the Ottoman army he claimed to have fought bravely on a number of fronts, was decorated and promoted, and came to the attention of war minister Enver Pasha. When Torosyan's family was being deported, he appealed to Enver, who ordered that the relocation law not be applied to the families of Armenian officers fighting in the Ottoman army. Salih Zeki Bey, the head of the district where the family resided, refused to obey Enver's order. The Torosyan family was duly deported, and his mother and father died during the deportation.[53]

This event suggests a number of possibilities. First, the regime in Istanbul may not have been strong enough to have its orders carried out in the provinces. After all, Kütahya was not so far from Istanbul, and its governor was in communication with the Porte. Had the Porte been determined to do so, it could have forced Faik Ali to obey its order to carry out the deportations or accepted his resignation. Second, the CUP was divided on this issue: many in the committee were opposed to the law. Faik Ali, though Süleyman Nazif's brother, was not so prominent a Unionist as to oppose Talat. But he may have had support in Istanbul so that local Unionists in Kütahya were unable to get their way. In the case of the Torosyan family even Enver Pasha seemed unable to force his orders to be obeyed.

The relocation was considered a temporary measure: the Interior Ministry ordered that records be kept of the property left behind by those who were relocated so that it could be given back to its Armenian owners when they returned to their homes. Such records exist in the Ottoman archives but are dismissed by skeptics as mere wartime propaganda. But Professor Jeremy Salt, who examined the problem, asks:

> If the Ottoman government was playing a double game—issuing orders for the protection of Armenians while formulating a policy of massacre—for propaganda reasons these orders surely would have been sent openly [and not in cipher], but they were not. They were only discovered by British intelligence officers raking through the Ottoman archives in the 1920s...If the Ottoman government really had ordered the massacres, why would it send confidential orders to provincial officials instructing them to safeguard the lives of the Armenians during the relocation?[54]

It should be emphasized once more that the war was not expected to last into 1918. A peace could have been negotiated at any time in 1915 or 1916, and deportees might have been allowed to return to their homes.

In mid-1915 the possibility of an Entente breakthrough at the Dardanelles was a reality. Admiral Georg von Müller, the chief of the naval cabinet, noted in his diary on July 2 that secretary of state Gottlieb von Jagow "was very low spirited as a result of the seriousness of the desperate situation at the Dardanelles, where the Turkish batteries are short of ammunition...The prospect of holding the Dardanelles is now very doubtful." A few days later Ambassador Morgenthau informed the State Department that the "Armenian issue" was "assuming unprecedented proportion," justified by the Porte on military grounds. He wrote: "The Moslem and Armenian populations have been living in harmony, but because Armenian volunteers, many of them Russian subjects, have joined the Russian Army in the Caucasus and because some have been implicated in armed revolutionary movements and others have been helpful to Russians in their invasion of Van district, terrible vengeance is being taken."[55]

The Unionists also feared a counterrevolution organized by Armenian revolutionaries. "They [the Unionists] admit that they will resort to any and every means to prevent their losing control of the Government. They say it is the Union and Progress Committee's nationalistic policy which they refused to modify even when Russia, France, and Great Britain threatened Ottoman Cabinet Ministers with personal responsibility."[56]

When the American Board of Commissioners for Foreign Missions asked the State Department to take measures to protect the Armenians, secretary of state Robert Lansing confessed that "efforts to aid Armenians are rendered more difficult by the fact that, according to reports received by the Department, large bodies of Armenians are in armed rebellion against the Turkish government, and that the Turkish Government claims that such measures as it has taken are only such as are necessary to its own protections."[57]

The situation of the Unionists was so desperate that on July 20 they surrendered territory to Bulgaria in order to bring Sofia into the alliance. The arrival of Prince Gottfried Hohenlohe to Istanbul may have been the German pressure necessary to force the Porte to make the concession. Earlier in May 1915 the Unionists even considered negotiating a separate peace with France, using Pierre Loti as the intermediary. But Russian setbacks and the stalemate in the Dardanelles foiled Loti's attempt.[58]

Throughout the war Armenian nationalists were proud of the contribution that they were making to the Entente's war effort. Arti, an Armenian nationalist writing from Nicosia, Cyprus, possibly with British prompting, told *Near East* readers:

> If there is anything soothing to the hearts of sorrow-stricken Armenians, it is the fact that over 50,000 of their gallant brothers, enlisted as regular soldiers under the Russian flag, are fighting gloriously in Poland and the Caucasus. And about 20,00 volunteers, supported chiefly by the gifts of Russian Armenians, under the "Dashnagist" and "Hunchagist" leaders, are marching side by side with the Russian soldiers from victory to victory. The whole vilayet of Van, one-third of the vilayet of Bitlis, one-fourth of the vilayet of Erzeroum are now in our hands. Antranik, the idol of the revolutionary Armenians, is marching on Mush. On the other hand, Baghos Nubar Pasha of Egypt, well known to the chancellors of the Allies, and enjoying their full confidence, at the head of the Armenian diplomatic delegation appointed by the Katholikos, is working in Europe to ensure the demands of four million Armenians.
>
> These things give us hope that very soon, with the help of the Allies, we shall conquer the land of our forefathers that has been ours for four thousand years; the land, every inch of which has been dyed red by the blood of its heroes. Yes, we shall conquer, and an autonomous Armenia shall no longer be a rosy dream.
>
> When the war broke out, big and small States had long, back and forth communications as to the future allotment of territories

and arrangement of frontiers. But Armenians, the world over made no bargains, had no hesitation in joining the Allies.[59]

The war in the Ottoman theater continued to go badly for the Ottomans. In August the kaiser was "very depressed by the news from the Dardanelles...Our boats [U-boats] have come too late." A British submarine had torpedoed the *Hayrettin Barborosa* in the Sea of Marmara, a serious blow to Unionist morale, though the incident was not reported in the press.[60]

A bright spot in the war for the Ottomans came when the Russians were forced to retreat from Van. Before the Ottoman forces entered the town the "bulk of the [Armenian] population withdrew with the Russian troops; the remainder were massacred." But within less than a month Van was again in Russian hands: with "the great advance of the Grand Duke Nicholas's army into Erzeroum and Mush and Bitlis, it seemed as if the final liberation of Armenia was secured."[61]

Not only were the Armenians of Istanbul not ill treated: even English enemy residents of the city, whose armies were invading the empire, were treated well. "Not a single case of really bad treatment of an Englishman has been reported from Constantinople; on the whole the English who have remained in Constantinople have not been seriously inconvenienced or molested by the Turkish authorities." A few days later the weekly *Near East* reported that "a large number of prisoners, English and French, had arrived in Istanbul recently, some of whom were wounded. But they were fairly well treated."[62]

In early September "unspecified sources" in the capital reported that the Turkish press was beginning to prepare public opinion for the loss of Armenia. *Tanin* and *Sabah*, in particular, devoted articles on the subject, preaching the idea that it was in Turkey's best interest to have a homogeneous population. The *Near East* wrote that the plight of Armenians in the Izmit region was terrible and that "only starvation and death appear to be before them." But the correspondent noted: "So far the Armenians have not been expelled from Constantinople...In Smyrna [Izmir] the Armenian inhabitants have not, so far, been molested; in fact, on the whole, Smyrna seems to be much better off than Constantinople...An Englishman who has just arrived from there states that perfect tranquility prevails, and both the Vali [Rahmi Bey] and the Military Governor continue to manifest a benevolent attitude towards the English and the French."[63]

Mehmed Cavid, the liberal Unionist, wrote in his diary that in September 1915 the Armenian question was heating up daily. Foreign ambassadors, the ambassadors of Germany and Austria, and neutral states like America reported that their public was perturbed and that the events were causing a bad impression abroad. When Ahmed Rıza raised the question in the Senate, an investigative committee was set up. The government refused to increase the committee's size and went as far as to threaten and intimidate the Senate. Not only Ahmed Rıza was speaking up, however: for the benefit of the investigative committee they invited some merchants. But those who were invited did not come forward because they were frightened or came forward and said nothing critical. Consequently the committee produced an extremely weak report. "When I saw the report I said: the mountain has given birth to a mouse [dağ sıçan doğurdu]."[64]

Talat and Enver let it be known that they would reject and return this report if it was presented it to them. "What a great constitution!" noted Cavid. "If they have any weapons to use against the Senate it is the threat of force."[65]

The Unionists were divided over what was happening to some Armenians even in the capital. Hüseyin Cahid, perhaps the most influential journalist and a prominent Unionist, told Talat that some deputies wanted to resign and even his supporters were cursing him. But Talat was in the minority in the Central Committee and had other pressing problems to deal with: he wanted to ignore the Armenian issue.[66] About the same time Cavid wrote that Krikor Zohrab's son came to see him: he said that his father and another deputy, Varteks Serengulyan, a revolutionary who had represented Erzurum before the war, had been arrested and sent to Konya "for interrogation." The son wanted Cavid to intervene with the government on their behalf. Cavid saw two prominent Unionist leaders, Halil and Talat. He complained to Talat about "the violation of the honor and dignity of two deputies for no reason" and said that he was unhappy about their ill-treatment. But Talat replied that he could do nothing and gave an explanation that Cavid does not record. Cavid concluded that "the poor man does not have the power to do anything."[67] Ten days later Cavid received a letter from Hüseyin Cahid about a visit from Krikor Zohrab's wife. Cavid commented: "If the purpose [of the arrests] was only interrogation, these men would not have been sent from Istanbul to Diyarbakır."[68]

The summer of 1915 was a critical period of the war for the Unionists. In June Prince Sabaheddin, who was in Athens conspiring with the British, discussed the situation in Istanbul with Mark Sykes. He proposed signing a separate peace after a successful coup had overthrown the Unionists. "His hope was to obtain assistance from the Allies, provoke a military revolution in Smyrna, extend it to Constantinople, overthrow the existing government and make separate terms of peace with the Allies; his idea being that with a revolution at the capital Turco-German resistance at the Dardanelles would collapse."[69] In July Ambassador Morgenthau also reported that the Unionists feared a counterrevolution organized by Armenian revolutionaries.[70] Fear of such a coup might explain the severe measures taken by the government against the Armenian revolutionaries. On June 15 twenty Armenians belonging to the Hunchak Party were hanged at Beyazit Square.[71]

Cavid discussed the Armenian question with Ambassador Wangenheim in September. He was told that the Germans were totally against Unionist policy and would definitely not defend the Porte in any peace conference. But they would remain silent.[72] Germany seemed to be preparing for the eventuality that Istanbul would be made to assume all responsibility for the deportations and massacres in the event of an early negotiated peace. That is why German archives on this question are unreliable; they too may have been doctored and purged to absolve Berlin of any responsibility. Wangenheim "instructed his consuls to collect any kind of information that would show that the Germans had tried to alleviate the lot of Armenians. These notices were to be published in a white book in hopes of impressing Entente and German public opinion."[73] The purpose was to support Germany's policy of deniability. Johannes Lepsuis's anti-Turkish campaign in Germany served the same purpose.

When the matter was discussed in parliament Talat said that the Germans would never interfere and even suggested that they would remain quiet about it. German public opinion and the press, he said, were not interested in the Armenian question, and the German government was obliged to give diplomatic notes to the Porte.[74]

The fear that the Entente would capture the capital had been the driving forces of the war for the Unionists. That fear receded in late 1915 after the Entente's failure at Gallipoli and the beginning of evacuation by British forces. The Porte's attitude toward the Armenians changed. "There was a noticeable relaxation of the attacks against Armenian refugees and an apparent willingness to permit relief activities among the survivors. Some officials were even co-operative. Whether Enver or Talat felt that they had accomplished the purpose of making 'Turkey for the Turks' a practical reality, or whether the vigorous and continuous protests of many countries, including the citizens of Germany, made a change of front expedient, history does not record." By the beginning of 1916 "there were a million or more Armenians who had survived in the Near East ... [and] the way had been opened for relief work, unhindered by the authorities."[75]

Though the threat from the West had receded, the Russian threat in the East was real and remained so until revolution in Russia in March 1917. The Russian offensive led by General Nikolai Yudenitich began on January 16, 1916. Erzurum was besieged on February 14, ending in the defeat of the Ottoman Third Army. The town, the greatest military base in Anatolia and the principal Ottoman fortress, fell after five days of heavy bombardment. The army that held Erzurum would command all the roads to the Armenian provinces, Iraq, and Persia and would possess a first class base for further offensives. The fall of Erzurum broke the spell of the success at Gallipoli and threatened the army's lines of communications in the region. The Russian army began to advance along the entire front from the Black Sea to Lake Van and soon threatened Rize. Reports said that the Muslim population of Trabzon on the Black Sea was preparing to evacuate the town.[76]

The situation in the empire was desperate. General Erich von Falkenhayn thought that Turkey (and Austria-Hungary) would not be able to carry on the war beyond the autumn of 1916.[77] The desire for a separate peace was strong even among the Unionists. Russia, too, wanted a separate peace with the Porte in order to focus its war effort against Germany, though no approach was made to Istanbul. What emerged later was Russia's willingness to double-cross Armenian revolutionaries and renege on promises made to them. Secret Russian documents released by the Bolsheviks in 1918 revealed that shortly after the Russian capture of Erzurum Prince Kurdachev, a diplomat attached to the tsar's retinue, sent a report to Minister Sazanov stating that he had held a conversation with Generals Alexiev and Danilov about the possibility of an armistice and a separate peace with Turkey. They considered renouncing their ambitions on Istanbul and offered to respect Ottoman territorial integrity, accept the abolition of the capitulations, and re-establish the status quo *ante bellum*. The publication of this document in March 1918 was to show that even in February 1916, when Armenian revolutionaries believed that their dream of a greater Armenia was about to be realized, their patrons were planning to abandon them.[78]

No offer of a separate peace was made, and the Russian advance continued. Bitlis fell on March 2, Rize on the Black Sea was occupied soon after, and Trabzon, some sixty miles away, was threatened. The capture of Bitlis aroused great enthusiasm among the Armenians of London, whose literary society organized a meeting to celebrate the occasion on March 4. "Mr. Karnigian, a journalist, who had just arrived from the Caucasian front, remarked that it was not realized that the Armenians were rendering valuable assistance to the cause of the Allies in many ways." Another speaker said: "The Armenians have drunk the cup of sorrow to the bottom, but the days of joy are at hand."[79]

The Third Armenian Volunteer Battalion, under Hamazasp Srvantsian, facilitated the capture of Bitlis by seizing Hizan, an important point on the road to Bitlis. "Many Armenians were liberated there, who then became the core of the newly organized regiments." Volunteers from the Hinis (Khinis) and the Erzincan regions reinforced these regiments. "In March 1918 these effectives participated in rear-guard fighting: these troops were then known as the Khinis Infantry Regiment and Erzindjan Cavalry regiment."[80]

The Armenian corps, operating in the Van region, was composed "almost exclusively of Armenians, either natives of Transcaucasia or refugees from the Turkish border provinces. In 1918 it was commanded by General Nazarbekoff and Major-General Vyshinskii was their chief of staff."[81] Even before the February Revolution in Russia, the Armenian volunteer battalions were gradually being transformed into regiments and formed into separate units. But it was too late in the day for them to be effective. That did not happen, because the tsarist government was frightened of separatism and did not want to set a precedent that other nationalities might try to follow. "In Tiflis, the Georgians watched with mistrust the forming of new Armenian units."[82]

In April the Russians carried out the first major amphibious operation and landed 16,000 troops at Rize to support their operations in Trabzon and the Caucasus. After consistent Russian bombardment from the sea Trabzon fell on April 18/19, 1916. Its capture facilitated the supply of Russian armies in Anatolia, because it was the principal port of the region. The Russians were now free to act against Erzincan and also threatened Bayburt in the south. Trabzon fell even though the Porte had sent reinforcements by sea, escorted by the *Breslau*.[83]

With the Russian advance along the Black Sea coast throughout the spring of 1916, measures were taken against the local Greeks in the region, who were considered a fifth column. Halil Pasha was furnished with Enver's intelligence reports claiming that the Russians were distributing guns to the Greeks. "More immediately, the Greek persecutions worried the Germans about what new crimes would be held [by the Entente] to their account."[84] But the Muslim population in all those towns occupied and threatened by the Russians also fled westward in large numbers in terror of their "traditional enemy." These refugees fleeing into western Anatolia were a problem for the wartime Ottoman government, confronted by the task of feeding even more people at a time when stocks of corn were insufficient for normal requirements. One effect of this emigration of Turks from eastern to western Asia Minor was to increase the hardships of the Christian populations in western provinces, especially the Armenians, who would be forced to make way for the Muslim refugees.[85]

In eastern Anatolia the Russian advance continued. Bayburt was captured in July, giving the Russian army control of the road between Trabzon and Erzurum. Erzincan was occupied on July 24. Though the town was not particularly large, it had huge military significance, providing military depth to the region. The Russian armies had made a major breakthrough in eastern Anatolia, described by the West as the "Armenian provinces." They were consolidating their gains in the triangle of territory that ran from Trabzon to Van through Erzincan and up to the Caucasus. Armenian refugees began returning with the Russian armies. American relief facilitated their resettlement. The Russians had completed the "conquest of Armenia" and began to plan an advance to Sıvas, 150 miles to the west.[86] There the climate was less harsh in winter and the campaign would be less hazardous. The Russian army had seized the initiative and was confident of advancing into the plain of Sıvas.

On September 29, 1916, the Unionists met in congress for the first time since the beginning of the war. Talat dealt with a variety of issues that the government had to cope with; his report dealt separately with the Armenian question. Talat emphasized the collaboration of Armenian revolutionaries with Russia, the Armenian bands, and the church. The deportations were intended to remove the bands from the fronts where the Ottomans were waging war, away from the railways and railway stations (*menzil*). He admitted that during the deportations certain illegal acts (*ifrarkarane hareket*) took place but said that the proper investigations followed and that the situation was put right.[87]

At the beginning of 1917 it seemed as though Ottoman Armenians in eastern Anatolia had been liberated by the Russians. An article in the *Westminister Gazette* on "The Resurrection of Armenia" proposed that the best future for Ottoman Armenians was to come under Russian tutelage. A. S. Safrastian, former British acting vice-consul at Bitlis, disagreed. He knew the region well and noted that, apart from towns such as Tiflis and Erivan, most of the peasants in the Russian Caucasus were a little better off than the average Ottoman Armenian peasant because of the prevailing system of land tenure, education, and some other causes.

Safrastian gave the example of Bulgaria, noting that Sofia had risen from being a filthy village to its present standing in less than forty years. It was therefore more reasonable to expect a thriving Erzurum, Van, or Trabzon to develop under self-governing Armenia than under Russia. Citing an article by a Professor Migulin in the November 1916 issue of *Novyi Ekonomist*, he discussed Russia's attitude toward the occupied provinces in Anatolia. Noting how Professor Migulin exhorted the Russian government to annex the conquered provinces in the interest of Russian industry, Safrastian asked how the Allies could allow Armenians to be subjected to Russia's industrial exploitation. He concluded that an autonomous Armenia, "guaranteed at least for a generation by the Allied Great Powers, would not only produce a resurrection of Armenia, but would also serve as the most trustworthy outpost of Russian Armenia on the south-western frontiers."[88]

Armenian revolutionaries would have preferred the Safrastian proposal had they not been totally dependent on the Entente. They became independent of Russia when revolution broke out in Petrograd in March 1917 and Russia's nationalities—the Finns, the Poles, and the Estonians, among others—demanded self-government or total independence. The Armenians proclaimed that the question of their future was of an international character; therefore they were waiting for the peace conference to settle it.[89]

After the February Revolution in 1917 the Georgians and the Armenians initially asked Alexander Kerensky's government to transfer all their military units in the Russian army on the Austrian and German fronts to the Caucasus so that they could form a national army corps. The Allies supported this demand, but Kerensky rejected it. At Brest-Litovsk the Bolsheviks tried to subvert tsarist troops with class rather than nationalist propaganda. But Georgian and Armenian troops disarmed Russian soldiers, and most of them left for the interior of Russia. The defense of Transcaucasia was left entirely to the Georgians and Armenians. When Ottoman troops began to reoccupy territory vacated by Russian troops and advanced on Erzurum and Trabzon, the Georgian and Armenian National Councils concluded a defensive alliance and fought against advancing Ottomans. The Georgians and Armenians operated together and mobilized the entire population of Georgia.[90]

As the Ottomans regained lost territory in eastern Anatolia they met resistance from Armenian militias. Massacres of Muslims occurred, and the Ottomans took revenge for the year of Russian occupation when Muslims had been persecuted and massacred. Muş was reoccupied in April 1917. The advance continued on the entire front from the Black Sea to Lake Van. We are told by Kemali that in some regions Armenian nationalists and Kurdish tribal chiefs, who had been at odds earlier, began to collaborate and fight against the advancing Ottomans.[91] After Soviet troops retreated from Anatolia, having signed the Armistice of Erzincan on December 18, 1917, Armenian forces were able to hold Erzurum for a few months. They were finally forced to abandon the town. The Ottoman forces reentered Erzurum on March 11, 1918, making it the army's headquarters in the east.[92]

Frederick Wirth, the U.S. consul, reported on the situation in the capital before he left for Switzerland in October 1917. In regard to the founding of the İtibar-i Milli Bankası (National Credit Bank) he "was informed on good authority that many rich Ottoman-Greek and Armenian merchants of Istanbul were practically compelled to subscribe to the stock of the bank in order that the undertaking might become a success...all the heads of the various departments of the bank are to be either Armenians or Greeks." He also wrote: "No further Armenian deportations have been reported during the past six months." Those who had withstood the awful trials of the first days of the deportations suffered considerably and were often reduced to poverty. But aid from the United States for Syrian and Armenian relief had accomplished a great deal of good:

> No attempt has been made by the Turkish authorities to prevent the distribution of these relief moneys—at least no attempt of a serious nature. Thousands of these poor wretches have starved to death and many more thousands have passed away from sheer exhaustion and exposure. It is reported, however, that many others are slowly recovering from the hardships resulting from their deportation and are endeavoring to reestablish themselves in other parts of the country in case they are unable to return to their former homes.[93]

Reports that the deportations had ended in 1916 after the evacuation of Gallipoli are found in a variety of sources. Armenians who had been expelled began to return to their former towns. But the atmosphere had been poisoned by the war: their homes and properties had been seized by local Muslims. As a result most found it impossible to resettle in their former provinces and left for Istanbul. Armenian members of parliament who did not belong to the Armenian Revolutionary Federation continued to play an active role in Istanbul. Artin Boşgeziyan, deputy for Aleppo, was critical of German loans that were made in paper not gold. "In my opinion, to borrow paper money is the same thing as borrowing nothing. As soon as paper money is put into circulation it loses value." He acknowledged that only after the war would the government be able to put into effect its democratic reforms and the special treatment proposed for the Arabian and Armenian districts, which had especially suffered during the conflict.[94]

By the spring of 1918 the war had still not been lost and the Unionists were optimistic about the future because Russia had been knocked out of the war. They wanted to repair the damage done to their relations with the Armenian community during the relocations of 1915–16. Finance minister Mehmed Cavid gave two interview, one to *Az Est* (Vienna) and the second one to *Berliner Tageblatt*. In the first interview on December 31, 1917, he adopted the ideas of Artin Boşgeziyan and said that the Young Turk regime would carry out democratic reforms and implement the special treatment proposed for the Arabian and Armenian districts only after the war. To the *Berliner Tageblatt* (n.d.) he said: "It will be one of the first tasks of the Turkish Government to find ways and means of making Armenians forget the suffering of the war."[95]

Following the revolution in Russia, on September 20 Armenians, Azeris, and Georgians formed an autonomous Transcaucasian republic. However, the republic had a short life. It was dissolved and divided into three separate republics on May 26, 1918. The newly created Armenian Republic laid claim to territories between Georgia and Azerbaijan and along the pre-1914 Russo-Ottoman border. The claim brought Armenia into conflict with the Ottomans, who had signed the Treaty of Brest-Litovsk on March 3, 1918. The Bolsheviks had agreed to evacuate territories that they occupied in eastern Anatolia and to give up Kars, Ardahan, and Batum, territories taken from Istanbul after the war in 1878.

The Republic of Armenia was forced to sign the Treaty of Batum on June 4, 1918, abandoning Armenian claims to Kars and restoring the 1878

Russo-Ottoman border along the Aras and Arpa Rivers. The treaty was never ratified because of the Ottoman collapse and the signing of the Armistice of Mudros in October 1918. Ottoman armies were soon forced behind the 1914 frontier.

After the revolution in Russia the Istanbul press began complaining about atrocities being committed by Armenian bands against Muslim villages. *Hilal*, the French-language counterpart of *Tanin*, wrote that irregular Armenian bands were devastating the country evacuated by Russian troops and that extensive massacres of Turks had taken place. The Russians were held responsible for not having taken necessary measures to ensure the safety of the inhabitants before retreating. The newspaper wrote that "the Russo-Turkish Commission set up after the armistice in order to establish a basis for the organization of the evacuated districts begged the Turkish Commander-in-Chief to send protection against these bands."[96]

General Kazim Karabekir later wrote that the recapture of Erzincan after the Russian occupation had cost only a few Ottoman lives. But he had been horrified at the sight of the massacre carried out by the Armenians. "Only a handful had survived from about 20,000 Turks who lived in Erzincan." The population had decreased from 6,000 households or about 22,000 people in 1914 to 1,600 households and about 9,000 people. The population of the province had been 135,000 in 1914 but was only 65,000 in 1919.[97]

Before restoring the three provinces—Kars, Ardahan, and Batum— to the Ottomans, the Soviets demanded that Ottoman Armenian refugees who had fled Ottoman territories into the Russian Caucasus, regardless of their religion, be allowed to return. It is a pity that the Soviets did not specify the numbers involved, but it is logical to assume that the figure would have been substantial. We do not know the number of the Armenian refugees who fled to the Caucasus. According to information received from a Swiss correspondent at the Porte, however, the number of Armenian refugees in Syria was 250,000. General James Harbord, who led a mission to Armenia in 1919, gave other figures. He reported that some 75,000 Armenians had been repatriated from the Syrian and Mesopotamian side:

> others are slowly returning from other regions, and some, from one cause or another, remained in the country. There are in the Trans Caucasus probably 300,000 refugees from Turkish Armenia, and some thousands more in other lands...We estimate a

total of perhaps half a million refugee Armenians as available to eventually begin life anew in a region about the size of New York, Pennsylvania, and Ohio, to which would be added those, not refugees, who might return from other lands…[Where] Armenians have returned they are gradually recovering their property, and in some cases have received rent for it.[98]

After the signing of the treaty of Brest-Litovsk the new states in the Caucasus refused to accept its terms. Istanbul had to negotiate with each state individually. At the Trabzon Conference the Armenian delegation demanded "self-determination for the Armenians within Ottoman borders." The Ottoman delegation, negotiating from a position of strength, refused to accept such a demand and declared that it could only sign treaties with states independent of Russia. Negotiations were broken off, with disastrous results for Georgia and Armenia.[99]

The Ottoman army resumed its offensive: Batum fell on April 1, 1918, and Kars on April 13. By the end of May the Armenian state was isolated, short of arms and ammunition, and on the verge of collapse. Therefore it decided to sign an armistice. On May 25 the Confederation of Transcaucasia was dissolved. Georgia declared its independence; Azerbaijan followed on May 27 and Armenia on May 28. On June 4 Istanbul signed treaties with each state at Batum. The Armenian Revolutionary Federation, which had established the Armenian Republic at Erivan, signed the treaty of Batum and abandoned all claims in Anatolia.

During this period of negotiations and war, the Unionist press claimed that it was the Entente that had inspired the Armenians with the idea of an independent Armenia. The English and the French were encouraging the Armenian separatist movement, furnishing it with arms and money. They had prevented the Armenian bands from leaving with the Russians after the armistice, inciting them to fight and even providing the officers. At the same time the Unionists tried to heal the wounds inflicted by the war. They emphasized the difference between Ottoman and Russian Armenians, just as they had done in 1913. The Unionists insisted on the difference between Armenians in the Balkans who had fought alongside the Bulgarians during the Balkan Wars and Ottoman Armenians in Anatolia, who were not to be held responsible for the sins of Russian Armenians. "The innocent suffer too often for the guilty when the people are in revolution. The Ottoman press deserves the gratitude of Ottoman Armenians for having insisted on the difference."[100]

In May the Sublime Porte issued an internal loan, which was given great publicity in the press. Articles in the press encouraged Ottoman Armenians to subscribe. *Jamanak*, the Armenian paper in Istanbul, suggested that subscribing to the loan was a magnificent opportunity to reestablish Armenian loyalty to the state after the unfortunate events in the Caucasus. All Armenians, rich and poor, were asked to subscribe.[101] *Sabah*, which was owned by Mihran Efendi, a wealthy Istanbul Armenian, also published an article on April 18 and wrote about the Armenian contribution to the internal loan. The article was received favorably by the capital's press: by *Tanin* on April 17 and by *Sabah* on April 18. The difference between the Armenians of Istanbul who belonged to the amira class or "bourgeoisie" and those of Anatolia was apparent.

By June 1918 it seemed as though relations with the Ottoman Armenians had been settled. Ahmed Emin (Yalman) noted that M. Haironian, president of the Armenian delegation to the Istanbul Conference, had declared that the Armenian Republic had no claim to interfere with the Armenian citizens of Turkey. That statement led to cordial relations between the press and the Armenian delegation. Ahmed Emin said: "If the Armenian government has realized the importance of our friendship, it will see the Armenian question in its historical light, and hereafter no power will come between ourselves and the Armenians." The Armenian press shared this view.[102] A few days later the French-language newspaper *Le Soir* examined Armenian evidence of loyalty to the Ottoman Empire, as set forth by four Armenian journals of Istanbul as well as by the Armenian delegation to the Istanbul Conference. It found the evidence most satisfactory.[103]

Not all issues had been resolved, however. On August 1 M. Hadisian, the Armenian minister of foreign affairs and a member of the Armenian delegation in Istanbul, visited Ahmed Nesimi, his Ottoman counterpart. He asked the Porte to facilitate the return to their homes of Armenian refugees who had left territories occupied by the Ottoman army. The Porte promised to grant the necessary orders before long. *Le Soir* (August 5) announced that the Porte was dealing with the repatriation of Arabs and Armenians "transferred elsewhere on account of the necessities of war." The Armenians would be repatriated as soon as interior minister İsmail Canbulat had concluded his inquiry into the matter. On August 8 *Le Soir* wrote that the Porte had decided on the repatriation of Armenians, though no decision had been arrived with regard as to the method. On August 10 *Le Soir* wrote that the repatriation of Armenian refugees from the Caucasus had now been decided upon, because of representations made by M. Hadisian; at present the return of Armenians from the region of Batum and Alexandropol had been sanctioned. M. Hadisian had declared categorically to *Vakit* that Armenia had no aim to reconquer Baku or any other town of Azerbaijan.

On September 3 and 4 *Vakit* set out the Porte's policy for the Caucasus, supporting the creation of an independent Armenian state:

> It is our interest more than any sentiment of friendship for the Armenians that prompts us to support an independent Armenia in the Caucasus. So long as the national aspirations remain unsatisfied, the Armenian element scattered everywhere will continue to agitate and be for us a source of embarrassment. In endowing the Armenians with a state we shall be rid of an irresponsible factor always ready to create disorder in our northeastern frontier, and of an element that may constitute a danger for us in the future. An independent Armenia would constitute no danger for us, for we would call it to account for anything hostile to us.
>
> Such an Armenia would be threatened by Russia and would therefore depend on Turkey for the safeguarding of its existence. We, in our turn, would profit by an Armenia as a barrier against the permanent danger that threatens us from the north.[104]

The Porte's policy would be decided as soon as Talat Pasha returned from Berlin, where he was discussing the situation with the Germans. But on his way back he learned in Sofia that Bulgaria had signed the armistice on September 29. On October 30 the Unionists themselves were also forced to sign the armistice. The Porte was no longer in a position to take the wishes of the Armenians into consideration. The future of the Armenians of Anatolia had become an international question left to the peace conference. Armenians in London held a meeting on November 11, the very day the war ended with the signing of the armistice with Germany. They met at the headquarters of the United Armenian Association to elect another delegate and prepared to participate in the Paris Peace Conference. James Malcolm, presiding, noted: "At the outset of the war, in the face of great dangers and in spite of most alluring promises, the Armenians had unhesitatingly and unanimously decided to throw in their lot with the Allies."[105]

The Ottoman parliament reconvened in Istanbul on November 18 and began to debate the Armenian question. Armenian deputies who had remained in Istanbul throughout the war denied that the Armenian community had any "national aspirations" and insisted that they were good Ottomans. That was true for the Istanbul Armenians but not for the nationalist revolutionary supporters of the Armenian Revolutionary Federation, who had led a national liberation movement against an empire. But after the enunciation of President Woodrow Wilson's "14 Points" in January 1918 the Armenians—like the Turks—were able to take umbrage based on the principle of self-determination. Thus when Ilyas Sami, deputy for Muş, accused Papazyan Efendi of giving an ultimatum to the Ottoman government in 1914 in regard to meeting Armenian demands, Dikran Barsamian (of Sıvas—a Unionist deputy at the time) explained: "We wanted the natural rights for the Armenians, we wanted Wilsonian principles."[106]

Ottoman deputies used British policy in Ireland, and the repression of Irish nationalists during the war, to justify Ottoman policy. Ottoman deputies like Ilyas Sami argued that the Armenians were responsible for the massacres because they sided with the Russians and attacked the Ottomans. Matyos Nalbandyan asked: if such incidents took place only in regions where Armenians collaborated with the Russians why did they take place in other regions where the Armenians had not collaborated?[107]

French forces occupied Adana on December 21, 1918. Lewis Heck, the U.S. commissioner in Istanbul, met Nabi Bey and Cavid Bey on January 15, 1919, to discuss the situation, describing both men as moderate. Nabi spoke of a committee of Turks that had been formed to uphold Turkish claims to the Adana district known as Cilicia. The local population was aroused over the landing of some 700 Armenian soldiers under French protection. They had taken over the local government and hoisted the Armenian flag. Nabi thought that this could cause friction with the Armenians.

Cavid discussed the question of repatriation of refugees and mentioned a point raised some time ago by Sir Adam Block, the British representative on the Public Debt Administration and financial advisor to the British High Commission. Block stated that Armenians were chiefly devoted to commerce and trade and that the Armenians of Constantinople would not go to Armenia, for example; nor would most of those who had emigrated to other countries desire to go back to primitive conditions and to real hardship. Lewis Heck also spoke to Avetis Aharonian, the leader of the delegation of the Erivan government to the Paris Conference. Aharonian had declared that "the real need of the [Armenian] nation was to take care of the hundreds of thousands of refugees in the

Caucasus and Turkey and to save especially the children, each of whom represents a future family."[108]

The British authorities in Istanbul wanted to draw America into the repatriation of refugees. But according to Bie Ravndal, "the Armenian Patriarch does not believe that the time is yet ripe for Armenians return to their homeland. America, in my opinion, should not undertake the pacification of any section of Turkey until after formally accepting a mandate."[109] On his return from Sıvas, however, James Harbord reported that Armenians were gradually returning to their homes and were encountering no violence and that there were no signs of any disturbance in the country.[110]

6

The Ottoman Jews

Unlike other non-Muslim communities, the Ottoman Jewish community was the least problematic nationality because it had no communal or "nationalist" demands. The Jewish community in the Byzantine Empire was given the right to live autonomously under its own leader, the chief rabbi (*hahambaşı/hakham bashi*), soon after the conquest of Constantinople. It too enjoyed shared sovereignty with the Ottoman administration, though as a junior partner. The years from 1453 until the seventeenth century marked the period of growth and prosperity, especially after the expulsion of the Jews from Spain in 1492. Many Spanish Jews (Sephardim) settled in the Ottoman Empire and changed the character of the community. The years of decline lasted until the 1850.

These years witnessed a Greek revival and modern education, with Ottoman Greeks ("Rum") becoming the dragomans at the Sublime Porte. These years also saw an Armenian renaissance that affected the position of the Jews adversely. Expanding European trade with the empire in the eighteenth century, with Greeks and Armenians acting as intermediaries, undermined the Jewish trading monopoly with the interior. For example, Ottoman Christians, as protégés of European powers, enjoyed the protection and privileges of the Capitulations, paying only three percent on imported goods while Ottoman Muslims and Jews were taxed at a higher rate. No Jewish Great Power existed, so Jewish merchants could not take advantage of the regime of Capitulations.[1]

At the beginning of the nineteenth century, during the rise of nationalism in the Ottoman Empire, the Jewish community was not affected by this trend and therefore sided with the Ottomans. At the outbreak of the Greek War of Independence in 1821 Jews joined the Muslims against the Greek Orthodox and "dragged the body of the wretched patriarch through the streets, to the delight of the mob, and hurled it into the sea." During the Armenian troubles of the 1890s Jews in several parts of the capital aided the Turks in attacking their Christian neighbors, "but their object was plunder."[2]

The founding of L'Alliance Israélite Universelle in the Empire led to the modernization of the Jewish community, especially as modern education became prevalent through the new schools.[3] The principal concentration of Sephardic Jews was the city of Salonika, although communities existed in Istanbul as well as in Izmir and western Anatolia. Salonika was the center of the clandestine activities of the Young Turk movement and remained so until November 1912, when the city fell to Greece. The Jews of Salonika were reputed to be active freemasons. Emanuel Karasu (aka Carasso), the grand master of the Macedonia Risorta lodge, which was protected by the Capitulations, promoted the activities of the Young Turk opposition by providing its members with a safe haven from the sultan's police. Mehmed Talat Bey, the interior minister who became grand vezir and pasha in 1917, joined the lodge in 1903. He established a lasting relationship with Karasu, who became Salonika's deputy—and after 1912 the deputy for Istanbul—in the Ottoman parliament and an influential member of Talat's inner circle.

Ottoman Jewry was too well integrated to seek a separate identity, having no desire to seek autonomy let alone an independent state. Therefore the Ottomans did not see them as a threat to the territorial integrity of the empire. The good relationship, described elsewhere as "special," had been established while the CUP was in opposition. The relationship was strengthened after the revolution when Haim Nahum Efendi replaced Mosheh Halevi as the acting *hahambaşı* after the fall of the Hamidian régime in January 1909. Mosheh Halevi had been closely associated with the old régime, while Nahum had developed a connection with the Young Turks while attending the rabbinical seminary in Paris (1893–97). He was a liberal with close links to the Alliance Israélite, an institution much respected by the Young Turks. Talat Bey, one of the most influential Unionists, had taught Turkish in the alliance school in Edirne and had been instructed in French by the daughter of the school director there. Nahum's election to the grand rabbinate on January 24, 1909, placed the relationship with the CUP on firm ground. His relationship with Talat remained very close until the end of the empire.[4]

While the Unionists struck political bargains with Greek and Armenian bodies prior to each election, they simply allotted seats to the Jewish community, knowing that its representatives were sympathetic to the Ottoman cause. It is worth emphasizing that relations among all the communities were based on mutual respect and interest at the time of the 1908 revolution, based on hostility to the Hamidian autocracy and a common desire to start afresh. That was particularly true for Turks and

Armenians and Turks and Jews. The Greeks, who were still very much under the sway of their patriarch and looked to Athens for redemption, were viewed with suspicion.

The Jewish supporters of the CUP and many Unionists also shared a similar professional profile. The four Jewish deputies who were elected to the 1908 assembly came from professional and business backgrounds, as did about 10 percent of the Muslim-Turkish representation. Vitali Faraci, who was elected from Istanbul in 1908 and 1912, was a leading lawyer in the capital. He also worked as the legal councilor at the Régie des Tabacs (Tobacco Administration). His portrait in the press reveals a cultivated, cosmopolitan gentleman of about fifty-five, dressed in a European suit, who would have been totally at home in a European setting. He died in 1912. Emanuel Karasu was also a lawyer. He was elected from Salonika in 1908 and 1912 and moved to Istanbul when Salonika was lost to Greece during the Balkan Wars. He represented the capital in the 1914 assembly. Though he was never a member of the CUP's Central Committee, he was part of the inner circle and a confidant of Talat and his faction. During the war Karasu was put in charge of food distribution and is reported to have made a fortune of 2 million liras. This, he told an unsympathetic correspondent of the *Times*, was "all honestly made out of my commission on purchase." During the armistice the sultan's anti-Unionist government confiscated half of this fortune. Karasu fled to Italy, where he died in June 1934.[5]

Nisim Mazliyah, described as Manısalı Nisim Mazliyah Efendi in the Izmir press, represented Izmir in all three assemblies. Apart from his legal training he also had commercial interests. Before 1908 he was in Salonika, where he became an active Unionist. According to Isaiah Friedman (who cites contemporary Zionist reports as his source of information), Mazliyah belonged to "the small group [of Jews] that funded the C.U.P." Abraham Galanté describes him as a member of the Commercial Tribunal of Salonika who was appointed professor of administrative law and Capitulations at the Police Academy. Hüseyin Hilmi Pasha, while inspector-general of the provinces of Salonika, Kosovo, and Manastır before the revolution, benefited from Mazliyah's legal expertise, especially when he had to deal with problems related to international law. That may explain why Mazliyah thought Hilmi Pasha could be "swayed" in favor of Zionism.[6]

As a committed Unionist Mazliyah was much respected in the organization. This rather than being Jewish accounted for his election from

Izmir, where, according to the yearbook (*Salname*) for the province of Aydın, the Jewish community in his district was not large enough to elect its own deputy. His district had only 25,002 Jews out of a population of 627,850, but 25,000 males over twenty-five were required for each deputy.[7] Mazliyah spoke Turkish eloquently, and the committee used his talents during election campaigns. He wrote for the Unionist press and founded the paper *İttihad* (Union) in Istanbul. He also served as secretary to the chamber in 1908–9. During the counterrevolution of April 1909 he spoke in the assembly to rally the demoralized Unionists, explaining to the counterrevolutionaries that their demands for the Sharia were incompatible with the constitution. In November 1912 Mazliyah was arrested by Kamil Pasha's government as part of its anti-Unionist purge and was released only after the Unionists seized power in January 1913. He was chosen to represent the government at the Stockholm Socialist Conference in 1917 and maintained contact with Talat Pasha until the latter's assassination in Berlin in 1921. According to Galanté, Mazliyah wrote *Le Parliament Ottoman* (n.d., n.p.) and published a political daily, *Hür Adam*, in 1930.[8]

Hasqaul Sasun (aka Ezechiel Sasoon) was deputy for Baghdad in the three assemblies. He came from a prominent family and was described as a businessman, at one time director of the Ottoman Steamship Company. After his election the CUP had him appointed undersecretary of state at the Ministry of Commerce. This was part of a Unionist strategy to penetrate the state structure and influence policymaking while they could not have Unionists in the cabinet. Friedman writes that the Zionist leader "Jacobson could hardly rely on Sasoon…whom he termed an 'Arab patriot.'"[9]

Ottoman Jews, especially in Salonika, also studied scientific farming. The government relied on them, as well as Armenians, to help in the modernization of the empire's economic infrastructure. Galanté writes that Vitali Stroumsa, who graduated from the school of agriculture in Montpelier, became director of the *école pratique* in Salonika, inspector of agriculture in Salonika and Kosovo, and secretary-general of the Financial Commission of the three provinces of Salonika, Kosovo, and Manastır. After he moved to Istanbul in 1908 he seems to have abandoned his interest in agriculture totally. He was appointed to the High Council for the reform of the empire's finances. During the war he was placed in charge of supervising the printing of Ottoman currency in Berlin.[10]

If the list of electors of the second degree in Izmir is an indicator of educational and professional trends among Ottoman Jews, then medicine came high on the list. Three of the four electors were doctors (Amado, Ishak, and Ishak Abuaf); the fourth, Mordechai Levi, is not identified by profession.[11] Generally speaking, the Jewish community (including women) participated in the expanding modern, commercial sector of the economy in cities such as Izmir and Istanbul. Writing in the March 1914 issue of *Kadınlar Mecmuası* (Women's Journal), Rhodie Tully, who described herself as "one of their [Ottoman women's] sincerest admirers," noted: "There are many large companies and institutions in Istanbul that would be too willing to employ women clerks could they but find good and accurate workers, but at present demand is far greater than the supply, and the field is almost entirely held by Israelites."

While Greeks and Armenians were willing to play a role in the economic revival of the empire, they were not keen to see the creation of a strong central state. That was the principal concern of the committee. This concern was shared by the Jewish political elite, the only non-Muslim, non-Turkish group to do so. Apart from the few members of the elite who have already been mentioned, the identities of many others who were active in the various arms of the bureaucracy. Two more names come to mind: Nisim Russo and Samuel Israel, who adopted the family name İzisel after the passage of the law of 1934.

Both men came from Salonika, where they were active Unionists, and moved to Istanbul after the revolution. Before the revolution Nisim Russo had served on Hüseyin Hilmi Pasha's staff in Macedonia, later working closely with Mehmed Cavid when he was finance minister. The career of Samuel Israel in the Ottoman secret police remains obscure. But we are told that he accompanied Enver Bey when he carried out the coup on January 23, 1913. After Mahmud Şevket Pasha was assassinated on June 11, 1913, Samuel Israel was himself shot and wounded while leading a detachment of special police against the assassins. The wound left him with a limp, and the Unionist government decorated him for bravery and valor in the line of duty. Samuel Efendi served the Unionist government throughout the war but was relieved of his post by the Istanbul government after the armistice of 1918. In the republic he was restored to his former post and remained in the police force until his retirement in 1947. After his retirement he taught law and French at the Police Academy in Ankara. Samuel Efendi died in 1949 at the age of seventy in Paris, where he had been sent by the government for medical treatment. As late as December 1971 he was remembered affectionately by his comrades and described as a brave and conscientious officer who had played an important role in the service of the Turkish secret police organization.[12]

The working relationship between the Committee of Union and Progress and the Jewish elite was apparent to observers of the contemporary political scene, especially to members of the intelligence communities of the Great Powers. The British embassy (and the *Times*), which supported the liberal faction of the Young Turks after July 1908, came to regard the Unionist movement as a Jewish-freemason conspiracy and went so far as to describe the CUP as the "Jew Committee of Union and Progress."[13]

Such a notion of politics reflected two European attitudes prevalent at the time: first, anti-Semitism and the theory of a Jewish conspiracy to control the world; and second, the conviction that non-Western peoples like the Muslims and Turks were incapable of modern government and required guidance from a European hand. Thus Ambassador Gerard Lowther informed the Foreign Office that the "Turk, devoid of real business instincts, has come under the almost exclusive economic and financial domination of the Jew ... The Jew can help the Young Turk with brains, business enterprise, his enormous influence in the press of Europe, and money in return for economic advantages and the realisation of the ideals of Israel, while the Young Turk want to regain and assert his national independence and get rid of the tutelage of Europe, as part of a general Asiatic revival."[14]

The ambassador's claims had no real basis. The Ottoman Sephardim enjoyed a religious identity unlike many Ashkenazim Jews of eastern Europe, who espoused Zionism as their national identity. Ottoman Jews may have initially looked with sympathy on the Zionist project, but they had no desire to work for the "realisation of the ideals of Israel." Isaiah Friedman writes that the Francophile Alliance Israélite Universelle, the nursery of the Ottoman Jewish elite, "became progressively more vociferous in criticizing Zionist ideology. That culminated in a speech made by Narcisse Levene, the Alliance's President, during a reception given to the Ottoman parliamentary delegation in Paris during the summer of 1909. The Turkish press picked up the theme, and consequently some of the Ottoman Jewish leaders damped down their earlier enthusiasm [for Zionism]. Those involved were closely linked with the Alliance, like Chief Rabbi Nahoum."[15]

Dr. Nazim, an influential and prominent Unionist, told Victor Jacobson that while he still favored Jewish immigration into Palestine he did not sympathize with Zionist aspirations, which he saw as separatist.

Zionism could undermine the harmonious relations with the Ottoman-Jewish community, which would be regrettable because the Jews were "a very valuable element." Because of growing Unionist hostility toward Zionism, Ottoman-Jewish leaders became more reserved, and Jacobson could no longer rely on their support. Jacobson, who knew Ottoman Jews intimately, described them as "largely materialistic and indifferent [to Zionism]."[16] Friedman concluded: "With their bitter experience in the Balkans fresh in their minds, they [the Ottoman Jewish community] could not risk creating a new nationality, however trustworthy. With the regime of Capitulations still in force and the majority of Zionist settlers in Palestine reluctant to adopt Ottoman nationality, the Porte had reason to be suspicious."[17]

Another feature of the special relationship was the question of military service. Ottoman Jews took the issue of military service seriously because they identified with the Ottoman state. Thus they enlisted and did not desert during the Balkan Wars even when the Ottoman army was being routed. An officer who kept a diary during the war noted how Christian soldiers deserted. But he paid Jewish soldiers the highest compliment he could think of: "A Jewish soldier if he is a regular, properly trained, serves like a Musulman. The effort and bravery of Sergeant Mişon from Mustafa Pasha in the Third Company really did his officers proud. Even though Sergeant Mişon is the son of a rich Jew, he did not pay the exemption tax. He commanded his troops at the most dreadful phase of the battle. He commanded a detachment."[18]

After the setback in the Balkans when the Porte feared a Greek invasion on the Aegean coast, Muslims and Jews in various districts under threat (such as Menemen and Manisa) were armed. In contrast the Armenian and the Greek communities of the region, considered unreliable and a potential fifth column, were not given arms. The Balkan Wars strengthened the bond between the Unionists and Jews. As Salonika was Hellenized many Jews left the city and settled in Izmir, Edirne, and Istanbul, where they played an important role in filling the vacuum in economic life left by Greeks who were forced to leave.[19] In March 1913, while Istanbul's situation was still dire, Lucien Sciuto, the editor of *L'Aurore*, wrote: "Our dearest dream—the dream of the whole of [Ottoman] Jewry—is to see a great and strong Turkey marching resolutely toward its future, parallel with a powerful Jewry also going freely to its destiny."[20]

The empire's special relationship with the leaders of its Jewish community proved to be an asset in the propaganda war that commenced with the outbreak of war in Europe in 1914. Arnold Toynbee, one of the principal architects of Great Britain's propaganda campaign against the Ottomans, wrote that Britain was greatly embarrassed by its Russian ally's treatment of the Jews in the Pale, knowing what an adverse effect that was having in the United States. That is why the British government decided to exploit the Armenian question, to neutralize the German campaign by exposing its ally's misdeeds.[21]

When the Capitulations were finally abrogated unilaterally in September 1914, the Turkish and Jewish communities welcomed the decision as deliverance from foreign control; the Christians mourned, uncertain as to their future.[22]

1914–1918

During the July crisis and the outbreak of war the Jewish community presented no problems for the Porte. In fact Ottoman Jews were also relocated and resided in the interior of western Anatolia until the end of the war as a precaution against Entente bombardments. During the course of the war the Jewish community actually benefited, for the commerce of Izmir and its hinterland passed entirely into Jewish hands. They replaced the Greeks and Armenians because of their "harmful political activity against the empire during the Balkan War of 1912," according to Galanté.[23] If the Jews had any problem, it was with the German embassy, which was unhappy about Nahum Efendi's "pro-French disposition." When Dr. Weber, the embassy's first dragoman, met Talat "and ventilated the German Embassy's displeasure," Talat advised Nahum to improve his relations with the Germans. When Weber and Nahum met later, Nahum "admitted that though he had been a Francophile, he was never a Germanophobe." In support of his argument he pointed to his "very good relations with the official [pro-German] Zionist representative in Constantinople."[24]

Though the CUP had no problems with the Sephardic community, it had problems with the Ashkenazim Zionists who had settled in Ottoman Palestine and retained Russian citizenship, refusing to abandon it for Ottoman citizenship. In 1914 the Zionist leaders were negotiating with the Porte in Istanbul about the naturalization of Russian Jews in Palestine. While negotiations were ongoing, on December 17, 1914, 500 Russian Jews were rounded up by the *kaymakam* in Jaffa and deported to Egypt. Arthur Ruppin complained to the authorities, but to no effect.

"That one kaimakam is able to destroy the work of so many years in a single day made me realize on what weak foundations all our efforts at settlement rest."[25] Kaymakam Bahaeddin Bey had been suspicious of Zionist
intentions for some time. In a newspaper article quoted by Ruppin he
claimed that the Zionists "want to establish their own government and
are already issuing stamps ... and bank notes ... What is worse, he actually
believes all this nonsense and told other officials, in all seriousness, that
the Zionists have already secretly formed their own government ... and
that we are only waiting for the arrival of the British for openly acknowl-
edging its existence."[26] Friedman attributes some of the decisions against
the Zionists to the decentralized character of Ottoman power or the
weakness of the central government. Kaymakam Bahaeddin Şakir, he
wrote, felt strong enough to take the law into his own hands and order
the expulsion of Russian Jews. But this was not an isolated case during
the war. Governors often acted independently of the Porte's orders.[27]
Ahmed Emin, a journalist who lived through the war and later wrote
about it, also emphasized the autonomy of provincial officials vis-à-vis
Istanbul. He wrote that Izmir's governor Rahmi Bey implemented "only
such measures as he saw fit." Bedri Bey, the prefect of police in Istanbul,
though close to Talat, frequently disregarded instructions.[28]

In 1914 fifty thousand Russian Jews lived in Palestine, as well as
German nationals and protégés. "By the end of 1915 the total figure of
those expelled in December 1914 and those who left of their own voli-
tion amounted to 11,277; the number of Jews who had adopted Ottoman
nationality amounted to 20,000."[29] While Germany remained the center for Zionist activity, Berlin exercised its influence on Istanbul and
prevented the large-scale deportations of Russian Jews from Palestine
to Egypt. Naturalization of foreign Jews had been the goal of the Porte
for decades. Ambassador Wangenheim reported that Talat Bey had the
"fullest understanding" of the political importance of this question. The
Porte had decided not to expel the Russian Jews. They were to be granted
facilities to acquire Ottoman nationality, and those liable to military service were to be given a further concession of deferment from conscription for one year. "Early in 1914 far-reaching facilities had been granted
in this respect but only twenty individuals had applied for naturalization ... [Talat] constantly drew the Zionists' attention to this failure ...
Chief Rabbi Nahoum fully concurred with the policy of naturalization."
But "the notorious maladministration and miscarriage of justice at the
hands of Ottoman officials made any foreign resident think twice about
jettisoning the advantage of consular protection."[30]

Cemal Pasha, who was appointed governor of Syria in 1914, did not want to have anything to do with foreign Jews and "hates Zionism, which he regards as the seed of future separatist tendencies," according to Ruppin.[31] Initially the Porte's policy had been against Russian Jews. But in January 1915 it became anti-Zionist. In his proclamation of January 25, Kaymakam Bahaeddin "referred to Ottoman Jews as 'our allies'" and the "true sons of the Fatherland." He contrasted them to the Zionists, who were branded as "wicked revolutionary elements," trying to create in the Palestinian region of the Ottoman Empire "a Jewish state...thus causing harm to the people of their own race."[32]

The Unionist government, however, used members of the Ottoman Jewish elite to represent its policy at home and abroad. Thus in January 1915 Leon Taranto, a relative of Isaac Taranto, legal councilor at the Foreign Ministry, was sent to neutral Greece to contact the British regarding the possibility of a separate peace. Emmanuel Karasu's advice was often sought in matters of foreign relations. In 1912 he had been sent on a secret mission to Rome to discuss the end of hostilities with Italy; in August 1915 he was one of the founders of the Ottoman-Israelite Union, the brainchild of Dr. Alfred Nossig. In July 1918 Karasu, along with Nahum and Mazliyah Efendi and three influential Unionists—Midhat Şükrü, Ziya Gökalp, and Dr. Nazim—formed the commissions to negotiate an "Ottoman Balfour Declaration" with German Zionists.[33] In the last months of the war Nahum went to the Netherlands and Sweden "to persuade his co-religionists throughout the world to back Turkey and the integrity of the Empire."[34]

The British used talk of Jewish persecution by the Ottomans to carry out anti-Turkish propaganda after Cemal Pasha's evacuation of Jaffa in March–April 1917. Istanbul was forced to counteract such propaganda lest it influence opinion in neutral states, especially America. The Istanbul press issued indignant denials about the persecution of Jews and only emphasized Ottoman Jewry's anti-Zionism. Two articles, representative of that sentiment, are worth quoting. In his *Tasvir-i Efkar* column of December 27, 1917, Ahmed Emin (Yalman) wrote:

> The spreading of news about supposed Turkish atrocities is not the only means that our enemies use to incite the Jews against us. Another way is exaggerated promises of territory, such as have been made to Italy, Serbia, Montenegro, and Greece. They try to create the belief in the Jews that the aim of a part of their people, namely an independent Jewish kingdom in Palestine, will now

be fulfilled...It is said that the former American ambassador at Istanbul [a reference to Henry Morgenthau] is to be sent to London for this purpose. The *New York Tribune* denies this fact in its issue of June 20...There is therefore no question whatever of the establishment of an independent Jewish state...What the Turkish Jews think about these efforts and how faithful they are to Turkey can be seen by the Note that the Grand Rabbi has sent to the government, as well as by the declaration of the Jewish associations, attached to the Note.[35]

The *Tasvir-i Efkar*'s editorial written after the Balfour Declaration was issued in November 1917 also accused England of "patronizing the Zionist movement so as to stir up the Jews everywhere against the Turks." It went on to say:

During the war Turkey has never persecuted the Jews and rumors to the contrary are false. Turkey has protected and provided shelter for Jews oppressed in other countries and is proud of its record. The majority of the Jews in the Ottoman Empire remain loyal and grateful. Talat Pasha also promises refuge to all Jewish immigrants who share this sentiment. But Zionism implies the separation of a part of the empire and is therefore repugnant to Turks, and naturally those who propagate it do more harm than good to the cause of the Jews.[36]

In conclusion, the editorial noted:

The Entente powers are currying favor with the Jews. But the Jews in Turkey remain loyal and others are welcome to join them when they come with the idea of becoming good patriots. Naturally we do not want elements hostile to our country...No country wants to be partitioned and therefore we cannot encourage Zionism. But as Jews in the Ottoman Empire have always been loyal to the State, there has never been a Jewish question in our empire.

If Nahum's opinions are any guide, these views were shared by the Ottoman Jewish elite. That is why the "special relationship" was based on such solid foundations. In February 1917, in his capacity as grand rabbi, Nahum informed the German ambassador in a private conversation that

Ottoman Jews regarded Zionism as "a foreign importation," which was being chiefly supported by Germany and America. He continued:

> The vocal and determined manner of the Zionist propaganda gave a false impression of their real influence among the Jews, but those in Turkey regarded it as an undesirable movement that endangered their interests... The Jewish people, thousands of years after the destruction of their political existence, had no cause to revive a Jewish state. The Jews should unconditionally and with no ulterior motives consider themselves nationals of the states in which they are domiciled and endeavor to identify themselves with their country's interests. This was the basic principle of Ottoman-Jewish policy. The Jews had always been on good terms with their state and had no intention of sacrificing this good relationship to any fantastic foreign ideas.[37]

By August 1918, the last German offensive having failed, the survival of the Ottoman Empire was in doubt. But even in these circumstances the Jewish elite did not desert the sinking ship. Nahum continued to speak for the Turks even after defeat; Nisim Mazliyah maintained relations with Talat Pasha in Berlin, hoping to bring about contacts between Talat and people like Hausmann so that they could learn about the situation in Turkey during the national struggle.

The Jewish political elite had never been monolithic, and its commitment to Ottomanism or Zionism would have been a matter for individual choice. Nahum's attitude may have been guided by his religious role as grand rabbi, while Karasu (in his own words) had "to reconcile his duty as a Turkish patriot with that of a nationalist Jew."[38] Others like Munis Tekinalp (Moise Kohen or Cohen) traveled beyond Ottomanism and supported ideas of Turkification—even adopting a Turkish name long before it was fashionable to do so. Suffice it to say, though never a ranking member of the elite, Tekinalp became one of the most important ideological voices among Turkish nationalists and led the way for the integration of the Jewish community into the new republic.[39]

The Arabs

Ever since the Ottoman conquest of the Arab world in 1516–17, the region had been divided into provinces and ruled from Istanbul. The empire had no separate Arab communities for the population—just like the other millets the Arab population was divided according to religions. Most Arabs being Muslims, they belonged to the Muslim millet. The same was true for the Greek Orthodox and other denominations. Egypt acquired its autonomy in the nineteenth century during the rule of Muhammad Ali (1801–49). But Egypt remained an Ottoman province in name until the British established a protectorate in 1914.

Nationalism did not come to Egypt with the French Revolution even though the French occupied the province between 1798 and 1801. Egypt's brief occupation of Syria under Muhammad Ali's son, Ibrahim Pasha, began the process of regional identity, strengthened by the Ottoman Law of the Vilayets in 1864. The law created new administrative units ruled by governors appointed by the Sublime Porte. The governors or valis worked with the local notables, who mediated between the population and the state, resulting in the phenomenon that the late Professor Albert Hourani popularized as the "politics of notables."[1] A broad-based notability identified with the landed interests of its own class rather than with the interests of the region that it purported to represent.

The next stage in the evolution of Arab elites came with the promulgation of the first Ottoman constitution in December 1876.[2] For the first time elections were held on the basis of local constituencies that were represented by deputies they elected. But the experiment in constitutional government was short-lived, ending in 1878 when Sultan Abdülhamid II shelved the constitution for the next thirty years. Thereafter the sultan co-opted many local notables by giving them sinecures at his court.

The restoration of the constitution in July 1908 was greeted with the same enthusiasm in the Arab provinces as in the rest of the empire. In Jerusalem, governed by Ekrem Bey, the son of Namık Kemal, one of the heroes of the 1876 constitution, the crowd in the main square and cheered while sheikhs, rabbis, and priests delivered speeches denouncing the old regime. Muslims, Christians, Jews, Samaritans, Turks, Arabs, and Armenians fraternized and formed processions proceeded by banners of liberty.[3]

People had great hope that the elections, held in November–December 1908, would bring about change, though few anticipated the kind of change that would occur. For the purpose of elections the empire was divided into 126 electoral districts, thereby creating a new political geography. People unwittingly adopted new local identities and began to see themselves in terms of the newly designated electoral districts. This was particularly true of the elites of these districts, who were elected by the primary voters and then, as secondary voters, elected the deputies from among themselves. The deputies (*mebus*), strictly speaking, were representatives of their geographical district and not of their communities. The Law of Association passed in 1909 did not permit communal (religious or ethnically based) organizations or parties. But in reality such bodies continued to exist. In the Republic of Turkey, the designation of elected representatives was changed from *mebus* to *milletvekili*, meaning representatives of the nation, not the district that they were elected from. In the last days of the empire the idea and even the vocabulary of nationalism was still underdeveloped. For most people *millet* meant their religious community, religion being more important than language in defining identity. It may be worth noting that the Ottomans used the term "Musevi" (followers of Moses) and not "Yahudi" for the Ottoman Jewish community. "Musevi" carried only religious connotations, while "Yahudi" tended to imply an international political body associated with Zionism. Only the small intelligentsia, conscious of the idea of nationalism, began to use the term *millet* for nation.

The Arab provinces were divided into the following electoral districts (broken up into four geographical units for convenience):

1. Greater Syria, including Lebanon and Palestine, was divided into the districts of Halep, Lazikiye, Hams, Humus, Havran, Cebel-i Lübnan, Trablusşam, Beyrut, Akka, Şam/Damascus, Nablus, Kudus, and Kerek.

2. Hijaz and Yemen included the districts of Hijaz, Jedda, Asir, Taiz, Sana, Hüdeyda, Mecca, and Medina.

3. Iraq was divided into the districts of Basra, Müntefik, Divaniye, Amare, Kerbela, Baghdad, Kerkük, Süleymaniye, and Mosul.

4. Libya had four electoral districts: Trablusgarb or Tripoli, Cebel-i Garbi, Fizan, and Bengazi.[4]

Each district elected a deputy for 50,000 primary voters. The Arab provinces, excluding Libya and Trablusgarb, elected about sixty deputies in 1908 and 1912 and eighty-four in 1914. It is not possible to be precise about the ethnic identities of the deputies because they were not elected on the basis of ethnicity, which foreign observers and later historians have tended to impose on the subject. We can identify some Kurdish deputies, though it is not clear that they would have identified themselves as such. For example, how did İsmail Hakkı Babanzade see himself? He came from a prominent Kurdish family of Iraq and was a well-known member of the Committee of Union and Progress, contributing a regular column on foreign affairs to the pro-Unionist *Tanin*. He was elected from Baghdad and was most vocal and articulate on local affairs, especially on the British penetration of Iraq. Yet at the end of the empire half of his family remained in the new republic, while the other half remained in Iraq.

The three electoral campaigns—1908, 1912, and 1914—also helped to strengthen the sense of localism not only among the elite but also among voters and the general public. Unionists and the Liberals competed for votes, often in bitter debates, and local issues were always in the forefront. Competition between the old notables and rising new class also occurred, which Samir Seikely describes so vividly in his essay "Shukri al-Asali: A Case Study of a Political Activist."[5] The lively press that emerged after the revolution in all parts of the empire was one of the principal instruments in the politicization of the regions; it introduced what Rashid Khalidi has appropriately described as "modern mass politics" in the Arab provinces.[6]

The debates in the Ottoman Assembly in 1908–18 give us a good sense of the growth of localism, and even proto-nationalism, in the Arab provinces. Hasan Kayalı has given us a glimpse of some of the issues discussed. For example, deputies who represented Iraq, excluding Mosul, were most perturbed about the Lynch affair, the surrender of the monopoly of riverboat traffic on the Tigris and the Euphrates to a British company. This issue was thrashed out in the assembly as well as in the streets of Baghdad and Basra, and the government in Istanbul was forced to resign to avoid giving the concession to the Lynch Company.[7] Then there was the case of Zionism, which mobilized the Syrian/Palestinian deputies who prevented the government from making serious concessions to the Zionists despite strong pressures.[8]

Apart from these dramatic issues in which the new elites participated were the day-to-day issues about budget allotments and the construction of public works in the districts of the various deputies. What is known in American politics as pork-barrel politics (fighting for money to be spent on an electoral district) was beginning to enter Ottoman political life. Deputies who wanted to be reelected had to show constituents that they had brought them some benefits during their stay in the capital. But in order to establish the extent of this kind of politics, more research on the parliamentary debates as well as the Arab press will have to be undertaken. So examination of the politics of Arab deputies shows not a radical growth of Arab nationalism, let alone separatism, but the growth of localism. This seems to have been missed by recent Arab scholars if we read most of the articles published in Rashid Khalidi's book of essays *The Origins of Arab Nationalism* (1991), which includes some of the latest scholarship on the subject. What case do today's Arab nationalist scholars tend to make?

The argument that is often made regarding the rise of "Arab nationalism" rests on a false premise: that it was a response to Turkish nationalism and the "Turkification" policies of the Committee of Union and Progress. This is based on the misreading of "Turkification." It is a problem that most scholars writing on this period are unable to use Ottoman sources and have only a cursory knowledge of late Ottoman history. Even if they knew modern Turkish, they would be hard put to find good histories in Turkish to guide them, because Turkish scholarship is trapped in its own myths, often adopted by Western scholars:

1. The Committee of Union and Progress was a powerful, monolithic body with a program that it was determined to implement.
2. This program was guided by a determination to Turkify all the non-Turkish elements of the empire.
3. The committee was all-powerful from 1908 to 1918.

When these myths are examined they are found to be devoid of content. It is true that the CUP emerged as the best-known single body when the constitution was restored in July 1908. But it was part of a movement and had no recognized leadership—it has been described as a party of leaders. While it was in opposition before July 1908 a number of communities—Turks, Albanians, Arabs, Armenians, Greeks, and Jews—came under its umbrella. In opposition they were politically divided and only agreed on the subject of combating Abdülhamid's autocracy and on restoring the constitution. The committee was a secret organization with centers in Europe and throughout the empire. Its leaders in exile, men like Ahmed Rıza and Prince Sabaheddin, played no significant role during the constitutional period except as external critics of the Hamidian régime.

Far from being a powerful body, the CUP came very close to elimination from power on one occasion and was ousted on the second occasion. During the counterrevolution of April 1909 it was saved by the military intervention of Mahmud Şevket Pasha and the high command. The generals were not Unionist though they shared some of the committee's reformist ideas. The CUP then played second fiddle to the generals until the military coup of July 1912, when it was ousted from power.

The 1912 coup was carried out by anti-Unionist junior officers who supported the Liberals. The Liberal governments began to purge Unionist organizations throughout the empire. If they had more time and the Balkan Wars had not intervened, the committee might well have been eliminated as a political force. But the disaster of the Balkan Wars and the failure of the Liberals to win British backing sounded the death-knell of Kamil Pasha's government. The Unionists carried out their own coup and seized power on January 23, 1913. That is when the CUP finally came to power.[9]

The government that ruled after crushing the counterrevolution of April 1909 was aware of Arab sensibilities. The daily *İkdam* (March 8, 1910) was suspended *sine die* owing to the publication of a letter from Yemen that the martial-law regime considered offensive to the Arabs. In the same way the Porte was unable to abandon Libya to the Italians, despite the cost of the war and the little benefit that Ottomans received from that province. As grand vezir, Hüseyin Hilmi Pasha pointed out to the British ambassador: "The Government, which is already being accused of being too Ottoman and too much inclined to neglect the interests of the other races of the Empire, especially the Arabs, could never agree to relinquish an Arab Province to a Christian Power. It would mean the rising en masse of all the Arab provinces of the Empire against the Government."[10] Italy in turn believed that that the local Arabs loyal to the Sanussi (the local religious leader) would join it to overthrow Ottoman rule. That was a miscalculation; instead Muslim religious leaders (*ulema*) proclaimed a jihad against the infidel invaders, beginning a bitter war of resistance.[11]

When the Porte was forced to make peace with Italy during the Balkan Wars and surrender Libya to Rome, an anti-Unionist deputy for

Damascus wrote in the Liberal Union's *Nevrah* (n.d.) that the committee and the Sublime Porte were responsible for losing Tripoli to the Italians. He accused the CUP of pursuing a negligent and deceitful policy, spending money on their members rather than buying arms and ammunition for the loyal Arabs who were struggling to recover the province.

The unnamed deputy also reminded readers that no Arab had been given high appointments under the new regime and that Arab officers who were not Unionist tools were removed from the army. The Porte was accused of causing dissension between Christians and Muslim Arabs, impeding progress and depriving the Arabs of their nationality. Zionism was being encouraged at the expense of Syria and Palestine. The author concluded that Arabs could escape this "post-constitutional despotism" by joining the Liberal Hürriyet ve İtilaf, whose aim was to establish real freedom and genuine constitutionalism.[12] Such complaints rather than national feeling were the source of Arab resentment against committee rule.

The disaster of the Balkan Wars so weakened the Istanbul government that members of the Arab elite—some of whom have been described as nationalists—began to call for reform under foreign supervision. A report from the American consulate in Beirut noted that

> there exists in this Vilayet (province), at the present time, an unprecedented movement in favor of reforms. The Syrians, particularly the Moslems amongst them, have now realized that the Turk can never become a proper administrator and is utterly unfit to continue the management of the affairs of the Empire... The Arab nationalists called for decentralization and the creation of an administrative council for the Vilayet with full power over its administration, and secondly, Arabic to be the official language of the Vilayet.[13]

On January 3, 1913, the council for the province of Beirut, hoping for concessions from the liberal cabinet of Kamil Pasha, proposed measures be taken toward decentralization. It asked that Arabic be recognized as the official language and that Arab recruits in the army be stationed locally. But on January 23 Kamil was overthrown by the Unionists. The government that came to power initially rejected these proposals for reform.

On February 22, 1913, Chaim Weizmann also wrote of an emerging Arab nationalist movement against the Zionists:

There is alarming news from Syria about the Arab national movement. With the weakening of central authority in Constantinople, the periphery of Asia Minor is beginning to totter. The Arabs
are beginning to organize, though in a very primitive manner.
They consider Palestine their own land and have embarked on
an intensive propaganda campaign in their semi-national, semi-
Christian, and semi-"anti-Semitic"—an expression that can
hardly apply to the Arabs—press against the selling of land to
"Zionists," the enemies of Turkey and the usurpers of Palestine.
We shall soon face a serious enemy, and it won't be enough to pay
just money for the land. In this connection, it's most important
to launch a strong propaganda drive for the transfer of Yemenite
Jews to Palestine as quickly as possible. It's more important than
ever to transfer sound and reliable Jewish elements to Palestine.[14]

After the catastrophe of the Balkan Wars the Unionist government
began to abandon its policy of "union and progress" in favor of limited
decentralization. So much for the so-called policy of Turkification. Finding itself ruling over an empire that had just lost most of its European
territories, it began to focus its attention on Anatolia and the Arab provinces. The Unionists even imagined using the Dual Monarchy model
for the Ottoman Empire. In February the Porte asked its ambassador
in Vienna to study and send a report on how that model worked. The
model was appealing because such an empire would rest on the shoulders
of Turks and Arabs, just as the Dual Monarchy rested on the shoulders
of the Germans and Hungarians.[15] The Unionists were convinced that
only a reduced empire would be able to survive the pressure of the Great
Powers. According to Halide Edib, a keen observer of Ottoman politics
throughout this decade, the empire "could be strong enough to resist the
overwhelming forces arrayed against it only through a close understanding between Turks and the Arabs. It is true that the Arabs were already
seized with the nationalist fever, but there was an idea ascribed to Mahmoud Shevket Pasha, himself of Arab origin, which was worth a trial. It
was the creation of a dual monarchy, Arabo-Turkish, with a seat of government at Aleppo."[16]

The idea of a Turkish-Arab "dual monarchy" also appealed to "Arab-
Ottoman nationalists" like Aziz Ali al-Misri (I have taken the term from
Mahmoud Haddad, though "Arab-Ottoman patriots" would be more
suitable). This idea of dual monarchy has not been taken seriously by

modern scholars, however, though Ahmed Tarabein mentions the idea in his article on 'Abd al-Hamid al-Zahrawi. He gives credit for this idea to Ottoman Liberals and not to the Unionists, though the Liberals were not in power at the time and therefore could hardly have proposed it.[17] The formula was never put into operation—not because the Unionists returned to power, as Tarabein claims, but because the First World War intervened in August 1914.

The provincial law (Law of the Vilayets), promulgated on March 26, 1913, went into effect on March 28.[18]

1. The law defined the powers of the governor (vali), who still enjoyed substantial authority.
2. It conferred the power of voting provisional budgets on Provisional Councils [controlled by Albert Hourani's notables], though the governor could veto decisions within three weeks of their adoption. Then the Council of State would mediate between the governor and his council.
3. The vali had the right to adjourn meetings of the Provisional Council for a week, after immediately advising the Interior minister, and to dissolve it in conformity with a decision of the Council of Ministers sanctioned by an imperial decree.
4. The Provisional Councils were forbidden to discuss political affairs or to pass any resolutions except with reference to taxation and local administration.

This law was an important measure toward decentralization, giving local administrations greater autonomy and financial independence. The powers of the vali were increased and defined. He became the highest executive official.

Writing in April 1916, Cemal Pasha described this law as a liberal measure that could have provided a degree of autonomy for the Arabs outside of military, financial, and foreign policy matters. But the Arab leaders, he asserted, were unable to trust the Unionist government. Therefore the new law could not be fully applied to the Arabs: "The Arabs prefer anarchy of their own to stable Ottoman government."[19]

When the Arab Congress met in Paris (June 18–24, 1913) the Unionists feared that this could be the prelude to French intervention in Syria. The committee had already tried to meet some Arab demands and could do little more than repeat its concessions. Cemal was convinced that French meddling in Syria would follow. Even before the congress convened, on May 6 *Tanin* attacked the organizers, questioning their motives and noting that they did not represent all Arabs: there were no delegates from Yemen, Baghdad, Egypt, and North Africa.[20]

Soon after the congress began its discussions the Unionists sent a delegation headed by Midhat Şükrü, a leading Unionist and the committee's secretary, to negotiate with the Arabs.[21] Negotiations later continued in Istanbul, and more concessions were made: administrative decentralization, use of Arabic in schools and in administration, and the appointment of Arab notables to the Senate and to the cabinet.[22]

Another measure designed to conciliate Arab opinion was the appointment of Said Halim Pasha as grand vezir and foreign minister, a measure that followed Şevket Pasha's assassination on June 11, 1913. Said Halim was a scion of the Egyptian khedival family and a veteran Unionist. His appointment was also a reminder that Egypt was still technically part of the empire. Another Arab in the cabinet was Süleyman al-Bustani, who was appointed minister of commerce and agriculture. This appointment was significant because Bustani was a Christian Arab, an intellectual highly regarded both in the Arab world and among Unionists.[23]

At the end of June the Porte recalled Hazım Bey, the governor of Beirut, described as "the uncompromising opponent of reform." His recall suggested that Istanbul was serious about reform and the concessions that had been made to the Arabs, especially after the Arab Congress. Hazım was replaced by Ali Münif (Yegane), a Unionist who belonged to the Talat faction and who could therefore be relied upon to follow instructions from the center. His transfer from Aleppo was seen as a positive step by the Arab reformers. Ali Münif arrived in Beirut on June 25, 1913, and was cordially received by the local press. Soon after he ordered the substitution of Arabic for Turkish in the courts, a decision that was praised in "some of the intransigent Arab nationalist organs," which hoped that this was the prelude to the application of the full program of reform.[24]

Before Hazım's recall 1,700 citizens of Beirut had sent a petition address to the Porte. They declared their loyalty to Istanbul but demanded:

1. The repeal of the new Law of the Vilayets.
2. The acceptance of their program of reforms previously presented to the old ministry.
3. The reopening of the Club of the Reform Committee.

"At the same time we wish to prove our solidarity and our complete accord with our brethren who, faithful to the fatherland and to the Government, are now assembled in Paris to deliberate on the all-important question of reform, and who have been prevented, by various well-known circumstances, from meeting together at Constantinople." The petition concluded that "our present statesmen cannot fail to realize that without the immediate application of radical reforms there can be no salvation for the country."[25]

On the basis of the agreement with the Arabs the Beirut press reported that the Porte had agreed that:

1. It would appoint Arabic-speaking officials to the Arab provinces.
2. Provincial councils would control expenditure in public works.
3. There were to be at least five Arab governors and three Arab ministers.
4. Arabic was to be the official language in the Arab provinces.[26]

The Istanbul press described this agreement as "one of the greatest achievements of the Committee Cabinet." It was perhaps the only agreement of any importance concluded with the Arabs that met with the full approval of all political parties and from which the country would derive the greatest benefit if the government proved as good as its word.[27]

Yusuf Akçura, perhaps the leading Turkish nationalist publicist, supported autonomy for the Arabs and urged the CUP to accept the "just demands of the Arabs for greater autonomy." He suggested that "the national evolution of a people who are able to constitute a nationality" not be prevented, provided that this was not contrary to Ottoman unity. That was "one of the fundamental tenets of the Turkish nationalists." Akçura was suggesting that there was no contradiction between Islam and nationalism: Islam was supranational and therefore could enable nations to live together in a union or federation.[28]

After the loss of the European provinces in the Balkans, the Unionists were determined to establish better relations with the Arabs. Initially they believed that this could be achieved not just through a policy of decentralization but by creating autonomous administrations with the governor at the head of a local council. That would mean that the old feudal order, thus far in the hands of traditional notables, would weaken while the councils composed of the more forward-looking Arabs would be strengthened. The old order may have been alarmed by such a policy, which may partially explain why the Arab nationalist movement during the First World War came to be led by tribal chiefs.

Toward the end of 1913 Wahib Bey (aka General Vehib [Bülkat]) was appointed governor and commander of troops, "with instructions to apply the (provisional) Law of the Vilayets and to extend the railroad from

Medina to Mecca." These moves met with resistance from Şerif Hüseyin, the amir of Mecca, and the tribes in the Hijaz. The Unionists considered deposing him, but Said Halim Pasha, a personal friend of the amir, intervened against the idea.[29] The Porte abandoned the idea of restricting the authority of the amir or extending the railway to Mecca for the moment.

The province of Syria may have been the heartland of an emerging Arab nationalism, but Iraq also called for reform. The Basra Reform Society, described by the *Near East*'s correspondent as "the Liberal Party of Irak as opposed to the Young Turkish Party," issued a manifesto. The document, observed the correspondent, represented "the interests of the well-to-do community in Irak," opposed to "the admission of foreign capitalists as concessionaires." Istanbul would "encounter very strong opposition if it endeavours to grant concessions to foreigners."[30]

The manifesto began by stating that "our kingdom shall be an entirely Ottoman empire under the Crescent flag, and no concession is to be given to foreigners. Our country must be protected from foreign intrigue and freed from foreign influence in every possible way." The third item noted: "The Imperial Ottoman Government is a Muslim kingdom under the sovereignty of the Muslim Caliph, the great Sultan, and is not an empire—as thought by unmanly people."[31]

In its remaining twenty-five clauses the manifesto went on to concede to the central government the direction of foreign politics, the army and navy, customs, postal and telegraph services, the making of laws, and the levying of taxes and rates. But the general council of the province was to have control of local matters. The governor would carry out the instructions of the central government and of the general council and appoint officials chosen by the council other than those who were elected.

The role of the general council was defined in some detail in clauses six to twelve. It was "to have supreme authority in all matters relating to the internal good of the vilayet." The council was not only to make laws but had the power to consult the governor and if necessary even ask for his dismissal. A census was to be taken and while *vakfs* (charitable foundations) were to be handed over to respective religious councils.

The powers of the Sublime Porte were severely restricted by the manifesto. While Istanbul could appoint the governor, he had to come from the province and have a thorough knowledge of the customs of the local tribes. Istanbul could also appoint other provincial officials but only in consultation with the general council and the governor. They too must have thorough knowledge of local Arabic dialects. Other officials had to be local appointees who knew the language and customs of the people. The general council would have to approve all appointments.

The revenue of the province levied from customs, postal, and telegraph departments and the military service tax would be sent to Istanbul, while the rest would be spent locally.

Other clauses dealt with legal matters. Again local Arabic was to be the official language of the court. Soldiers recruited locally would serve in their own towns in time of peace, though the Porte could send them wherever necessary in time of war. Farmers were to be exempted from military service for twenty years and "house builders" for thirty. Arabic was to be the language of instruction, but the study of Turkish and of religion was to be encouraged. Finally, Muslim "women must be absolutely prohibited from committing adultery."[32]

If David Ben-Gurion's memory of his meeting with Arab students at Istanbul University in late 1912 is reliable, then the students were not interested in independence. In his memoirs he wrote:

> It seemed strange to me that these intellectual young Arabs did not see the future in terms of their struggle for independence from Turkish rule. None of them spoke at the time of independent Arab states, let alone working towards such a goal. On the contrary, most of them looked forward to a vaster and more grandiose Turkish Empire, offering grander opportunities for administrative posts which they, Arabs educated at Turkey's mother university, would be asked to fill. For them, in such posts, stretched a life of ease, between luxury and material honours. As a matter of fact, very few of them took any part later in the movement for Arab independence.[33]

The attitude of the Arab students was not surprising given that the idea of nationalism had yet to develop in the Arab world (or even among the Turks). As the students told Ben-Gurion, the elites sought "grander opportunities for administrative posts" in the empire. That is precisely what the elites in all provinces asked for. Apart from administrative posts, the Arabs also wanted—and received—a larger representation in the 1914 parliament, in proportion to their population. On the basis of the prevailing political climate, the *Near East* reported that that "the Arabs will play a far more important role in the next Parliament, which will contain a far smaller proportion of Turks... The Arabs formed less than twenty-five per cent of the last Chamber. They will form nearly a third of the next."[34]

The accord that the Unionists had reached with the Arabs was regarded as an important achievement following the losses in the Balkans. It promised to guarantee what remained of the Ottoman Empire. In February 1914, however, the arrest of Aziz Ali al-Misri, an Arab nationalist in the Ottoman army, threatened the reconciliation. He was arrested ostensibly on the charge of embezzling money during the Tripoli war. But George Antonius claimed that the real reason was political. Aziz Ali had played a prominent role in Arab secret societies, whose aim was said to be to win autonomy for the Arab provinces. More recently he had formed a new society called Al-Ahd (The Covenant) among Arab officers, particularly Iraqis, who were the most numerous in the Ottoman army. He was known to be a leader of the group of young Arab officers who were unhappy with the government.[35]

The Unionists were aware of this society and were unlikely to have been bothered by the demand for autonomy, as they were already in the process of making concessions. The reason for Aziz Ali's arrest was said to be his anti-Ottoman intrigues with the notables of Iraq, the khedive of Egypt, and the British in Cairo; his brother-in-law was the governor there. Unable to bring out these issues out into the open, the Unionists tried Aziz Ali in camera, ostensibly for crimes such as embezzling army funds, surrendering Cyrenaica to the Italians for a bribe, and having attempted to set up an Arab kingdom in north Africa.[36]

Philip Stoddard interviewed Salih Basha Harb and Aziz Ali years later. He was told that Aziz Ali was one of the organizers of the resistance forces in Libya after the departure of most of the Turkish officers at the outbreak of the Balkan Wars. Aziz Ali said that he left for Egypt in the fall of 1913 and took with him as much equipment as he could as well as, according to Salih Basha Harb, most of the money that Enver had left to pay Bedouin volunteers. He allegedly left the money in Alexandria and went to Istanbul, where he was arrested, tried, and convicted of embezzlement and treason. Aziz Ali denied these charges and described the affair as "another of Enver's plots against me."[37]

There may have been some truth to the conspiracy theory. While Aziz Ali was under arrest, some of his friends informed the British ambassador that they were planning an insurrection in Iraq that would involve Kuwait and even Abdul Aziz Ibn Saud.[38] But evidence for such a plot was never presented. On April 15 it was announced that Aziz Ali had been sentenced to death but that his sentence had been commuted to fifteen years of hard labor.[39]

Thanks to the intervention of the British ambassador, Aziz Ali was pardoned on April 21 and left the next day for Cairo. After his departure Charles Marling noted: "The Aziz Ali agitation, which moved Arab opinion over a wide area, and in connection with which my action was purely humanitarian, was rendered liable to misconstruction by indiscreet violence and partisanship of *The Times.*" It was the conviction of the grand vezir that Aziz Ali had been employed by the khedive in connection with his endeavors to persuade the sheikh of Senoussi to make peace with the Italians: "it is not impossible that the Turkish government may have some sort of evidence to support this supposition. Being at peace with Italy, they could not object openly to such action on the part of Aziz Ali, but they certainly resented the Khedive's intrigues with the Senoussi…The Turkish Government suspects H.M.G., or at any rate, the Egyptian Government, and His Highness's [the khedive's] activities, which they may regard as a further indication of British interference in Arab politics."[40] The *Times's* involvement in this affair on Aziz Ali's behalf would only have confirmed Unionist suspicions about British interference.

In order to strengthen their position in the Arab provinces the Unionists sent two Ottoman airmen—Fethi Bey and Sadık Bey—to fly to Syria to counter the propaganda of the French airmen who had flown to Syria on February 15, 1914. The Ottoman pilots were sent the following week and "were lionised by the population." Their daily flights and maneuvers overshadowed all other questions of public interest. The flight of the French airmen had created a sense of inferiority, signaling the "scientific triumph of the Christian West as compared to the Mohammedan East." The flight of Ottoman airmen made up for this. The pilots left Damascus on February 26, when their aircraft crashed near Lake Tiberias, killing both men. That was a blow for Ottoman aviation. Though the pilots were buried in Damascus, the War Ministry decided to erect a monument in their memory. In April Enver Pasha and other members of the cabinet, as well as members of the German military mission, laid the foundation stone of a monument in the Fatih district commemorating the two airmen's flight to Egypt.[41]

If the Ottomans had strengthened their position in Syria and Iraq, their position in the Hijaz had weakened. By 1911 Ambassador Mallet thought that the committee had lost control of the Hijaz. Reporting on the 1912 general election, he wrote that in "other conflicts with the CUP the Amir [of Mecca] always seemed to get the better of them." By 1911 the Unionist clubs in Mecca had "died a natural death." In the 1912 elections Sharif 'Abdullah was reelected from Mecca and his younger brother from Jedda. "The Ottoman governor no longer counted for much and the Amir was in full control."[42] In 1911 Hacı Adil, an influential Unionist leader, had proposed replacing Şerif Hüsayin with 'Ali Haydar, his rival from another clan. But war minister Mahmud Şevket Pasha had refused to support such a proposal.[43]

In March 1914 Talat was still optimistic about the government's position in the Arab provinces. On being asked by the British ambassador about the "disposition of Sayid Talib" in Basra, Talat replied that Talib was now on good terms with the government and that Sheikh Khazal and Sheikh Mubarak were also friendly and would help them settle matters with Ibn Saud. Talat claimed that the Porte "had come to a satisfactory arrangement with the Arabs about representation in Parliament" and that the Arabs were now quite satisfied. A new Arab senator had been appointed that very day, which had given satisfaction. Talat added that the Porte was "nowadays very wise and prudent, and that they meant to settle their differences peacefully in future and not by the sword."[44] Talat was right about Sayyid Talib. In August the *naqib* (head notable) of Basra visited Mubarak in order to persuade him to pursue a more cooperative policy vis-à-vis Istanbul.[45]

Viscount Herbert Kitchener explained the "Arab animosity" as being aroused by the policy of centralization adopted during the last few years, "and more especially by the proposal to push forward railway communications, which would cause great pecuniary loss to the Arabs who live on their camel hire."[46] Kitchener had a point, for Talat had made an important offer to Şerif Hüsayin in March. In return for the completion of the lines from Median to Mecca, from Jidda to Mecca, and from Yanbu to Medina, he was to have complete control over one-third of the revenues of the railroad. In addition the force necessary for the execution of the project was to be commanded by the amir, who was to have a quarter of a million guineas to spend among the tribes. Finally, the amirate was to be Hüsayin's for life and be hereditary in his family. C. Ernest Dawn concluded that "such modernizing measures as the extension of the railway and the prohibition of slavery created solid tribal support for the Amir by endangering tribal interests in a way in which his heavy hand never does."[47]

By 1914 the Unionists wanted to abandon the Hamidian policy of relying on the tribal chiefs and the "sheikhly" families of Iraq for support. Hanna Batatu wrote that in the 1914 parliament only one out of thirty-four deputies representing Iraq descended from such a family and was "himself by birth and ideas a townsman." The deputy in question was 'Abd-ul-Majid ash-Shawi of the ruling family of the 'Ubiad tribe. Two other deputies, 'Abd-ul Muhsin as-Sadun and his brother 'Abd-ul-Karim, came from the Sadah tribe that dominated the Muntafiq confederation, but both had become wholly urbanized by education in Istanbul.[48]

Such was the situation of Ottoman–Arab relations when the July 1914 crisis broke out. Initially it was only an Austro-Serbian war, the third Balkan War. But by the beginning of August it had become a world war, and the Unionists and the nationalities were forced to reconsider their options in the Arab world.

1914–1918

When Germany signed the secret alliance with the Sublime Porte, one of Berlin's aims was to revolutionize the Islamic world, according to Fritz Fischer. The alliance "was concluded with an eye to the unleashing of a pan-Islamic movement, which was to lead off with a 'Holy War.'" While Istanbul was to exercise "a constant threat against Russia's southern flank, she was also meant to act as a springboard from which Germany should attack Britain at her two most vulnerable points, India and Egypt."[49] Liman von Sanders, who led Germany's military mission to the Ottoman Empire, said much the same: "Turkey was expected not only to defend the straits and protect her frontiers at immense distances, but conquer Egypt, make Persia independent, prepare the creation of independent states in Trans-Caucasia, threaten India from Afghanistan if possible, and in addition furnish active assistance in European theatres."[50]

Even before Istanbul had become a belligerent, while it was only mobilizing, there was talk of jihad in Iraq. Letters written from Baghdad on August 9 spoke of a pamphlet on "Holy war" that had been suppressed because of British, French, and Russian intervention. But the general feeling in Baghdad was anti-British. In early August the state of siege was declared and conscription was in full swing. The local authorities were spreading the news of a jihad, while news of German victories was broadcast around the town. The concept of jihad was also being used to mobilize the tribes.[51] On the same day consul Charles F. Brissel reported that

an order of the Fourth Army in Syria, commanded by Cemal Pasha, to
the vali of Baghdad asked him to appeal to Islamic sentiment to encourage military service in the army.[52]

That was the situation until the Porte entered the war in November.
Then the press, writing under strict military censorship, reflected what
the government wanted to publicize. Thus *Sabah* reported on November 5 that the first consequence of the war with the Entente would be the
expulsion of the British from Egypt. Istanbul, it emphasized, had never
renounced its rights over Egypt, which were specified and enumerated
in the imperial edicts of investiture of the khedive. The newspaper also
declared its solidarity with the aims of the Egyptian nationalist Mustafa
Kamil's patriotic party, the Hizb-i Vatani (Patriotic Party). On the same
day the British proclaimed martial law in Egypt and annexed Cyprus;
Egypt became a British protectorate on November 19.

The Entente controlled all the seas around the Ottoman Empire,
which feared that the port cities like Beirut and Izmir would be bom-
barded. That is why Cemal Pasha issued a warning to the Entente that for
each Muslim killed in a bombardment of Beirut three English or French
subjects would be shot, while all material losses would be compensated
by Entente subjects. "I decline to accept all responsibility if the bombardment of an open city provokes a massacre of Christians."[53]

The Ottomans and the Germans could do little to defend the Arab
provinces at this point. Thus on November 20, 1914, British forces began
to occupy the province of Basra, formally entering the town on November 22. Nakibzade Seyyid Talib abandoned the Ottomans and joined the
British. He came from a family of notables that traditionally provided the
naqib al-ashraf (leader of notables) for Basra. By marriage he was allied
to the family of Abu'l Huda al-Sayyidi, who had exercised great influence
under Abdülhamid. After 1908 Seyyid Talib had been elected to all three
parliaments but had resigned on June 3, 1914, when he began to play a
double game with the British.[54] Needless to say, Seyyid Talib's defection
was a setback for the Ottomans in Iraq.

Cemal Pasha's Expeditionary Force left Beersheba on January 14,
1914, with about 25,000 men. He planned to storm Ismailia after con-
fusing the British with feints on other targets along the Suez Canal.
But surveillance aircraft warned the British of the impending attack on
the canal and robbed Cemal Pasha of the element of surprise. He was
forced to abandon his attack on the canal and return to Beersheba in
mid-February. His prestige was damaged by his failure to take the canal. For the moment the Ottomans were forced to concentrate on their

position at Gallipoli under attack by the Anglo-French fleet.[55] The first canal campaign had lasted a month, from mid-January to mid-February 1915; a second attempt was made in June 1915. Though both campaigns were unsuccessful, they forced the British to station thousands of troops in Egypt who would have been more usefully employed in the European theaters of war.[56]

Before leaving for Egypt Cemal made a proclamation to the people of Palestine:

> Palestine is directly in line of the operation of the Imperial army that has been entrusted with the task of emancipating Egypt with the help of the Almighty. The population of Palestine has therefore, to a greater extent than that of other regions, the duty of taking part in the defense of the fatherland and in the sacred Jihad.
>
> This duty includes establishing and maintaining cordial relations and indissoluble ties among all Ottoman elements. The least act that might cause injury to such amicable relations will be severely punished. I therefore order the Muhammedan races who form the majority, to make proof of their patriotic sentiments by cordial relations with the Israelite and Christian elements of the population. The subjects of our allies and those of friendly and neutral States, who are living in Palestine, are respected guests. At a time when we are engaged in a life-and-death struggle, we are under obligation to manifest as regards these persons a better attitude than ever. Character shows itself most clearly of all in grave and difficult crises; and since it is to our national interests to secure the friendship and sympathy of the races of the country, we can secure this end only by conduct such as this. The goods, the life, the honor, and especially the individual rights of the subjects of the States at war with us are also under the guarantee of our national honor. I therefore shall not allow the least aggression against these either. I call the attention of the whole population of Palestine to this proclamation. May God give success to Islam.[57]

On February 12 the press published the text of the sultan's proclamation to the Egyptian people, entitled "My Egyptian Children," saying much the same.[58]

Just as the British had established a protectorate over Egypt and annexed Cyprus, now the Ottomans unilaterally denounced Lebanon's Organic Law, established in agreement with the Great Powers. This was done by the sultan's edict read by the Ali Münif, the newly appointed governor of Lebanon. Ali Münif declared that the Porte had put an end to all foreign interference in the affairs of the Lebanon. But while privileges to foreigners had been abolished the government would not abandon its policy of generosity conferred on the Lebanese for centuries without any foreign intervention.

The Lebanese, alarmed by the repeal of the Organic Law, were assured that the privileges granted to them would not be abolished. There would be no addition to the fixed taxes levied in lieu of the tithes, the tax on property (*temettu*); nor would the arrangement regarding the exemption of the Lebanese from military service be altered. Moreover, the Porte would continue to respect sectarian privileges and traditions.

The governor added that the government eventually would have to introduce certain necessary modifications in the system of administration of Mount Lebanon. The administrative and judicial departments and the gendarmerie would be reformed in such a manner as to ensure the security and welfare of its inhabitants and, by an equitable dispensation of justice, safeguard their rights and liberties within the limits of the constitution. The appointment of governors and officials would be made according to personal merit, with the Lebanese of course enjoying the right of priority.

Furthermore, the government promised to consider new schemes in regard to education, which had so far been almost exclusively directed by foreigners. Special attention would be devoted to the development of agriculture and industry and the devising of means to increase the population's wealth by works of public utility. The Imperial Treasury would provide special grants to cover any deficit in the local budget. "And, whoever may be at the helm, whether it be myself or any of the *Mutessarifs*, my successors, it behooves the Lebanese to co-operate with them for the better fulfillment of their duties, with a view to their happiness, and to work hand in hand with the Government for the better attainment of their ends." The speech confirmed what had been repeated in earlier correspondence: the Lebanese would not be called up for military service. It adopted an unexpectedly friendly and conciliatory tone in the hope of restoring the Lebanon as a province that would be administered on purely Ottoman lines after the war.[59]

News of the failure of the first canal campaign was spread throughout Syria as enemy propaganda. Cemal Pasha denounced such rumors as false reports. The campaign was described as "offensive reconnaissance undertaken last month by a part of our army and which was crowned with great success." The Ottoman army was preparing for another campaign: he asked the "nation, on whom the army reposes its confidence, to be impressed with the sense of its victories and conquests." The Arabs were praised for their proven "historic nobility by their fresh acts of valor that they have accomplished in this war. The Arab blood that mingles with the waters of the canal and which tomorrow will invade the heart of Egypt…will by the grace of God announce to the universe the victory of the Mohammedans at Cairo and the conquest of the beloved city. Let everyone be certain that I shall oversee the conquest of Egypt, beginning with the place where are rising the cries of 'Allah! Allah!'"[60]

For the moment the principal concern of Istanbul (and Berlin) was to defeat the Entente invasion in the Dardanelles. Not fearing a rebellion in Syria, Ottoman forces, along with the German officers, were sent to the capital, leaving behind a garrison of six thousand to eight thousand troops.[61]

As a warning to Syrian nationalists on May 6 Cemal Pasha hanged eleven Arab notables in Beirut and twenty-one more in Damascus. "Curiously enough," noted *the Near East* correspondent, "the list of hanged does not include the name of a single Christian." Those hanged were leading members of notable families of Tripoli, Beirut, Damascus, and Nablus.[62] In his justification published in 1916 as *The Truth regarding the Syrian Question* Cemal Pasha justified the executions on the basis of documents from 1913, seized from the French consulates of Beirut and Damascus when France became an enemy power. The documents revealed that after Ottoman defeat in the Balkans Syrian notables appealed to France to pressure the Porte into granting reform and a measure of autonomy. Correspondence on this matter followed, and the Syrians even held their conference in Paris. This was seen as treason and the betrayal of the Ottoman Empire.[63]

The Unionists had responded to the Paris Congress by making such significant concessions as recognizing the use of Arabic in the Arab provinces, reforming the provincial administration, and giving administrative positions to some of the notables. The notables had been appeased for the moment. But with the outbreak of war and the prospect of having France as an enemy, Cemal saw the notables as a potential threat, especially while the enemy fleet controlled the coast off Syria. Members of some families were therefore banished to Anatolia, while others were executed.

No executions of nationalists took place in Iraq, for the province was

a backwater as far as the idea of nationalism was concerned. Iraqi officers trained in Ottoman military schools played a significant role on
various fronts. Some defected only after the Hashemite rebellion in June
1916. But in April 1915 only the people of Najaf rebelled and expelled the
Ottomans from the city. Each of Najaf's four quarters became independent and continued to enjoy that status until the coming of the British
in August 1917.[64] Iraq saw no other rebellion. In fact the province was
the scene of one of the few Ottoman triumphs of the war: the capture of
the town of Kut ul-Amara on April 29, 1916, along with General C. V. F.
Townsend's army. The siege began on December 7, 1915, and lasted over
three months. It was lauded in the press and made great propaganda.[65]

The capture of Kut was one of the few bright spots of the war in the
Arab provinces. Thereafter it was downhill all the way. Perhaps the major
setback was the Hashemite revolt on June 10, 1916, described in British
propaganda and later scholarship as the "Arab revolt." In fact there was
no Arab revolt, only the revolt of some tribes in the Hijaz under Hashemite leadership. That was a major setback for the Ottomans, however,
for the Hashemite revolt was led by a prominent religious figure, the *şerif*
of Mecca, the guardian of Mecca and Medina, the holy cities of Islam.
Şerif Hüseyin's rebellion therefore made a mockery of the Ottoman jihad. The Porte maintained a news blackout until July 1, when Şerif Ali
Haydar, who belonged to the Zayd clan (rivals to Hüseyin's Awn clan),
was appointed amir of Mecca, replacing the "rebel" Hüseyin. Ali Haydar
had been loyal to the Ottomans and was therefore appointed a senator
and elected first vice-president of parliament.[66]

Şerif Hüseyin's political authority depended on his position in the Islamic world, because he hailed from the family of the Prophet and was
the guardian of the holy places. For the British his revolt was important:
he could be a focus of an anti-Ottoman movements, especially as the
Unionists were described in British propaganda as anti-Islamic secular
"Turkifiers." Hüseyin had also established contacts with the Arab nationalist movement Al-Fatat in Damascus. His importance grew as tension
between the nationalists and the Ottomans sharpened after Cemal Pasha's execution of nationalists in Damascus in the spring of 1916.

The British knew of Şerif Hüseyin's ambitions to lead the Arabs once
he became independent of the Ottomans. In the spring of 1914 they exploited and manipulated him, especially after the visit of 'Abdullah—
Hüseyin's second son—to Lord Kitchener, commander-in-chief of the
Egyptian army. Thereafter links between the Hashemites and the British

were developed, and British arms were shipped across the Red Sea in preparation for the rebellion. Moreover, the Hijaz was also dependent on British India for some of its food, and Istanbul found it difficult to continue supplying the region during wartime.

Even though the Ottomans and Germans were aware that the preparations for revolt were underway, they were unable to prevent British arms from reaching Hüseyin. Hüseyin's sons, Ali and Faysal, launched the rebellion on June 5, 1916, and cut off the railway to the north of Mecca. In the south Hüseyin attacked Mecca, taking the town after a short siege of three days. The port of Jedda was also captured thanks to the role of the Royal Navy seaplane carrier; by late July Hüseyin's forces had captured most of the Hijaz. Hüseyin had himself declared "King of the Arabs," but under British pressure he was forced to adopt the title "King of the Hejaz." His army grew when Arab officers in Ottoman service defected in large numbers, transforming a tribal into an "Arab army."

Fahrettin Pasha's skillful defense of Medina destroyed some of the momentum of the rebellion. He repaired the railway to Damascus, and 16,000 troops were able to reach the town by November 1916, supported by a few German aircraft. Fahrettin Pasha failed to break out of the city. But he was independent enough to ignore Enver's instructions to evacuate Medina in early 1917. The siege continued until Fahrettin surrendered in January 1919, having held out until his starving troops mutinied.[67]

Under Faysal's leadership, now joined by Colonel T. E. Lawrence (aka Lawrence of Arabia), as well as other British officers, the rebellion concentrated its forces in northern Hejaz and Palestine, pinning down large numbers of Ottoman troops. In July 1917 Arab forces captured Aqaba with British support. Aqaba became Faysal's main base. His northern army became the main strike force, while other troops contained Fahrettin Pasha in Medina. Thereafter Arab forces played a divisionary role by using guerrilla tactics against the Ottomans while British forces under the command of General Edmund Allenby (later Viscount Allenby, 1861–1936) advanced into Palestine. By early 1918 the revolt had prevented some 23,000 regular Turkish army troops from participating in the Palestine campaign and was responsible for an estimated 15,000 Turkish casualties (including losses to illness).[68]

The Ottomans naturally saw Şerif Hüseyin's revolt as treachery, a betrayal of the legitimate government from which he had enjoyed a salaried appointment. Hüseyin's revolt has continued to be seen as a stab in the

back by both Turkish journalists and present-day scholars. The nationalist historian İsmail Hami Danişmend, for example, described the rebellion in graphic terms: "Hüseyin, the Şerif of Mecca, having been bought
off by the British, revolted against the Ottoman state which had protected Islam and whose bread he had eaten, betraying the Turkish nation
and the institution of the Caliphate."[69] Today the revolt ought to be seen
as an event in the process of the decolonization of the Ottoman Empire,
which was heading for defeat. In fairness to Şerif Hüseyin, he had held
back from rebellion until June 1916 instead of rebelling while the Ottomans were at their weakest during the Dardanelles campaign throughout
1915. Mecca had always been dependent on external aid in order to feed
both its indigenous population and pilgrims who came for the annual
Haj. The pilgrimage was an essential element in the economy of the region: the money spent by pilgrims was essential for the survival of the
inhabitants of Mecca. By 1916 the pilgrimage had virtually dried up as a
result of the First World War. Istanbul found it impossible to maintain
supplies essential to its upkeep. Consequently Mecca became even more
dependent on the British. Moreover, Hüseyin, though hardly a nationalist, was ambitious and saw himself as the leader of a restored Arab empire
or at least an Arab federation. That is how he interpreted British promises, and the British played along.[70]

"The Hashemites," wrote Uriel Dann, "adhered to the brand of nationalism which emerged during the 'Great Arab Rebellion' (or *thawra*)
of 1916 led by Sharif Husayn." They believed that they had a historic
claim to Arab national leadership and that their mission was to work
for Arab unity under their guidance within the Arab Peninsula and the
Fertile Crescent. According to their perception Egypt was not genuinely
Arab and north Africa was too far away. "This mission was first claimed
by the Hashemites as male descendents of the Prophet's daughter Fatima
and through their guardianship of the holy places at Mecca and Medina
for almost a millennium."[71]

For the Ottomans the situation in the Arab provinces continued
to deteriorate. In February 1917 General Sir Stanley Maude recaptured
Kut despite stubborn resistance. Ottoman forces retreated to Baghdad,
pursued by General Maude, who never gave them the opportunity to re-
group their shattered army. Enver's uncle, Halil (Kut) Pasha, with a force
of around 10,000 men including the Baghdad garrison and the survivors
from Kut, wavered as how best to save the city. Two divisions of around
20,000 men under Ali Ihsan Bey were recalled from northern Iran. But

given the poor communications by both roads and railways, troops in the Caucasus were too far away to be of any help. Baghdad fell to Maude's army on March 11, 1917, and the Ottoman position in Iraq and the Arab provinces became weaker.[72] The defeats in Iraq had an impact in Istanbul. The press emphasized that Ottoman troops were also fighting in Galacia to support the Germans while they could not hold their ground within the empire itself. Military strategy was still being made in Berlin.

Soon after the capture of Baghdad General Sir Archibald Murray (commander of the British army in Egypt) attacked Gaza on March 26 with the hope of opening the road to Palestine. An Ottoman force led by Friedrich Kress von Kressenstein foiled his advance. But that proved to be only a temporary setback for the British advance. In July Arab forces led by Faysal and Lawrence captured the port of Aqaba, establishing a direct link with the British in Egypt. Aqaba became the center of British logistic support and the Gulf of Aqaba headquarters of Faysal's northern army.

British forces continued to advance into Palestine, and Jerusalem fell on December 9, 1917. General Allenby entered the city on foot on December 12. The British celebrated December 9 as the day of Jerusalem's liberation. The conquest of "Jerusalem was widely seen in Britain as a closing victory of the crusades…of colonialism [, which] is a kind of a Crusade, all Western manners and customs are 'Christian,' and any 'Christian' writer may justly be called a 'Crusader.' A two-page photograph of Allenby entering the city was headed: 'Cross Replaces Crescent in Holy City for Which Crusaders Fought and Died.'"[73]

Though the British were advancing in all the Arab provinces, Arab-Ottomans such as Emir Şekib Arslan clung to the hope that the Ottomans could still regain the provinces as part of the empire. He tried to win back Arab allegiance with an article published in Germany entitled "Syria's War Aims" about the relationship between Syria and Istanbul. He wrote that Syrian loyalty was conditional on the Arabs being able to retain their own language, laws, and customs. Though there was a small separatist party in Syria, the majority in the country wished to retain the connection with Istanbul, with either total political autonomy or autonomy in internal matters. Everyone agreed on wanting the revival of Arabic customs and language. The Arabs were filled with a desire for progress and civilization; but, before all else, they were Muslims. They were prepared for any sacrifice in the defense of Islam. This feeling, shared by the Turks, brought them together in an indissoluble union. The Arabs did not wish to be separated from the Turks, for they feared that they might share the fate of Tunis, Algeria, or Morocco.[74] Arslan proved to be very perceptive.

Turning to the ideological trends among the Unionists in Istanbul, Şekib Arslan noted two groups—the Ottomans and the Turanists—with differing views toward the Ottoman Empire. He described the Turanists as "Turkish chauvinists," who spoke of the "Mongol race" and bragged about the heroic deeds of Genghis Khan, Hulagu, and Timur. They preferred to call themselves Turanian rather than Ottoman and wished to revive pre-Islamic mythology and rid the Turkish language of Arabic words. To this group the Arabs were no more than the inhabitants of a colony. England gained many friends in Syria thanks to these people and put itself in direct opposition to the principles of Islamic unity. There could be no greater service to the Entente than the success of the efforts of the Turkish nationalist faction, which was playing into the hands of the enemy.

But an Arab had only to contemplate the possibility of being under French control to become violently pro-Turk. Pro-English Syrians tried to point out the benefits of British rule, but such propaganda had the effect of making Syrians more pro-Turkish than ever. The general feeling in Syria was that the country would remain Turkish after the war, with slight alterations only in the present regime.[75]

Despite the military setback in the Arab provinces the Unionists were far from pessimistic about the future. Russia had collapsed in the midst of revolution and was suing for peace. It signed a peace treaty in March 1918. The Unionists allied with Germany still believed in victory and a negotiated peace based on strength. In such a peace Istanbul hoped to regain the lost Arab provinces as well as Egypt and Cyprus. When Khedive Hüseyin Kamil died in October 1917, Istanbul's press announced that Egypt was an international question; the Ottoman province had been under British occupation since 1882 but had to be vacated when peace was made. Until 1914 Britain had been a hegemonic power. But the war had ended British hegemony, and "the world would be freed from the British yoke." The loss of Egypt would be a great blow to British imperialism, undermining its position east of Suez.[76]

An interview with Sheikh Esad Sükair Efendi, the mufti and the supreme religious head of the Fourth Army in Syria, reflected views similar to those of Istanbul. Asked about relations between Arabs and Turks, he said that the Arabs had always remained faithful to the Ottoman Empire. The talk of an Arab question was the work of some Arab agitators who, "in order to fulfill their personal ambitions have endeavored to raise the standard of revolt." They had followed the advice of French agents and organized the Arab Congress in Paris, which was to have prepared the revolution of the Arab population. When the Central Committee of the Young Turks invited the organizers of the Arab Congress to Istanbul, the leaders of this movement endeavored to obtain high positions. This agitation was the beginning of the Arab question. "You may be sure the Arab chiefs will refuse all interference of foreigners in their internal affairs, and that all important matters will be decided in perfect agreement with the Turks." Asked about Şerif Hüseyin, the sheikh said:

> The false Emir of Mecca revolted against the Turks at the instigation of the English to assure the autonomy of his country, and to obtain succession in his family. England hoped that all Mohammedans would join the rebel chief. With this aim, Hussein Pasha sent an appeal to all Mohammedans asking for their aid. But the religious Chiefs of Palestine, Syria, and other lands replied by a *fetva* condemning his revolt against the Padishah, and thousands of copies of this *fetva* were distributed in all Mohammedan countries. At the present time, Hussein can only count on two tribes, who remained faithful to him as he provided them with money and rice. Once these gifts cease, they too will abandon him.[77]

In January 1918 parliament, still confident of an ultimate German victory, began to discuss the bill to reorganize Iraq by creating the *sancak*s (provincial subdivisions) of Sincar, Habur, and Cezira between the Tigris and the Euphrates. Anarchy was said to reign in the region, so order and justice had to be restored if the region was to progress and develop its natural resources. The tribes living in the plains oppressed and levied supplies from the towns and villages of the region between harvests, with the result that the sedentary and agrarian populations were never sure of their lives and property. These people, finding that the state could not protect them or punish the plunderers, had become demoralized and had surrendered themselves to the whims of the tribal chiefs and sheikhs. After some discussion parliament passed the law that was to go into effect in March 1919.[78]

In March the Yıldırım Force, commanded by Liman von Sanders and supported by German aircraft stationed at Dera, was able to defend Amman. On March 30 Ottoman reinforcements arrived to foil the British

advance, marking a rare Ottoman victory on the Palestine front.[79] In parliament foreign minister Halil Bey reported on the peace treaties with
Russia and Ukraine and promised that England would be driven out of
Egypt, which would then be restored to Turkey. Emir Şekib Arslan, deputy for Havran, then declared that the Porte's first duty was to concentrate the nation's forces against England, henceforth Turkey's sole enemy,
and to defend southern portions of the empire. He recalled the recent
declarations of prime minister Bonar Law and foreign secretary David
Balfour that England would never leave Egypt. Protesting vehemently in
the name of the Arabs and Egyptians against this declaration, Şekib Arslan declared that the Egyptians and Arabs were Ottoman subjects and
wished to remain Ottoman. His speech was warmly applauded amid cries
and curses against England.[80]

Ottoman propaganda seems to have an effect in the Arab provinces,
for on June 16 the British issued a declaration that henceforth Arab territories liberated from the Ottomans would be governed with the consent
of their inhabitants. This suggested that Ottoman propaganda among
the Arabs had to be countered.[81] By the summer of 1918 everything depended on the success of Germany's final offensive. While everything was
in the balance Şekib Arslan wrote another article on Ottoman war aims
and the future of the empire and the Arab provinces. He noted that it
was a question of whether Turkey and Germany would allow England
to realize its gigantic plans in the East—the domination of Egypt, Iraq,
and Syria and the protectorate over the Hijaz—or whether they would
strike a critical blow in Palestine, retake Jerusalem, and drive the English
back to the Suez Canal. "We are convinced that our rulers have never lost
sight of the fact that the regaining of the Arab provinces occupied by the
enemy is a vital question for the Ottoman Empire."[82]

The death of Sultan Mehmed Reşad and the investiture of Mehmed V
Vahdettin on August 31, 1918, were an opportunity for the Istanbul press
to highlight the role of the caliph, "the great representative of the religion
of which he has become champion." The arrival of Libyan leader Sheikh
Ahmed al-Sanussi from his exile in Vienna for the ceremony of Vahdettin's investiture "was seen as evidence of the Muslim world's attachment
to the caliphate, especially the Muslims of north Africa, long alienated by
Anglo-French-Italian intrigue."[83]

By August 1918 the German offensive had failed, the Ottoman Empire had been defeated, and its Arab provinces had been lost. The Ottomans had no other card to play than Islam and the Caliphate. At this

point Şekib Arslan, formerly the Ottoman-Arab patriot, reinvented himself as a Syrian nationalist. On October 4 *Osmanischer Lloyd* published his telegram to all belligerents and neutrals, protesting against the partition of Syria between England and France according to a secret agreement that they had signed during the war that had been revealed by the Bolsheviks. That was sufficient proof, argued Şekib Bey, that the war that the Entente fought had been a war of conquest and annexation. He proposed that, in conformity "with the well-known and oft-proclaimed principles of President Wilson, Lloyd George, and other Entente statesmen, a plebiscite be taken, freely and uninfluenced by any power. All measures taken contrary to the true will of the Syrian nation will necessarily contain any germs of future wars."[84]

8

Postscript

Ottoman Defeat and the Aftermath

When war ended in total defeat the Ottomans had lost virtually all their empire outside Anatolia. A de facto border was negotiated during the armistice of October 30, 1918. But even this territory was not secure: Britain, France, and Italy, which had signed secret treaties during the war, contested the terms of the armistice. The Armenian nationalists and Greece also hoped to fulfill their national aspirations at the expense of the now prostrate Ottomans. Had the Treaty of Sèvres of August 1920 been imposed on the sultan's government, the postwar Ottoman state would have been a truncated monarchy in the center of Anatolia; the Armenian Revolutionary Federation would have won the state it had fought for; and Greece would have redeemed much of its subject population in Anatolia. The future of Anatolia was to be decided at the Paris Peace Conference.

Richard Hovanissian is correct to note that "Turkish publications during the World War referred to the Armenian decision at Erzerum [in 1914] as proof of disloyalty." That was to be expected from publications of an imperial power, especially one at war and under strict censorship. It is more surprising that many writers in Turkey today, long after the fall of the Ottomans, continue to see the struggle of the nationalities as betrayal and a stab in the back rather than as nationalist struggles and the decolonization of an empire.[1] Other scholars view the struggle during the war as a civil war. Arif Erzen, in his introduction to Erich Feigl, *A Myth of Terror*, describes the events of the war years as a "civil war": "the Armenian minority was in a 'state of war' with its own Ottoman government."[2] Civil wars (for example, the American Civil War, the English Civil War, the Russian civil war after the Bolsheviks seized power in November 1917, and the Spanish Civil War of 1936–38) were fought between citizens of the same country. They are not wars within empires, even if the Ottomans passed a citizenship law in the late nineteenth century. Thus no one today describes the American Revolution of 1776 against the British as a civil war, because it was a war of independence. But the war between the American North and South in the 1860s was a civil war. Postimperial writing on the Ottomans fails to see the struggle of nationalities as the effort to create national liberation movements against a dynastic empire in the process of decolonization. The final such conflict against the Ottoman dynasty was Turkey's own national struggle, in which the nationalists were led by Mustafa Kemal Pasha. That was described by the Istanbul government as the betrayal of the sultan-caliph. In April 1920, while the nationalists were fighting against the Greek advance, the sultan's Şeyhülislam issued a religious edict declaring that the killing of rebels on the orders of the sultan-caliph was a religious duty. The fetva argued that the nationalists had rebelled against the sultan-caliph and that the nationalist forces were bandits who were attacking and robbing the loyal subjects of the sultan and therefore deserved to be killed. The fetva failed to have the desired effect. Soon afterward the nationalists liberated the territories within the armistice lines of 1918 that formed the borders of the "national pact." Few today dispute the legitimacy of Turkey's national struggle or describe the nationalists as traitors.

After the restoration of the constitution in 1908 the Armenian nationalists initially worked side by side with the Unionists, hoping to achieve a measure of reform. But once the empire seemed to be on its last legs during the Balkan Wars a Dashnak faction led by Antranig Pasha fought alongside the Bulgarians, hoping to achieve statehood after the collapse of the empire. When the empire did not fall in 1913, most Ottoman publications took care not to denounce all Armenians as disloyal—only the Armenians of Thrace who had supported Antranig Pasha. The Ottomans hoped that the Armenians of Anatolia would continue to remain part of the empire alongside Turks, Greeks, Jews, and Arabs. When the First World War broke out, Armenian revolutionaries again anticipated the end of the Ottoman Empire if the Unionists entered the war on the German side. They calculated that the Entente would defeat Germany. By siding with England, France, and Russia they saw their opportunity to create their own state. That was a rational choice that any nationalist movement might have made.

The First World War had been predicted to be a short war. Even though that did not turn out to be the case, its final outcome remained uncertain until the summer of 1918. The nationalities remained hopeful that they would fulfill their hopes of liberation. Soon after the Kerensky government came to power in Russia in March 1917, the question of nationalities in the Russian Empire came to the fore. Nationalities of the Russian Empire advanced their claims for self-government and even total independence. The Armenians, however, stated that the question of their future was of an international character. Therefore they waited for the peace conference to settle their claim.[3] Russia's Armenians were considering not only their status in Russia but also their kin in the Ottoman Empire. After the Entente victory in 1918 Armenian and Greek nationalists relied on the Great Powers in Paris to fulfill their ambitions. Before the peace conference opened, Baghos Nubar Pasha (president of the Armenian National Delegation representing the Armenians of Anatolia) wrote to France's foreign minister, Stephen Pichon, on October 29, 1918, and claimed the status of belligerent for the Armenians. Even when the Ottomans entered the war in 1914 the Association Franco-Arménienne asked the French government to recognize Armenia as a belligerent. Nubar Pasha expressed grave disappointment to the *Times* in his letter published on January 30, 1919. He complained that the Allies had not invited the Armenian Revolutionary Federation to the peace conference. "The fact is well known," he wrote, "that ever since the beginning of the war, Armenians have been belligerents 'de facto' since their indignant refusal to side with the Turks...; our volunteers fought in Syria and Palestine...After the breakdown of Russia, the Armenian legions were the only force to resist the advance of the Turks whom they held in check until the armistice was signed."[4]

The situation must have seemed hopeful when the French general Franchet d'Esperey made his official entry into Istanbul on a white horse on February 2, 1919, wildly cheered by the Greeks, Armenians, and Levantines. Though the Armenians were not given the status of a belligerent, they were allowed to present their case before the Supreme Council at the conference. The Armenian delegation under Nubar Pasha began to argue its case on February 26, 1919. He asked for an Armenian state that would include Cilicia (including Alexandretta/Hatay) and the six provinces of Erzurum, Bitlis, Van, Diyarbakır, Harput, and Sıvas, with a portion of Trabzon in order to give the Armenian state access to the Black Sea. Nubar Pasha did not claim the entire province of Trabzon because of its Greek majority. Ottoman Armenians continued to put forward territorial claims, with ports on both the Mediterranean and the Black Sea.[5]

Avetis Aharonian was co-leader of the delegation. He was president of the Republic of Armenia and head of the Dashnak government, while

Nubar led a delegation of Armenian Liberals, chosen by the patriarch in 1912. Aharonian presented his case on February 28. Both he and Nubar emphasized that the Unionist government had offered the Armenians autonomy but they had refused, preferring to join the Entente. Their devotion to the Entente, Nubar maintained, was one of the reasons for the massacres and deportations. They had therefore been belligerents; the "tribute of life paid by Armenia is heavier than that of any other belligerent nation."[6] Professor K. K. Krikorian, another delegate, defended the demand for a large state, declaring that it would be "the only important oasis in the Moslem desert in the future struggle of western civilization with Moslem militarism."[7] Nubar appealed to the historic past of the Armenians in the region, the persistence of their Christian church, Armenian service to the Allies, and Allied promises. The area he claimed for an Armenian state stretched from the Caucasus to the Mediterranean; he also asked for the protection of the Great Powers.[8]

After the Armenian delegation had made its case, everything depended on a Great Power taking the mandate for the Armenian state to be created in eastern Anatolia. While the Allies were committed to such a state, Britain, France, and Italy did not want to be directly involved in its creation. Such a state would require a mandate, which "promised to be a very expensive headache with little or no material of strategic benefits to recompense the mandatory power."[9] On March 14, 1919, Colonel Edward M. House had assured Lloyd George and Georges Clemenceau that the United States would "undoubtedly take on a mandate." While the British were delighted because that would keep the French out of the region, the French were unhappy, for they believed that Cilicia, which had been promised to France by the Sykes-Picot Agreement, would go to Armenia in a U.S. mandate.[9] The question of Armenia came before the Council of Four on March 14. "President Wilson agreed to accept a mandate, subject, he added, to the consent of the American Senate." The French were displeased with the prospect of an American mandate that would give Washington control of territory from the Black Sea to the Mediterranean.[10] They were so frustrated by Armenian claims that on December 19, 1919, Clemenceau is said to have rebuked Nubar Pasha with the words: "We are fed up with the Armenians already."[11]

The Great Powers in Paris favored the creation of an Armenian state in Anatolia, though they disagreed about its size. But they were faced with another dilemma: "in no area of Asia Minor did the Armenians constitute a distinct majority of the population, and their total in any sizable state would run as low as 30–35 percent." Thus despite Wilson's call for self-determination, the principle of a majority being given this right could not be applied to the Armenians in Anatolia or to the Zionists in Palestine.[12] Meanwhile the Istanbul government bent over backward to appease the Great Powers in order to win their support. On February 12, 1919, the Porte formed a military tribunal and began to try Unionists involved in the Armenian deportations and punished those found guilty of crimes against Armenians. On April 10 Mehmed Kemal Bey, former governor of Bogazliyan and Yozgat, was found guilty of such crimes and sentenced to death by court-martial. He was hanged in Beyazit Square on April 10. His funeral the next day turned into a protest against the government and the Allied occupation.[13]

The Istanbul daily *Entente* reported on May 7, 1919, that the sultan's government was compensating Greek and Armenian deportees who were returning to Thrace and Anatolia. A bill was to be passed to provide compensation to deportees whose houses and goods had been destroyed. On the same day *Pontus* reported that the minister of the interior had offered the posts of Governors of Sıvas, Diyarbakır, Mamuret-ul-Aziz, and Van to Armenians.[14] But such measures on the part of the Istanbul government were unlikely to appease the Armenian nationalists who were looking to America to take the mandate for their state. When the Senate discussed the question of a U.S. mandate for Armenia, the *Commercial Appeal* of Memphis noted: "The Armenians were unfortunate that they did not live in an oil field. Then we would have protected them to the last man!" The U.S. Senate rejected the proposal to accept the mandate on June 1, 1920.[15] The Treaty of Sèvres of August 10, 1920, recognized Armenia as a free and independent state whose boundaries in the provinces of Erzurum, Trabzon, Van, and Bitlis were to be decided by President Wilson. On November 22, 1920, Wilson assigned some 40,000 square miles of Anatolia to Armenia, including Trabzon, Erzincan, Erzurum, Muş, and Van.[16] Had the Treaty of Sèvres been enforced, the new Turkey ruled by the sultan-caliph would no longer have had control over the Straits or a Mediterranean coastline and would have had a truncated Black Sea coast and no Armenian or Kurdish territory in northeast Anatolia.

Without Great Power willingness to enforce the treaty the survival of the Armenian state was uncertain. The nationalist parliament in Ankara declared war on the Republic of Armenia on September 24, 1920, and its army launched an offensive on September 28, capturing Sarıkamış and Kars on September 30 and Gümrü on November 7. An armistice was signed on November 17. On December 2 the Bolsheviks, the allies of the

Turkish nationalists, overthrew the Dashnak-Menshevik Armenian government, took Georgia, and became Turkey's neighbors.[17] Meanwhile Mustafa Kemal Pasha, the leader of the Turkish nationalists, met Stéphen Pichon in December 1920 to discuss France's role in southeastern Anatolia. After the negotiations France abandoned the Armenians who had thrown in their lot with the French forces in Cilicia. But after signing the agreement with France the nationalists tried to win over the Armenians of Cilicia by granting an amnesty to those who had participated in the French campaign.[18] The Soviet-Turkish Treaty, signed in Moscow on March 16, 1921, sealed the fate of an independent Armenia in Anatolia. Batum was ceded to the Soviets and Kars and Ardahan to Ankara. On December 2, 1921, Armenia signed the Treaty of Gümrü with the nationalists and accepted all their terms.[19] The Treaty of Lausanne of July 23, 1923, gave international recognition to an independent and sovereign Turkey. By the terms of this treaty the Armenian citizens in the new Turkey were to be protected as a minority, with complete security of life and liberty without distinction of birth, nationality, language, ethnicity, or religion. The tragedy of Armenian nationalism had been its failure to find a Great Power to take the mandate and to provide protection while the Armenian nation and state developed.

GREECE

On October 20, 1918, the signing of the Armistice of Mudros on Admiral Arthur Calthorpe's flagship, the *Agamemnon*, named for the mythical Greek hero of the Trojan War, may have been seen as an omen by the Greeks. Now that the Ottomans had been soundly defeated, Greek ambitions would be fulfilled. A U.S. Near Eastern Intelligence Report from Geneva dated December 31, based on the Athenian press, noted that the Greek destroyer *Lion* had debarked a detachment of Greek marines at Izmir who were welcomed by the Greek population and by Armenians and Greeks in the Ottoman Empire favoring collaboration. The Greek patriarch broke off relations with the Porte on March 9, 1919, and asked his flock not to participate in the coming elections. A few days later the Greeks of Istanbul, led by the patriarch, demonstrated and hoisted Greek flags over their churches, severed relations with the Porte, and renounced their civic responsibilities as Ottoman citizens.[20]

In Paris Greek prime minister Eleftherios Venizelos appeared before the peace conference on February 3 and 4, 1919. On the basis of population he made the Greek case for the acquisition of the Aegean and the Dodecanese Islands as well as Thrace and western Anatolia. He made no demand for Cyprus but hoped that Britain, having offered the island to Greece during the war, would now surrender it. Venizelos also made no request for Constantinople, though "in reality it was a Greek town." *Spectateur d'Orient* (May 3, 1919) published the population of Istanbul as reported by the general directorate of registration. According to the city's demography, it was not a "Greek town" as Venizelos claimed. The 983,358 inhabitants included 608,884 Muslims, 219,567 Greeks, 78,294 Armenians, 55,593 Jews, 10,950 Catholic Armenians, 1,350 Evangelicals, and 8,280 Latins, Bulgarians, Syrians, Chaldeans, and Gypsies. Venizelos proposed internationalizing the city—including the districts of Izmit, Gallipoli, Biga, and parts of Bursa—and placing the entire region under the League of Nations. He suggested that the sultan should be required to leave Istanbul and go to Konya or Bursa, while a small Turkish state should be confined to Anatolia. He argued that that his claims were based on Wilson's twelfth point, calling for self-determination, as well as on "the geographical and historical unity of the country and the Greek majority." The majority in western Thrace, however, was Turkish. But, as Helmreich notes, "it was apparent that Turks did not count."[21]

Not everyone was convinced of the validity of Greek claims. When Professor Sir W. M. Ramsay, an expert on the geography of Anatolia, was asked to comment on Greek claims in Asia Minor, he answered that he would like to see Greek claims based on trustworthy maps. So far as he had seen or heard, all maps submitted by the Greeks showed that the distribution of population on the western edge of Anatolia and the eastern coast of the Aegean had been falsified to a marked degree. Margaret MacMillan also found that Venizelos's "statistics were dubious." The American experts did not support Greek claims on demographic grounds either.[22]

The Greeks and Armenians at Paris collaborated against the Turkish delegation. Prime Minister Venizelos spoke for Armenians when he declared that their state should include the six "Armenian vilayets" united with Russian Armenia, plus Trabzon and Adana. After Venizelos had finished presenting his case, Lloyd George, who was enamored of the Greek prime minister, describing him as the greatest Greek since Pericles, moved that Greek claims be examined by an expert committee to be composed of two Americans and representatives of the British Empire, France, and Italy. This committee made its recommendations on March 6. The American, British, and French members accepted Greek demands, but the Italians were opposed. The committee made no recommendations in regard to the partition of western Anatolia, claiming that the settlement could not be separated from the overall settlement for Asia Minor. In short, Greek claims clashed with those of Italy. The Italians believed that they had secured Izmir and Antalya by the secret treaties of 1915 and 1917. The British representative, Sir Eyre Crowe, who favored Athens, had already informed the Italians on March 1, 1919, that the 1915 agreement referred only to Antalya, while the 1917 agreement was invalid due to lack of Russian approval.[23] In order to preempt unilateral action by Greece, on March 23 the Italians landed troops at Antalya in order to secure the land promised them by Britain and France. On April 29 an Italian warship entered Izmir, again to forestall a Greek invasion. In the weeks after the occupation of Antalya, the Italians secured the area from Antalya to Bodrum and inland as far as Konya.[24]

The Italians began to take matters into their own hands, much to the chagrin of Britain, France, and America. On May 5 Lloyd George announced that Italy had occupied the harbor at Marmaris as a coaling station, while a battalion was at Konya and troops had landed at Antalya. On the same day the Council of Three in Paris—composed of Britain, France, and America, because the Italian delegate was away—approved the occupation of Izmir by Greek forces. On the following day President Wilson announced that the United States would not be sending troops to Turkey, because it had not been at war with that country.[25] On May 13 Admiral Calthorpe informed the Ottoman governor and the military commander of Aydın that the Allies would occupy the fortification and defenses of the city the next day. After the forts had been occupied the governor was told that Greek forces would be landing on May 15, according to article 7 of the Armistice of Mudros. The governor acquiesced under protest, and next morning the Greeks began their occupation of Izmir.[26]

The Greek army occupied Izmir under the cover of British, French, and American ships, while the English, French, and Italian troops occupied the forts. Greek troops entered a defenseless town amid cheers of the local Greek population. They pillaged the governor's residence and government offices. All that the local government could do was file a long report to the War Ministry in Istanbul, noting that the Greek army of occupation had taken over control of the administration. The Istanbul press wrote on May 27 that the Greek invasion was in full swing and that Menemen and Manisa had also been occupied. *Sabah* (May 27, 1919) added

Çeşme and Nispet to the list of territories occupied by Greek forces. The newspaper asked: "What the Turks want to know is, where will they stop? What is the frontier allotted to them at the Conference?"[27] When Andrew Kalmykov, the Russian consul, returned to Izmir in October 1919, he found that the Greeks had taken possession of the city. It was not a temporary military occupation like that of Constantinople under an allied force. "The Greeks had come to stay for good."[28] "In committing itself to a full-fledged support of Greek ambitions in Asia Minor, Britain was gambling that Greece would permanently supplant Turkey as the dominant force in the eastern Mediterranean area."[29]

Prime Minister Venizelos, seeing the passive response of the governments in Istanbul, believed that the Turks were on their knees and would not offer any resistance to a Greek advance. His intelligence may have informed him of the *Moniteur Oriental* report of May 29 that Turkish officers of the reserve army had held a protest meeting in Istanbul against the Greek invasion. They had then presented a memorandum to the sultan, vowing to sacrifice their lives for the national cause. But the sultan had replied: "God willing [*Inshallah*], there would be no need to sacrifice their lives for the fatherland!"[30]

Having consolidated the Greek position in the province of Aydın, Greek forces began to advance inland. In June 1920, with Lloyd George's blessing, Greek forces began to move beyond the Milne line; as a quid pro quo Venizelos agreed to send troops to support the Allied occupation of Istanbul. By August the Greeks had advanced 250 miles into Anatolia.[31] The Greek advance created a crisis in the Nationalist Assembly in Ankara, and many believed that Turkey could be saved only through European intervention. Little did they realize that Europe stood firmly behind Venizelos. When the Treaty of Sèvres, "supported with interest by Britain," was signed on August 10, 1920, it seemed as though Venizelos's ambition of a "greater Greece" had been fulfilled. Elizabeth Wiskemann wrote: "They [the Greeks] hoped not only to drive the Turks out of Europe, bag and baggage, but also incorporate parts of Asia Minor where Greeks had lived from times immemorial."[32]

After further consolidation the Greek army in Anatolia resumed its advance on March 23, 1921. The Greeks suffered a serious setback, however, at the Battle of İnönü on March 31. But Athens was not deterred and was determined to advance. To boost the morale of his army prior to the next offensive King Constantine arrived in Izmir on June 12. The offensive was launched on July 12, and Eskişehir and Kütahya fell on July

17.[33] But the Greeks had extended their lines too far into Anatolia, succumbing to the Turkish counteroffensive of July 21. At the start of the Greek invasion of Anatolia war minister and general John Metaxas, future dictator of Greece, had been right when he warned Venizelos: "The Greek state is not today ready for the government and exploitation of so extensive a territory."[34] After the defeat at the Battle of Sakarya on September 13, the Greek army began to retreat. On May 25, 1922, General Anastasios Papoulas resigned as commander-in-chief and was replaced by General George Hazianestis, marking a serious decline in Greek morale. Generals Nikolaos Trikoupis and Kimon Digenis finally surrendered on September 2/3, and the Turkish army entered Izmir on September 9. Thus ended Greece's Anatolian Catastrophe.[35]

After the nationalist victory only the fate of the Greeks of Turkey remained to be decided. At Lausanne it was agreed that the Greeks of Anatolia, except those residing in Istanbul, would be exchanged for the Muslims of Thrace. The Lausanne Convention of January 30, 1923, stipulated that the transfers were to begin on May 1. Between 1923 and 1930 an estimated 1.25 million Greeks were sent from Turkey to Greece and a somewhat smaller number of Turks from Greece to Turkey. The persons to be exchanged were described as "Turkish subjects of the Greek orthodox religion residing in Turkey" and "Greek subjects of the Muslim religion residing in Greece."[36]

The other nationality that remains to be discussed is the Ottoman Jewish community, usually described as "Musevi" (followers of Moses), in contrast to the European Zionists, who were described as "Yahudi," a term that generally carried political connotations. With the end of the Ottoman Empire, the Jews had no demands to make; as with the non-Muslims who remained in the republic after the signing of the Treaty of Lausanne in 1923, they were given the status of a protected minority. But most Turks continued to see them as a community well integrated into Turkish society. In May 1919 the Istanbul government announced that Christians would no longer have to do military service but Ottoman Jews, who were considered "integrated with Muslims," were not included in the decision and would therefore have to serve in the army.[37]

The fact that Jews were not included in the decision evoked an outcry from the Jewish community. At a sitting of the Jewish National Council on May 10 a resolution was passed, protesting the distinction drawn as being calculated to contravene the principle of equality of rights of all non-Muslim nationalities of the Ottoman Empire. The Jews should also be included in the exemption. But such a decision undermined the 1908 constitution that had proclaimed equality of all Ottomans. While the decision to exempt Jews from military service was welcomed by the French-language press on May 3, it received a mixed reception from Turkish-language newspapers that continued to describe the Jewish community as Ottoman. They wrote that the constitutional revolution of 1908 had come full circle. The document had proclaimed the equality of all Ottoman citizens before the law and ended the humiliation that enabled non-Muslims to buy themselves out of military service. That privilege was being restored.

On February 19, 1920, the Ottoman parliament in Istanbul began discussing the terms "Turk" and "millet." The consensus arrived at suggested that the term "Turk" included only the Muslim elements—Turk, Kurd, Laz, Circassian, and Arab. But then why not use the term "Islamic elements" (*anasir-i Islamiyye*) asked the cleric Abdülaziz Mecdi Efendi. In the discussion Hüseyin Bey, deputy for Erzurum, declared that the term "Turk" should also include Jews, suggesting that the use of "Islamic elements" would not be appropriate.[38] The Istanbul government's discussions and declarations in the Ottoman parliament were academic. Neither institution had long to survive. But they do tell us something about the attitude that postimperial Turkey had toward the Jewish community.

Notes

CHAPTER 1. INTRODUCTION

1 L. S. Stavrianos, *The Balkans since 1453*, 49ff. Benedict Anderson, *Imagined Communities*, 72, notes that by the mid-eighteenth century German, French, and English scholars had made "a firmly pagan ancient civilization" available to "a small number of young Greek-speaking Christian intellectuals." Such intellectuals would have played an important role in the anti-Ottoman movement that developed. See also Hans Kohn's classic work *The Idea of Nationalism*; and Charles Jelavich and Barbara Jelavich, *The Establishment of the Balkan National States, 1804–1920*.

2. Üner Turgay, "Nation," in *Oxford Encyclopedia of the Islamic World*, 233–34.

3. While the excellent collection *Empire to Nation* edited by Joseph Esherick, Hasan Kayalı, and Eric Van Young has an entry in the index on "colonization," it has no entry for "decolonization." I would have thought that the two processes go together.

4. Stavrianos, *Balkans*, 238–47. "None took up arms against the rule of the sultan.... Rather, they fought against the troublemakers [the janissaries] who were flouting the sultan's authority" (245–46). Ainslee Embree, "Imperialism and Decolonization," provides a useful account of the process for the twentieth century but neglects to discuss the Ottoman case.

5. Ibid., 211, n. 14.

6. Erdoğan Göçer, *Türk Tabiyat Hukuku*; Alexis Alexandris, *The Greek Minority of Istanbul*, 24–25 (quotation).

7. Max Weber, *General Economic History*, 233.

8. Göcer, *Türk Tabiyat Hukuku*; and Feroz Ahmad, "Ottoman Perceptions of the Capitulations, 1800–1914."

9. E. E. Ramsaur, *The Young Turks*; M. Şükrü Hanioğlu, *The Young Turks in Opposition*.

10. Vice Consul Dickson to O'Conor, Van, March 2, 1908, Foreign Office (hereafter FO) 371/533.

11. Louise Nalbandian, *The Armenian Revolutionary Movement*, 176–78; William Langer, *The Diplomacy of Imperialism, 1890–1902*; Justin McCarthy, *Death and Exile*, 119–22.

12. Murat Bardakcı, *Hürriyet*, November 17 and 22, 2003.

CHAPTER 2. THE ARMENIAN COMMUNITY

1. Sarkis Atamian, *The Armenian Community*, 159ff., 165.

2. *Puzantion*, October 9, 1909, 164; and *Azadamard*, October 13 and 14, 1909, quoted in Atamian, *The Armenian Community*, 165.

3. Djemal Pasha (Ahmed Cemal Pasha), *Memories of a Turkish Statesman, 1913–1919*, 252–53; Ahmed Cemal Paşa, *Hatıralar*, 345–46.

4. Fitzmaurice to Lowther, Nov. 30, 1908, FO 195/2281; the conversation took place on November 30. Kevork Pamukciyan, *Biyografileriyle Ermeniler*, 254–55, provides a useful biography of the patriarch and some other Armenian personalities of this period.

5. Surtees to Lowther, no. 42, Constantinople, May 16, 1909, FO 371/776/19401; and *Tanin*, November 2, 1909.

6. Assembly debates for June 16 and 21 and July 21: *Tanin*, June 17 and 22 and July 22, 1909. When the Balkan Wars broke out in October 1912, the Armenian patriarch noted that 8,000 Armenians were serving in the army and more were enlisting. The patriarch had appointed fifteen chaplains, "provided for the spiritual needs of Armenian troops," *Near East*, November 8, 1912, 4.

7. E. J. Dillon, "The Reforming Turk," *Quarterly Review* 210 (1909): 247.

8. Lowther to Grey, no. 36 confidential, Pera, January 18, 1909, FO 371/762/3123.

9. Lewis Heck to Secretary of State, Constantinople, January 17, 1919, United States, Department of State, *Foreign Relations of the United States* (hereafter *FRUS*), 867.00/846. Adam Block had been the former chief dragoman at the British Embassy before the revolution then British representative on the Ottoman Public Debt Administration, as well as financial advisor to the British high commissioner at Istanbul after the armistice. He arrived in Istanbul in November 1877 as a student interpreter. See G. R. Berridge, *Gerald Fitzmaurice (1865–1939)*.

10. On the counterrevolution in Istanbul and the incidents in Adana, see Feroz Ahmad, *The Young Turks*, 14ff., 43. For a comprehensive analysis of the counter-revolution, see Sina Akşin, *Şeriatçı Bir Ayaklanma*. On *Trosag*, see Murat Koptaş, "Armenian Political Thinking in the Second Constitutional Period: The Case of Krikor Zohrab" (MA thesis, Boğazici University, Istanbul, 2005), 63, n. 30.

11. Lowther to Grey, no. 324C, Constantinople, May 4, 1909, FO 371/772/1775.

12. *Tanin*, May 13 and 16, 1909.

13. Consul-General Barnham to Lowther, no. 52, Smyrna, June 5, 1909, FO 371/776/22033.

14. Lowther to Grey, no 566C, Therapia, July 20, 1909, FO 371/773/28029; H. C. Yalçın, "31 Marttan sonra İdamlar karşısında," *Yakın Tarihimiz* 1 (1962): 170–71.

15. On the agreement, see *Tanin*, September 16, 1909, quoted in Esat Uras, *Tarihte Ermeniler ve Ermeni Meselesi*, 584–85 (576–77 in 1976 edition). Biographies of Noradunghian (rendered Kapriyel Noradunkyan) Kapriyel and Bedros Halaciyan (Hallacyan), see Pamukciyan, *Biyografileriyle Ermeniler*, 334 and 238, respectively.

16. C/108-47 Western Bureau–Turkish Section circular number 14 to ARF, April 16, 1911, quoted in Dikran Kaligian, "The Armenian Revolutionary Federation under Ottoman Constitutional Rule, 1908–1914," 141.

17. Dikran Kaligian, "Agrarian Land Reform and the Armenians in the Ottoman Empire," 32.

18. Lowther to Grey, Constantinople, January 22, 1911, FO 424/226/65, quoted in Kaligian, "Agrarian Land Reform," 24.

19. *Near East*, June 24, 1911, 47.

20. Kaligian, "Agrarian Land Reform," 33–34, citing Marling to Grey, Constantinople, July 4, 1911, FO 424/228/16.

21. *Near East*, June 28, 1911, 167; see also June 21, 1911, 143.

22. "Our Armenian Letter," dated January 11, 1912, *Near East*, January 19, 1912, 328. For a brief biographical note on Arşaruni, see Pamukciyan, *Biyografileriyle Ermeniler*, 39.

23. "Armenian Letter," dated January 26, 1912; *Near East*, February 1912, 394.

24. Ibid.

25. "Armenian Letter," dated February 23, 1912, *Near East*, March 1, 1912, 534.

26. *Near East*, February 16, 1912, 462; Aykut Kansu, *Politics in Post-Revolutionary Turkey, 1908–1913*, 331.

27. *Times*, March 19 and 22, 1912.

28. For work done by the reform commission in the vilayet of Kosovo, see *Times*, May 28, 1912.

29. On the so-called big stick elections of 1912, see Ahmad, *The Young Turks*, 91; for details, see Tevfik Çavdar, *"Müntehib-I Sani"den Seçmene.*

30. *Near East*, March 22, 1912, 639, and March 29, 675; Alan Bodger, "Russia and the End of the Ottoman Empire," 81ff.

31. Andrew D. Kalmykov, *Memoirs of a Russian Diplomat*, 250. Charykov, however, seems to have become a Turcophile. After the Bolshevik revolution he preferred to live and die in exile in Istanbul rather than Paris.

32. *Near East*, May 10, 1912, 3; Philip Mosely, "Russian Policy in 1911–12," 69–86, wrote: "In dealing with a Turkey in the process of renewal, it [Russia] hesitated between a policy of outright hostility and partition, and one of veiled protectorate, modeled on Unkiar-Skelessi [Treaty of Hünkar İskelesi of 1833]." For Russian attempts to secure the opening of the Straits in 1911, see 71–72.

33. "Armenian Letter," dated May 3, *Near East*, May 10, 1912, 3.

34. Harry N. Howard, *The Partition of the Ottoman Empire*, 22–23.

35. Murat Koptaş, "Armenian Political Thinking in the Second Constitutional Period," 71, n. 47.

36. *Near East*, September 13, 1912, 547.

37. *Near East*, February 14, 1912, 547.

38. *Near East*, September 27, 1912, 620.

39. G. P. Gooch, *Recent Revelations of European Diplomacy*, 216.

40. *Near East*, November 8, 1912, 4. On Antranig Pasha (Antranig Özanian, aka Baruyr), see Koptaş, "Armenian Political Thinking," 57, n. 33. Antranig Pasha also fought alongside the Russian army during the First World War and was decorated by the tsar.

41. *Near East*, January 17, 1913, 301.

42. "Another Letter by an Armenian Student," *Near East*, April 18, 1913, 670.

43. H[asan] Cemal, *Tekrar Başımıza Gelenler*, 123. Richard Hovanissian wrote: "In 1912 Balkan Armenians responded by forming a volunteer unit to assist the Bulgarians against Turkey, while the Armenians of Transcaucasia again agitated for Russian involvement in Ottoman affairs": Richard G. Hovanissian, *Armenia on the Road to Independence, 1918*, 30–31. Leon Trotsky, who covered the Balkan Wars as a journalist, interviewed Ottoman prisoners of war and describes the attitude of Greek, Armenian, and Muslim prisoners in *The Balkan Wars, 1912–13*, 57–352. See my review article on this book: Feroz Ahmad, "Leon Trotsky's Writings on the Ottoman State," in *From Empire to Nation*, 85–100.

44. C/117-1/ARF Self-Defense Body to Troshag Editorial Board, October 27, 1912, 326; Kaligian, "The Armenian Revolutionary Federation," 237, n. 157.
45. Kaligian, "The Armenian Revolutionary Federation," 248, n. 5, quoting a document from the Russian Foreign Policy Archives in Manoog J. Somakian, *Empires in Conflict*, 58; see also *Near East*, November 15, 1912, 40.
46. Memoirs of Baron Beyens, *Deux ans à Berlin*, cited in Gooch, *Recent Revelations of European Diplomacy*, 335–36. Alfred von Kiderlen-Wachter (1852–1912) was foreign minister at the time.
47. *Hansard Parliamentary Debates*, House of Commons, vol. 56, 1913, 2311.
48. *Times of India*, February 14, 1913, quoted in Azmi Özcan, *Pan-Islamism, Indian Muslims, the Ottomans and Britain, 1877–1924*, 164–65. British policy toward the Armenian question also changed during the Balkan conflict—the Foreign Office began to think in terms of foreign control. Kaligian, "The Armenian Revolutionary Federation," 249–50; and Joseph Heller, *British Policy towards the Ottoman Empire, 1908–1914*, 83.
49. Michael Llewellyn Smith, *Ionian Visions*, 30–33. On Muslim refugees and territories lost during the Balkan Wars, see Arnold Toynbee, *The Western Question in Greece and Turkey*, 138; and McCarthy, *Death and Exile*.
50. Lowther to Grey, 986C, Constantinople, November 23, 1912, FO 371/1484/50520 with the enclosure of the Şeyhülislam's proclamation in *Liberté*, November 19, 1912.
51. *Near East*, May 24, 1912, 74. The exodus increased during and after the Balkan Wars.
52. Kaligian, "The Armenian Revolutionary Federation," 297–98.
53. Ibid., 299, n. 141.
54. C/118-29/ARF Self-Defense Body to U.S. Central Committee in Kaligian, "The Armenian Revolutionary Federation," 273.
55. *Tanin*, April 27, 28, and 29 1913; see also Yusuf Hikmet Bayur, *Türk İnkılabı Tarihi*, vol. 2, part 4, 304–7; Stephen Longrigg, *Iraq: 1900–1950*, 47–51; Rommily to Secretary of State, Constantinople, April 29 1913, no. 480, *FRUS*, 876.00/530.
56. Kaligian, "The Armenian Revolutionary Federation," 293, nn. 123 and 124, citing Lowther's reports to the Foreign Office.
57. Ibid., 285.
58. Ibid., 285, n. 103, citing Vice-Consul Molyneux-Seel's report to Lowther, dated Van, April 4, 1913.
59. *Near East*, May 16 and 23, 1913, 30 and 59, respectively.
60. *Near East*, May 23, 1913, 59.
61. *Near East*, May 16, 1913, 30; Kaligian, "The Armenian Revolutionary Federation," writes about the explosive situation in the Adana region, with fears of massacres. A consular report (Vice-Consul Matthews to Lowther, Adana, March 29, 1913) noted that the "end of the war invited reprisals against the Christian population by disbanded troops and embittered muhajirs [refugees]," 283, n. 97; *Near East*, May 23, 1913, 59; the Molyneux-Seel report is quoted in Kaligian, "The Armenian Revolutionary Federation," 293–94, n. 125.
62. *Near East*, May 16, 1913.
63. Molyneux-Seel to Lowther, Van, July 9, 1913, in Kaligian, "The Armenian

Revolutionary Federation," 294–95, nn. 126 and 127: "The vali of Van also responded forcefully in July when the Norduz and Beir-ul-Shebab tribes again
raided Armenian villages."
64. Ibid. See also *Near East*, July 11, 1913. 274: "The Future of Armenia." *Near East*,
November 11, 1913.
65 *Near East*, July 11, 1913, 280.
66. Ibid.
67. Ibid.
68. *Near East*, July 18, 1913, 299, and November 21, 1913, 65. Wyndham Deedes (aka
Deedes Bey, 1883–1956) joined the Ottoman gendarmerie in 1910 and served until
the outbreak of war in 1914. He returned to the British army and proved useful as
an intelligence officer through his knowledge of Turkish and the Ottomans during
the Gallipoli campaign. See John Pressland, *Deedes Bey*.
69. "Armenian Reform," *Near East,* January 23, 1914, 39.
70. Major General Sir Charles E. Calwell, *Field-Marshal Sir Henry Wilson* (London:
Cassell, 1927), 1:128ff., quoted in Alfred Vagts, *Defence and Diplomacy*, 197.
71. Count Leon Ostrorog, *The Turkish Problem*, xi. Ostrorog was a Pole of German
origin whose family left Poland in the nineteenth century and settled in France.
The family then came to the Ottoman Empire after the Crimean War and settled
in Polonezköy. Educated at the Paris law school, Ostrorog acquired a doctorate
and came to Istanbul in the early 1890s at the invitation of the Sublime Porte to act
as financial advisor. He also taught law in Istanbul. In 1908 he helped to write the
program of the Ottoman Liberal Party (Ahrar Firkası). In 1909 he was appointed
to the Justice Ministry and published *Pour la réforme de la justice* (Istanbul: F.
Loeffler) the same year. Ostrorog was an expert on Islamic as well as Western law,
having translated the works of such a significant jurist as Maverdi (974–1058).
Before he died in London in 1930, he asked to be buried in Istanbul at the Feriköy
Catholic Cemetery.
72. *Stamboul*, October 31, 1913. On an Armenian point of view regarding the coming
elections, see Tigrane Zaven in *Stamboul*, December 7 and 12, 1913; and negotiations with the Armenian leadership, *Stamboul*, December 13 and 15, 1913. See also
Kaligian, "The Armenian Revolutionary Federation," 307–8.
73. Kaligian, "The Armenian Revolutionary Federation," 304, n. 162: C/61-72/West-
ern Bureau to the U.S. Central Committee, November 9, 1913.
74. Ibid., 295–96, n. 129: C/61-72/Western Bureau to the U.S. Central Committee,
November 9, 1913.
75. *Tanin*, November 24, 1913. On the Dashnak position on the coming elections, see
Kaligian, "The Armenian Revolutionary Federation," 305–7. They wanted to unite
all Armenian parties and to boycott the election unless they were given proportional representation.
76. *Times*, February 26, 1914. On the ARF position on the coming elections, see Kaligian, "The Armenian Revolutionary Federation," 305–7.
77. Smith to Mallet, January 10, 1914, quoted in Heller, *British Policy towards the
Ottoman Empire*, 110.
78. *Orient* 22, June 3, 1914, 212.
79. Vice-Consul Smith to Sir Louis Mallet, Van, January 10, 1914, in Mallet to Grey,

Constantinople, January 30, 1914, FO 424/251/117, quoted in Kaligian, "The Armenian Revolutionary Federation," 311, n. 4.

80. *Orient* 3/13, April 1, 1914, 123.

81. *Le Réveil* (Beirut), cited in ibid.

82. *Orient* 3/13, April 1, 1914; Bayur, *Türk İnkılabı Tarihi*, vol. 2, part 3, 116; and Kamuran Gürün, *The Armenian File*, 182–85, gives the text of the agreement to resolve the Armenian question between the Porte and Constantin Gulkevitch, the Russian chargé d'affaires. Because this agreement was signed with Russia, it was seen as the supervisor; the other powers had left Russia a free hand in the eastern provinces. Djemal Pasha, *Memories of a Turkish Statesman*, also gives the text, 272–74; *Tanin*, February 11, 1914; *Orient*, 5/7, February 14, 1914, 61–62.

83. Kaligian, "The Armenian Revolutionary Federation," 313, n. 12; C/62-34/Western Bureau to U.S. Central Committee, Constantinople, April 8, 1914.

84. Ahmed Emin Yalman, *Turkey in the World War*, 58.

85. Bodger, "Russia and the End of the Ottoman Empire," 96; Hovanissian, *Armenia on the Road to Independence*, 31–39.

86. *Orient* 14, April 8, 1914, 131; Bayur, *Türk İnkılabı Tarihi*, vol. 2, part 3, 188–89; Feroz Ahmad, "Unionist Relations with Greek, Armenian, and Jewish Communities," 424; Kaligian, "The Armenian Revolutionary Federation," 334; Western Bureau-Turkish Section to *Troshak* editors, March 17, 1914.

87. *Orient* 5/15, April 15, 1914, 148.

88. *Orient* 5/22, June 3, 1914, 212.

89. Ibid.; and *Orient* 5/51, December 23, 1914, 462 (quotation). Cemal Pasha wrote in his memoirs that it was part of the Russian scheme "to stir up the Kurdish Beys and, more important still, the influential sheikhs to resistance against the Government and the Armenians." Djemal Pasha, *Memories of a Turkish Statesman*, 275–76.

90. Kaligian, "The Armenian Revolutionary Federation," 318.

91. Ibid., 317–18.

92. Ibid., 319–20. The issue of appointing Armenian officials became a bone of contention in the negotiations between the patriarchate and the Dashnak. The patriarchate wanted to limit the influence of the Armenian revolutionaries.

93. *Tanin*, July 14, 1914; and *Orient* 529, July 22, 1914, 281.

94. Kaligian, "The Armenian Revolutionary Federation," 321–23; *Orient,* July 28, 1914, 281.

CHAPTER 3. THE OTTOMAN GREEKS

1. Lowther to Grey, Pera, November 23, 1908, FO 371/546/41691.

2. Lowther to Grey, no. 541 C, Therapia, September 2, 1908, FO 371/559/31787. The ambassador's discussion was with Talat and Bahaeddin Şakir, who described themselves as secretaries of the internal and external branches, respectively, of the CUP. On the opposition of the Greek community, see Hasan Taner Kerimoğlu, *İttihat-Terakki ve Rumlar 1908–1914*.

3. Ahmad, *The Young Turks*, 38. The declaration of the Greek Political Association supported the counterrevolutionary army, whose aim was to overthrow the constitution. Veremis and Boura, quoted by Umut Özkırımlı and Spyros Sofos, *Tormented by History*, 20; and George Leon, *Greece and the Great Powers*, 4.

4. Alexandris, *The Greek Minority of Istanbul*, 46. See also Vangelis Kechriotis, "The Modernization of the Empire," 53–70.

5. *Times*, February 29, 1912.

6. Caterina Boura, "The Greek Millet in Turkish Politics," 193–206.

7. Bayur, *Türk İnkılabı Tarihi*, vol. 2, part 1 (1943), 245–47, cited in Alexandris, *The Greek Minority of Istanbul*, 41–42.

8. Alexandris, *The Greek Minority of Istanbul*, 42, citing a book by Paul Karolidis published in Athens in 1913.

9. "Notes from Smyrna," dated March 21, 1912, *Near East*, March 29, 1912, 676.

10. *Times*, July 12, 1912.

11. *Near East*, October 25, 1912, 724.

12. Smith, *Ionian Visions*, 30–31 (quotation); Toynbee, *The Western Question*, 138–39; Harry J. Psomiades, *The Eastern Question*, 68, wrote that "some four million left Greece or areas occupied by Greece." Toynbee gave figures taken from the Ottoman Ministry of Refugees for Muslim refugees from all territories lost in the Balkan Wars: 177,352 refugees and 68,947 square km of territory were lost to Greece in 1912–13; 120,566 refugees and 53,718 square km in 1914–15 (138).

13. Howard, *The Partition*, 33; Carnegie Endowment for International Peace, *The Report*, 418.

14. McCarthy, *Death and Exile*, 135–36.

15. T. A. Culoumbis, J. A. Petropoulos, and H. J. Psomiades, *Foreign Policy Interference in Greek Politics*, 35 (quotation); Howard, *The Partition*, 25–26; Paul Helmreich, *From Paris to Sèvres*, 329–31.

16. C. F. Dixon-Johnson's letter, "Greece and Turkey," *Near East*, October 10, 1913, 663.

17. Cüneyd Okay, "İki Çocuk Dergisinin Rekabeti ve Müsluman Boykotaji," 42–45. Even children were mobilized.

18. Aubrey Herbert's letter dated June 30, 1913, *Near East*, July 4, 1913, 247. Herbert was a member of parliament for Somerset.

19. Dixon-Johnson's letter, "Greece and Turkey," 663. The Ottoman Association in London sent a letter to Sir Edward Grey on the same issue dated January 28, 1914. See FO 371/2128/4327, cited in Salahi Sonyel, *Minorities and the Destruction of the Ottoman Empire*, 278–79.

20. Dr. Charles Vamvacas, "Constantinople and the Straits," *Balkan Review* 1 (1919): 353–57. Yorgi Boşo Efendi was also a deputy of Serfice in Albania.

21. Acting Vice-Consul Harris to Sir G. Lowther, Dardanelles, March 26, 1913, report enclosed in Lowther to Grey, Constantinople, April 9, 1913, in Bilal Şimşir, *Ege Sorunu*, 574–75, 591–94.

22. Randolph S. Churchill, *Winston Churchill*, 624 (quotation)–27. Ironically, in August 1914 Britain's failure to deliver the two ships ordered by the Porte pushed Istanbul into closer relations with Germany.

23. *Tanin*, December 10, 1913.

24. *Tanin*, December 11, 1913.

25. "Constantinople Letter," *Near East*, July 18, 1913, 299.

26. Hilmi Uran, *Hatıralarım*, 65–67. In writing his memoirs in the 1950s Uran was probably exaggerating for political reasons because of the growing Cyprus crisis.

27. Victoria Solomonides, "Greece in Asia Minor," 14–15, citing Greek archival documents. I have used only her dissertation, which was published in 2010 as *Greece in Asia Minor, 1919–1922*.

28. Izmir correspondent, "Constantinople Business Letter," dated February 12, 1914, *Near East*, February 20, 1914, 516.

29. Consul-General Barnham to Sir Louis Mallet, Smyrna, February 18, 1914 in Mallet to Grey, Constantinople, February 26, 1914, FO 424/251/188. It was probably the local branch of the CUP and not the leadership in the capital that directed such boycotts.

30. Wangenheim to Foreign Ministry, June 15, 1914, in Frank G. Weber, *Eagles on the Crescent*, 56; and "Minorities in the Balkans," *Near East*, April 17, 1914, 755.

31. Solomonides, "Greece in Asia Minor," 17; Toynbee, *The Western Question*, 70; Ahmed Emin Yalman, *Gördüklerin ve Geçirdiklerim*, 199.

32. "Constantinople Letter," dated April 3, 1914, *Near East*, April 10, 1914, 723–24.

33. Mallet to Grey, Constantinople, April 15 and 30, 1914, FO 424/252/55 and 74.

34. Kalmykov, *Memoirs*, 258.

35. *Near East*, April 17, 1914, 787 and 819.

36. "Report from İzmir," *Near East*, May 22, 1914, 73.

37. "Constantinople Letter," *Near East*, May 29, 1914, 99 and June 5, 1914, 135 (quotation). Alexandris, *The Greek Minority*, 23, writes that Germanos V was the last patriarch to receive a *berat* (an imperial title) from Sultan Reşad, acting "in some way like a Byzantine emperor… Even the privilege of using Greek as the official language in its relations with the Sublime Porte was granted to the Patriarchate."

38. Alexandris, *The Greek Minority*, 36–37.

39. *Near East*, June 5, 1914, 135.

40. Wangenheim to Foreign Ministry, June 8 and 13, 1914, in Weber, *Eagles on the Crescent*, 55–56. The patriarch had resorted to the closure of churches in Istanbul in 1890. Because this protest attracted international attention Sultan Abdülhamid decided to restore the traditional privileges of the Greek millet. Alexandris, *The Greek Minority*, 35.

41. *Orient* 5/25, June 24, 1914, 241; and excerpts from the Istanbul press, cited on 241–42.

42. *Tanin*, May 15, 1914, 1.

43. *Tanin*, May 20, 1914, 14; Jacob Landau, *Pan-Turkism in Turkey*, 47.

44. Excerpts from the Istanbul press in *Orient*, June 24, 1914, 241–42.

45. Weber, *Eagles on the Crescent*, 56–57, citing German diplomatic documents for June 14, 15, 16, and 17, 1914; Heath Lowry, *The Story*, 33 (Morgenthau quotation).

46. "Letter from Smyrna," June 16, 1914, *Near East*, June 26, 1914, 273 and July 3, 1914, 303; Weber, *Eagles on the Crescent*, 57.

47. "Constantinople Letter," July 5, 1914, *Near East*, July 10, 1914, 399.

48. *Orient* 5/30, July 29, 1914, 298–99.

49. "The Situation in Anatolia," July 13, 1914, *Near East*, July 17, 1914, 381.

50. "An Occasional Correspondent" writing from Izmir, *Near East*, July 24, 1914, 412.

CHAPTER 4. THE ALBANIANS

1. Stavro Skendi, "The History of the Albanian Alphabet," 264–72; George W. Gawrych, *The Crescent and the Eagle*. In Turkish one of the best and most detailed discussions of the topic is Bilgin Çelik's *İttihatçılar ve Arnavutlar*.
2. Piro Misha, "Invention of a Nationalism," 33.
3. Ismail Kemal, *The Memoirs*, 8–9ff.
4. Gawrych, *The Crescent and the Eagle*, 1ff.
5. Stavro Skendi, "Albanian Political Thought and Revolutionary Activity," 8; see also Isa Blumi, "The Role of Education," 49ff.
6. Consul Heathcote to Barclay, Monastir, July 8, 1908, in Barclay to Grey, Therapia, July 15, 1908, FO 371/544/25086. On Albanians and the rebellion in Macedonia, see Gawrych, *The Crescent and the Eagle*, 149–55.
7. Ali Cevat, *İkinci Meşrutiyetin İlanı*, 44–45; *Tanin*, April 7, 1909.
8. Skendi, "Albanian Political Thought and Revolutionary Activity," 19.
9. Ibid., 23.
10. Skendi, "The History of the Albanian Alphabet," 277.
11. Ibid., p. 279.
12. Pallacini to Aehrenthal, Constantinople, March 16, 1910, quoted in ibid., 283.
13. *Times*, April 12, 1909.
14. *Tanin*, April 27, 1909.
15. Vice-Consul Geary to Lowther, Monastir, June 2, 1910, in Lowther to Grey, no. 366, Constantinople, June 7, 1910, FO 371/1010/20903.
16. Tarık Zafer Tunaya, *Türkiye'de Siyasi Partiler,* 199; and M. S. Anderson, *The Eastern Question*, 276.
17. *Times*, 3 May 1911.
18. *Tanin* and other Istanbul papers, June 6, 1911, and later extensive coverage of the sultan's tour. The occasion was commemorated with a special issue of Ottoman stamps. See Ahmad, "Postage Stamps, Politics and Ideology in the Late Ottoman Empire"; Kristo Frasheri, *The History of Albania*, 169–70; and Erik Jan Zürcher, "Kosova Revisited."
19. Count Leon Ostrorog, *The Angora Reform*, 51–52; Halil Menteşe, "Eski Meclisi Mebusan Reisi Halil Menteşe'nin Hatıraları," İsmail Hami Danişmend, *Izahalı Osmanlı Tarihi Kronolojisi*, 383–84; Frasheri, *The History of Albania*, 169–70. Ali Canip Yöntem, "Bizim Selanikte bir Gezinti," 328–30 (quotation).
20. Wilfred Scawen Blunt, *My Diaries* (June 11, 1911, entry).
21. *Times*, July 3, 1911.
22. *Times*, June 10, 1911, and August 13, 1912 (demands); Frasheri, *The History of Albania*, 266ff.
23. *Times*, May 28, 1912.
24. Hüseyin Cahid, "Harbiye Nazirinin Nutku," *Tanin*, July 2, 1912.
25. Vice-Consul Peckham to Consul-General Lamb, Üsküb, June 29, 1912, enclosure in Lowther to Grey, 565C, Constantinople, July 3, 1912, FO 1481/28728.
26. *Times*, December 18, 1912.

27. Cemal Paşa, *Hatıralar*, 263, and the English translation: Djemal Pasha, *Memories of a Turkish Statesman*, 355.
28. *Times*, August 13, 1912.
29. *Times*, November 29 and 30, 1912; Frasheri, *The History of Albania*, 174–79.
30. Essad Pasha, "My Policy for Albania," 330; *Stamboul*, April 2, 1913.
31. Frasheri, *The History of Albania*, 187–89.
32. Prince Karl Max Lichnowsky's memorandum "Delusion or Design?" in *1914: Delusion or Design?* ed. John Röhl, 88–89.
33. *Tanin*, May 20, 1914; Landau, *Pan-Turkism*, 47, described this speech as irredentism.

CHAPTER 5. THE GREEKS AND ARMENIANS

1. *Near East*, July 10 and 17, 1914, 38.
2. Farrar, *Short War Illusion*, 21–22ff., 31.
3. Bodger, "Russia and the End of the Ottoman Empire," 90.
4. Farrar, *Short War Illusion;* Bodger, "Russia and the End of the Ottoman Empire"; Gilbert, *The First World War*, 79.
5. Gilbert, *The First World War*, 78.
6. Quoted in Richard Norton-Taylor's report in the *Guardian* (London), June 15, 1998. Roger Casement was hanged in Pentonville prison on August 3, 1916. As yet there was no Irish nationalist movement. That was formed in January 1919 with the Irish Revolutionary Army (IRA), which declared the "Irish war of independence" and began to wage a guerrilla war against the British Empire. See Richard English, *Armed Struggle*.
7. Feroz Ahmad, "1914–1915 Yıllarında Istanbul'da Hint Milliyetçi Devrimciler."
8. Isaiah Friedman, *The Question of Palestine*, 38–39, citing Salo W. Baron, *The Russian Jew under Tsars and Soviets*, 189–90. Ansky was a witness to the persecution and expulsions and wrote a moving account of what he saw: S. Ansky, *The Enemy at His Pleasure*.
9. Friedman, *The Question of Palestine*, 48.
10. Toynbee, *Acquaintances*, 149–52ff.
11. Ibid. The chapter is titled "Lord Bryce." Friedman, *The Question of Palestine*, 202ff., discusses the importance of American Jewry and how the December 1915 expulsion of Russian Jews from Palestine was also exploited by British propaganda (215–16). On propaganda and the war, see Grattan, *Why We Fought*.
12. Mine Erol, *Osmanlı İmparatorluğu'nun Amerika Büyük Elçisi*, 21–26, gives the statement in Turkish translation; the original is in *FRUS*, 1:71–72.
13. C/103-30/Arshag Vramian to Western Bureau, August 17, 1914, in Kaligian, "The Armenian Revolutionary Federation," 344. Kaligian's source on the 1914 meeting in Erzurum is Vramian's internal report to his bureau, cited as C/103-30/Arshag Vramian to Western Bureau, August 17, 1914 (344, n. 74); C/103-30/Arshag Vramian to Western Bureau, August 17, 1914. See also Hikmet Çiçek, *Bahaeddin Şakir*, 120–22.
14. Kaligian, "The Armenian Revolutionary Federation," 345–46.
15. Ibid., 346–47 (quotations); Çiçek, *Bahaeddin Şakir*, 122. Bahaeddin Şakir is said to

have noted that the Armenian delegates were in constant touch with the Russian consulate in Erzurum and was surprised at their openness. In Istanbul Talat expressed his disappointment to the revolutionary Armen Garo (aka Karakin Pastirmaciyan) and added that the CUP would draw its own conclusions from that.

16. *Orient* 5/28, July 15, 1914, 279.

17. "Notes from Tabriz," *Near East*, November 6, 1914, 6.

18. The *Birzhevyya Vedomosti*, May 16/29, 1916, article was translated in Great Britain, War Office, *The Daily Review of the Foreign Press* (hereafter *DRFP*), June 20, 1916; as well as in Bryce, *The Treatment of Armenians*, 80–82; B. Bareilles, *Les Turcs*, 290–92.

19. Papazyan, in Bareilles, *Les Turcs*, 276–79.

20. Ibid., 276–79.

21. Ibid.

22. *Stamboul*, August 28, 1914.

23. *Moniteur Oriental*, November 16, 1914.

24. Hovanissian, *Armenia on the Road to Independence*, 42 (quotation); *Die Welt des Islams* 23 (1941): 14.

25. *Die Welt des Islams*, xxiii, 1941, 12; Hovanissian, *Armenia on the Road to Independence*, 41 (quotation). It is worth emphasizing that the Jäschke article was published in Germany in 1941 when Adolf Hitler's armies were invading Soviet Russia. The Nazis therefore emphasized "Enver's Pan-Turanism" in order to influence that very trend in Turkey and win Turkish support for the German invasion. But in November 1914 the Unionists had declared jihad and were focusing on Islam rather than nationalism in their propaganda. The circular that Jäschke cites called for the "unification with all Turkic peoples in the Moslem world's struggle for the liberation from the infidel oppressors," a call to pan-Islam and pan-Turkism.

26. The Istanbul fetva against the nationalists was declared on April 11, 1920. See Akşin, *İç Savaş*, 18–19; Mahmud Kemal İnal, *Osmanlı Devrinde Son Sadriazamlar*, 2054–55.

27. Osmanlı Devleti, Dahiliye Nezareti, *Ermeni Komitelerinin Emelleri ve İhtilal Hareketleri* (reprinted in modern Turkish under the same title), 126ff. This book was originally published in 1916 to explain to the world at war why the Armenians were relocated.

28. Ibid., 130–31.

29. *Tanin*, December 8, 1914.

30. Samih Nafiz Tansu, *İki Devrin Perde Arkası* (the memoirs of Hüsameddin Ertürk, a member of the Teşkilatı Mahsusa during the war), 112.

31. "The Armenian Volunteers in Action," dated January 3, 1915, *Near East*, January 22, 1915, 381.

32. Morgenthau to Lansing, private and confidential, November 18, 1915, *FRUS*, 867.00/798.

33. Rafael de Nogales, *Four Years beneath the Crescent*, 45.

34. *Orient* 6/3, January 20, 1915, 23.

35. Cavid's diary entries of February 19 and 21, *Tanin*, December 19, 1944; and "News from Turkey," dated Athens, March 12, 1915, *Near East*, March 26, 1915, 570.

36. Dan van der Vat, *The Ship That Changed the World*, 210.

37. *FRUS*, 1915, supplement, 963. Ziya Sakir (*Son Posta*, October 5–6, 1934) confirms Morgenthau's telegram. Field Marshal Colmar von der Goltz had suggested Konya as the capital of the empire even in 1897 as a part of his idea to create a "nation-in-arms" (*la nation armée*). See M. Larcher, *La guerre turque*, 21, n. 1. See also Dr. Harry Stuermer, *Two War Years*, 85; and Liman von Sanders, *Five Years in Turkey*, 53.

38. Frank Caleb Gates, *Not To Me Only*, 213–14; W. W. Gottlieb, *Studies in Secret Diplomacy*, 309, n. 17.

39. "Bombarmanin esrari," *Tanin*, March 11, 1915.

40. Gottlieb, *Studies in Secret Diplomacy*, 83, quoting Churchill.

41. Lowry, *The Story behind Ambassador Morgenthau's Story*, 227.

42. B. H. Liddell Hart, *The Real War*, 159–60.

43. Morgenthau to Secretary of State, cipher telegram, Constantinople, March 30, 1915, *FRUS*, 867.00/764. Morgenthau's information was based on reports from his consul at Aleppo.

44. Brissel to Secretary of State, Bagdad, April 1, 1915, *FRUS*, 867.00/760.

45. Türklaya Ataöv, *A British Source,* 14. Lewis Einstein, *Inside Constantinople*, 68 and 88, wrote of Armenian excesses at Van, along with the Russian army in which many were fighting. See also "Armenian Massacres" and "Caucasian Front," in Pope and Wheal, *Macmillan Dictionary*, 34–35 and 105, respectively.

46. "The Siege of Van (from our Correspondent lately in Tabiz), Tiflis (Caucasia)," July 10, 1915, *Near East*, September 17, 1915, 551–52. Ambassador Morgenthau confirmed that Armenian contingents were part of the invading Russian armies and that Ottoman Armenians were fighting alongside the Russians. Morgenthau to Lansing, November 18, 1915, in *FRUS*, 1:767–78; Gottlieb, *Studies in Secret Diplomacy*, 110. For a detailed account, see Justin McCarthy, *The Armenian Rebellion at Van*.

47. Mirza Firooz Khan, "Armenian News," *Near East*, May 14, 1915, 39. Franz Werfel immortalized this event in his *Forty Days on Musa Dagh*.

48. Oran, *Türk Dış Politikası,* 102–3; Gürün, *The Armenian File*, 204ff.

49. Solomonides, "Greece in Asia Minor," 32.

50. Ibid., 22–23, citing E. Emmanouilidis, *Ta Teleftaia Eti Tis Othom Anikis Afokratoris* (Athens, 1924), 339–75, 376–91.

51. Barton, *Story of Near East Relief,* 46.

52. Sarkis Seropian, "Vicdanlı Türk Valisi," 47, quoting Stephan Stepanyan, who was one of the eyewitnesses for Arsak Alboyaciyan's *Husamadayan Gudinahayeru* (Beirut: Donikyan Basimevi, 1961), 218–28.

53. Yüzbaşı Sarkis Torosyan, *Çanakkale'den Filistin Cephesi'ne*. Though the veracity of Sarkis Torosyan's memoir has been questioned, I find that his account of Enver Pasha is quite believable, given the weakness of the central government.

54. Jeremy Salt, "The Narrative Gap," 22.

55. Walter Görlitz, *The Kaiser and His Court,* 90; and Morgenthau to Secretary of State, Constantinople, July 10, 1915, *FRUS*, supplement, 982–84.

56. Morgenthau to Secretary of State, Constantinople, July 10, 1915, *FRUS* 982–84.

57. Secretary of State to Board of Commissioners of Foreign Missions (Rev. James L. Barton), Washington, July 19, 1915, *FRUS* 1915, supplement, 984–85.

58. Lesley Blanch, *Pierre Loti*, 307.

59. Arti's letter was dated August 7. *Near East*, September 3, 1915, 493.

60. Görlitz, *The Kaiser*, 99–100, diary entry dated August 8, 1915; Pope and Wheal, *Macmillan Dictionary*, 217.

61. The *Near East*'s editorial of August 18, 1915, 376.

62. "News from Turkey," report sent from Athens on August 25, 1915, *Near East*, September 3, 1915, 489, and September 17, 1915, 548.

63. Bryce, *The Treatment of Armenians*, 390, n. 16, on "unspecified sources"; and report from Athens, dated September 6, 1915, *Near East*, September 17, 1915, 548.

64. Mehmed Cavid, "Memoirs," *Tanin*, February 3, 1945.

65. On Ahmed Rıza's opposition on the Armenian question in the Senate, see Bayur, *Türk İnkılabı Tarihi*, vol. 3, part 3, 46ff.

66. Cavid, "Memoirs," *Tanin*, January 10, 1945.

67. Cavid, "Memoirs," *Tanin*, January 8, 1945.

68. Cavid, "Memoirs," *Tanin*, January 10, 1945.

69. Mark Sykes's interview with Prince Sabaheddin, in Mark Sykes to Major-General C. E. Calwell, C.B., Director of Military Operations, No. 4 Secret, Athens, June 1915, FO 371/2486. I owe this information to my friend Hasan Kayalı.

70. Morgenthau to Secretary of State, Constantinople, July 10, 1915, *FRUS*, 1915, supplement, 982–84.

71. *Tanin* and the Istanbul press, June 16 and 17, 1915.

72. Cavid, "Memoirs," *Tanin*, February 2, 1945.

73. Foreign Ministry to German Embassy, Constantinople, July 4, 1915, in Weber, *Eagles on the Crescent*, 150–51ff. On how German documents were purged after the war in order to deny the "war guilt" clause imposed by the Allies at Paris and to show that Britain not Germany was responsible for causing the war, see John Röhl's introduction in *1914: Delusion or Design?*

74. Cavid, "Memoirs," *Tanin*, February 2, 1945.

75. Barton, *Story of Near East Relief*, 59, 42.

76. *Near East*, February 25, 1916, 462 (article "Erzeroum-Kut-Baghdad").

77. Görlitz, *The Kaiser*, 129, diary entry of January 24, 1916.

78. *Tasvir-i Efkar*, March 14, 1918 ("Rus Vesaik hafiyesinde: Rusya'nin iki sene evvelki tesviratı").

79. *Near East*, March 10, 1916, 501.

80. Kayaloff, *The Battle of Sadarabad*, 46.

81. Ibid., 72.

82. Ibid., 75–76.

83. Pope and Wheal, *Macmillan Dictionary*, "Rize Landing," 393.

84. Weber, *Eagles on the Crescent*, 200.

85. "News from Turkey," dated Athens, May 31, 1916, *Near East*, June 16, 1916, 149.

86. *Near East*, July 21, 1916, 270–73.

87. The Central Committee's report was published in the Istanbul press on September 29 and 30, 1916. It may also be found in Abram Elkus to Secretary of State, Constantinople, October 14, 1916, *FRUS*, 867.00/791; *Tarih ve Toplum* (September 1986): 6–10 gives the text with an introduction by Zafer Toprak on the occasion of "70. Yıldönümünde İttihat ve Terakki'nin 1916 Kongresi." The text of the pamphlet on the 1916 congress in modern Turkish in found in Tuncay, *Cihat ve Tehcir*, 56–84, with an article from *Tanin* on the congress.

88. A. S. Safrastian's letter on "The Resurrection of Armenia," dated February 14, 1917, *Near East*, February 23, 1917, 391.

89. "The Russian Campaign in Nearer Asia," *Near East*, February 23, 1917, 481.

90. D. Ghambashidze, "The Caucasus," part 3, *Near East*, April 19, 1918, 323–24.

91. Ali Kemali, *Erzincan*, 120ff.

92. Bodger, "Russia and the End of the Ottoman Empire," 100.

93. Frederick Wirth's report, on the situation in Turkey, dated November 27, 1917, in Consul-General to Secretary of State, Athens, October 27, 1917, *FRUS*, 867.00/807; and George Horton to Secretary of State, Salonica, December 7, 17, *FRUS*, 867.00/811.

94. The debate on a new German loan of 50 million liras took place on November 29, 1917: *Tanin*, November 30, 1917.

95. The *Berliner Tageblatt* interview would have been given before January 4 1918; quoted in *DRFP*, January 4, 1918.

96. *Hilal*, February 9, 1918, 1.

97. Karabekir, *1917–20 Arasında*, 102–3, 123–24.

98. Harbord, *Report*, 7–8; and *Le Soir*, citing Swiss papers, September 3, 1918.

99. Zeki Arikan, "Mühittin Birgen," 46–53. The text of the treaty is in Wheeler-Bennett, *Brest-Litovsk*, 403–8; Bayur, *Türk İnkılabı Tarihi*, vol. 3, part 4, 103–4.

100. *Vakit*, March 14; and "Imperialist politika," *Sabah*, March 16, 1918 (quotation).

101. See "Dahili istikraz," *Tanin*, April 14, 1918, 3; and "İtibar-i Milli Bankası," *Tanin*, April 14, 1918, 3, and "Dahiliye istikraz ve Ermeniler: *Jamanak*'in bir makalesi"; François Georgeon, "Le premier emprunt intérieur."

102. Ahmed Emin, "Ermeni meselesinin tesfiye hisabı," *Vakit*, June 27, 1918.

103. *Le Soir*, August 1, 1918.

104. "Our Caucasus Policy and Armenia," *Vakit*, September 3 and 4, 1918.

105. "London Armenians and the Peace Conference," dated November 9, 1918, *Near East*, November 15, 1918, 925.

106. *Meclisi Mebusan Zabit Ceridesi*, vol. 1 (Ankara: Türkiye Büyük Millet Meclisi Basınevi, 1992), 157. No "Wilsonian principles" had been established in 1914—they had yet to be developed. But in 1918 non-Muslim deputies claimed that "we wanted our natural rights, we wanted Wilsonian principles." For a detailed discussion of this question in the assembly, see Ayhan Aktar, "Son Osmanlı Meclisi ve Ermeni Meselesi."

107. *Meclisi Mebusan Zabit Ceridesi*, 156ff., 158, column 2, and 160–61.

108. Lewis Heck, Constantinople, January 17, 1919, *FRUS*, 867.00/846.

109. Bie Ravndal, American Commissioner, July 1, 1919, *FRUS*, 867.00/894.

110. Undated telegram from Stanav at the American Mission (in Istanbul), undated, to Secretary of State, sent via Paris on October 3, 1919, *FRUS*, 867.00/943.

CHAPTER 6. THE OTTOMAN JEWS

1. Feroz Ahmad, "Ottoman Perceptions of the Capitulations"; Abraham Galanté, *Histoire des Juifs d'Anatolie*; Abraham Galanté, *Role économique des Juifs*.

2. Davy, *The Sultan*, 392–93.

3. Aron Rodrigue, *French Jews, Turkish Jews*. The Porte was also "annoyed by the Zionist demand that Hebrew be recognized in the Ottoman Empire" soon after

it was recognized by the Italians in Libya in 1911 after they annexed the Ottoman province. See Jacob Landau, "Relations between Jews and Non-Jews in the Late Ottoman Empire," 356.

4. On the "special relationship," see Feroz Ahmad, "The Special Relationship"; and Esther Benbassa's biography of Nahum Efendi: *Un grand rabbin sépharade*.

5. *Times*, June 8, 1934. Karasu's obituary was entitled "Carasso Effendi: A Parasite of the Young Turks." See also Ronni Margulies, "Emanuel Karasu," *Toplumsal Tarih* 4/21 (September 1995): 24–29.

6. Isaiah Friedman, *Germany, Turkey, and Zionism*, 143.

7. Fevzi Demir, "İzmir Sancağında 1912 Meclis-i Mebusan Seçimleri," 158.

8. Abraham Galanté, *Türkler ve Yahudiler*, 127–29. Jewish deputies were so closely associated with the Unionists that when the anti-CUP government arrested members of the committee in 1912, it also arrested Karasu and Mazliyah. See Manuel Karasu and Nesim Mazliyah, "Hatıralar," *Tanin*, February 14, 1944; and *Times*, November 11, 18, and 20, 1912.

9. Friedman, *Germany, Turkey, and Zionism*, 143.

10. Galanté, *Türkler ve Yahudiler*, 116–17; Ahmad, "Unionist Relations with Greek, Armenian, and Jewish Communities," 428.

11. Demir, "İzmir," 176.

12. Galanté, *Türkler ve Yahudiler*, 123–24; Güngör Gönültaş, "Mahmut Şevket Paşa'nın Katillerini Vuran Polis Samuel Efendi Anıldı," *Milliyet*, December 27, 1971; Ahmad, "The Special Relationship," 24.

13. Elie Kedourie, "Young Turks, Freemasons and Jews," 89–104.

14. Ambassador Lowther's reports quoted in ibid., 99–100.

15. Friedman, *Germany, Turkey, and Zionism*, 146.

16. Ibid., 141–44. Jacob Landau, citing Esther Benbassa's research, noted that the "tensions grew between the Ashkenazi community in Istanbul, supported by Zionist groups, and *Hahambaşı* Rabbi Nahum, supported by the Alliance Israelite Universelle and the Ottoman state leadership": Jacob Landau, "The Ashkenazi Community in Istanbul during the Last Generation of the Ottoman Empire," in Jacob Landau, *Exploring Ottoman and Turkish History*, 364.

17. Friedman, *Germany, Turkey, and Zionism*, 148.

18. H[asan] Cemal, *Tekrar Başımıza Gelenler*, 122–23, diary entry of December 29, 1912.

19. Mark Mazower, *Salonica City of Ghosts*, discusses "Making the City Greek" in part 3.

20. Neville Mandel, *The Arabs and Zionism*, 146, quoting a cutting from *L'Aurore*, an enclosure in Ambassador Lowther's dispatch. Lowther described these sentiments as "a picture of what might be styled an alliance between Pan-Judaism and Pan-Islamism in Turkey."

21. Toynbee, *Acquaintances*, 149ff.

22. Ahmad, "Ottoman Perceptions."

23. Galanté, *Histoire des Juifs*, i; *Les Juifs d'Izmir (Smyrne)* (vol. 1 of *Histoire des Juifs*), 4.

24. Friedman, *Germany, Turkey, and Zionism*, 210.

25. Arthur Ruppin, *Memoirs, Diaries, Letters*, 153.

26. Ibid., 155.
27. Friedman, *Germany, Turkey, and Zionism*, 213. Kaymakam Bahaeddin was not the same person as Bahaeddin Şakir, the powerful figure in the committee, as Friedman seems to think.
28. Ahmed Emin Yalman, *Turkey in the World War*, 105–6.
29. Friedman, *Germany, Turkey, and Zionism*, 190ff., 218, and 222 n. 113.
30. Ibid., 191–200, 208–9.
31. Ruppin, *Memoirs*, 152–54.
32. Israel Cohen, *The Turkish Persecution of the Jews* (London: Alabaster, Passmore, 1918), appendix 1, 116–17. Cohen's book is described as Wellington House or British wartime propaganda against the Turks. See Pat Walsh, *Britain's Great War on Turkey* (Belfast: Athol Books, 2009); Friedman, *Germany, Turkey, and Zionism*, 219–20.
33. Friedman, *Germany, Turkey, and Zionism*, 347ff.; and Ahmed Emin, "Filistin Meselesi," *Sabah*, August 27, 1917 (quotation).
34. Ahmed Emin, "Osmanlı Devleti ve Museviler," *Tasvir-i Efkar*, December 27, 1917.
35. Ibid.
36. Ibid.
37. Friedman, *The Question of Palestine*, 298.
38. Galanté, *Türkler ve Yahudiler*, 86–87. See the brief article by Haim Nahum on the Ottoman Jews, 86–97, especially the note on 86 giving his activities after 1908. After the armistice he was named "Plenipotentiary to the United States, but permission was denied him to leave the continent."
39. Jacob Landau, *Tekinalp*.

CHAPTER 7. THE ARABS

1. Albert Hourani, "Ottoman Reform and the Politics of Notables." This formative article was originally published in *Beginning of Modernization in the Middle East: The Nineteenth Century*, ed. William Polk and Richard Chambers, 41–68.
2. Robert Devereux, *The First Ottoman Constitutional Period*.
3. *Times*, August 11, 1908.
4. Feroz Ahmad and D. A. Rustow, "The Parliament of the Second Constitutional Period, 1908–1918."
5. Samir Seikaly, "Shukri al-Asali." Ömer Kürkçüoğlu discusses the Arab independence movement against the Ottoman state during the constitutional era: Kürkçüoğlu, *Osmanlı Devleti'ne Karşı Arap Bağımsızlkı Hareketi (1908–1918)*.
6. Rashid Khalidi, "Ottomanism and Arabism in Syria before 1914," 64.
7. Kayalı, *Arabs and Young Turks*. The issue of selling state lands to foreigners was also debated, which the central government wanted to do in 1913 because it was strapped for cash. But local forces in Iraq prevented that from happening. Both issues are discussed in Mahmoud Haddad, "Iraq before World War One."
8. Mandel, *The Arabs and Zionism*, 1976.
9. Ahmad, *The Young Turks*, 14–120; William L. Cleveland, *Islam against the West*, 19–21.
10. Lowther to Grey, 893C, Pera, December 4, 1911, FO 371/1259/49376.
11. Lowther to Grey, no. 918 confidential, Constantinople, December 12, 1911, FO 371/1263/50573; Bosworth, "Italy," 60.

12. Lowther to Grey, no. 918 confidential, Constantinople, December 12, 1911.

13. Quoted in Kaligian, "The Armenian Revolutionary Federation," 252–53, nn. 14 and 15.

14. Hanna Weiner and Barnet Litvinoff, eds., *The Letters and Papers of Chaim Weizmann*, 394–95.

15. Bayur, *Türk İnkılabı Tarihi*, vol. 2, part 4, 407–9. In his 1887 article General Colmar von der Goltz, the German military adviser to the Porte, had suggested that the Ottoman capital be moved to Anatolia so that it would exercise equal influence "over the chief components of the Ottoman population," Turk and Arab: Kayalı, *Arabs and Young Turks*, 33. Goltz "contemplated an Austro-Hungarian model for the Ottoman Empire" (136).

16. Halide Edib, *Conflict of East and West in Turkey*, 73. The book was based on lectures given at the Jamia Milia College in Delhi in 1935.

17. Ahmed Tarabein, "'Abd al-Hamid al-Zahrawi," 102. Majid Khadduri, "Aziz Ali al-Misri," 149; Mahmoud Haddad, "Iraq before World War I: A Case of Anti-European Arab Ottomanism," in *The Origins of Arab Nationalism*, ed. Khalidi et al., 120–50.

18. The Law of the Vilayets was promulgated on March 26, and went into effect on March 28, though still to be ratified by the assembly. See *Tanin*, March 26, 1913, and later issues.

19. Cemal's letter to Esref Kuşçubaşı, quoted in Philip Hendrik Stoddard, "The Ottoman Government and the Arabs," 137.

20. *Tanin*, May 6, 1913; Djemal Pasha, *Memories of a Turkish Statesman*, 58–59; Tag Elsir Ahmed Mohammad Harran, "Turkish-Syrian Relations," 301.

21. Djemal Pasha, *Memories of a Turkish Statesman*, 58–59; George Antonius, *The Arab Awakening*, 116.

22. Bayur, *Türk İnkılabı Tarihi*, vol. 2, part 4, 314, and vol. 2, part 3, 244ff.; Mandel, *The Arabs and Zionism*, 161, citing Zionist archives, describes the concession made by Talat after his meeting with 'Abd al-Karim al-Khalil, a leader of the Arab nationalist group in Istanbul.

23. *Tanin*, June 13, 1913; Kayalı, *Arabs and Young Turks*, 139.

24. *Near East*, July 25, 1913, correspondent's report in his "Notes from Beyrout," dated June 28. On Hazım's unpopularity among the Beirut reformers, see Kayalı, *Arabs and Young Turks*, 132. On Ali Münif, see Feroz Ahmad, "Ali Münif Yegana."

25. *Near East*, July 25, 1913, 333.

26. *Near East*, August 8, 1913, 387.

27. "Constantinople Letter," dated August 9, 1913, *Near East*, August 15, 1913, 415. Rashid Khalidi wrote: "By the end of 1913, however, it had become clear to many educated and politicized young Arabs that the Turkish-dominated C.U.P. had no intention of granting the reforms demanded by the Arabs, of decentralizing the Empire, of sharing political power": "'Abd al-Ghani al-Uraisi," 42–43. Unfortunately Khalidi gives no citation from any contemporary source, not even from *al-Mufid*. In February 1914 the Unionists had already appointed an Arab, 'Arif al-Mardini, governor of Damascus. See Kayalı, *Arabs and Young Turks*, 131.

28. Yusuf Akçura, "1329 senesinde Türk dünyası," *Türk Yurdu*, quoted in David Thomas, "The Life and Thought of Yusuf Akçura," 145. Celal Nuri (İleri) also

urged decentralization for the Arab provinces as a way to preserve the empire's unity: see Kayalı, *Arabs and Young Turks*, 142.

29. C. Ernest Dawn, *From Ottomanism to Arabism*, 17–18 (quotation); Djemal Pasha, *Memories of a Turkish Statesman*, 227–28; George Stitt, *A Prince of Arabia*, 142–44.

30. *Near East*, October 10, 1913, 661.

31. "Busreh [Basra] Reform Party: An Arab Manifesto," *Near East*, October 10, 1913, 661 (all further citations of this manifesto are from this source).

32. Ibid.

33. Perleman, *Ben Gurion Looks Back*, 46–47; the interviews took place in 1964.

34. *Near East*, November 14, 1913, 35. Because of the gains the Arabs were making, Armenian nationalists, citing *al-Muqattam*, July 12, 1913, complained that the Syrians and the Arabs were getting more than they were, "although we struggled for longer than they."

35. Antonius, *The Arab Awakening*, 110ff.

36. Ibid., 119–20.

37. Stoddard, "The Ottoman Government," 92–93, 201–2.

38. Mallet to Grey, 117C, Constantinople February 24, 1914, FO 2131/9033; see also enclosures of the Mallet-Kitchener correspondence.

39. Mallet to Grey, 335C, Constantinople, May 12, 1914, FO 371/2124/22042; see also Mallet to Grey, 153 TC, Constantinople, March 9, 1914, FO 371/2131/10697; and Antonius, *The Arab Awakening*, 120–21. In 1916 Aziz Ali wrote to Kitchener "thanking for the help." Jukka Nevakivi, "Lord Kitchener," 318, n. 7.

40. Mallet to Grey, 335 C, Constantinople, May 12, 1913, FO 372/2124/22042 (quotation); Antonius, *The Arab Awakening*, 120; Khadduri, "Aziz Ali al-Misri"; David Thomas, "The First Arab Congress," 325.

41. "Aviation in Syria," *Near East*, February 25, 1914, and March 6, 1914, 564; "Constantinople Letter," dated April 2, 1914, *Near East*, April 10, 1914, 723. In her paper "The First Ottoman Airplanes in the Sky of Syria" read at the Türk Hava Kuvetleri Tarih Sempozumu, February 8, 2011, Professor Khairia Kamimeh described how the achievement of the Ottoman pilots was celebrated throughout the Arab world and even became the subject of Syrian poets.

42. Mallet to Grey, March 18, 1914, in Gooch and Temperley, *British Documents*, vol. 10, no. 2, 829.

43. Stitt, *A Prince of Arabia*, 137; Kayalı, *Arabs and Young Turks*, 148, 168–69; Dawn, *From Ottomanism to Arabism*, 16.

44. Mallet to Grey, 205 Very Confidential, Constantinople, March 25, 1914, FO 2128/13883 (quotations); Djemal Pasha, *Memories of a Turkish Statesman*, 97.

45. Briton Cooper Busch, *Britain and the Persian Gulf*, 145, n. 46, and 196, n. 25. Sayyid Talib had been mutassarif of Najd in 1903.

46. Viscount Kitchener to Grey, 58C, Cairo, April 4, 1914, 2128/15883; Dawn, *From Ottomanism to Arabism*, 19, for 'Abdullah's conversation with Talat.

47. Dawn, *From Ottomanism to Arabism*, 19–20, 33.

48. Hanna Batatu, *The Old Social Classes*, 95 and n. 161. Batatu took the list of Iraqi deputies to the assembly from Faidi, *Fi Ghamrat-in-Nidal*, 4.

49. Fritz Fischer, *Germany's Aims in the First World War*, 122.

50. Liman von Sanders, *Five Years in Turkey*, 326.

51. "Baghdad and the War," dated August 9, 1914, *Near East*, October 16, 1914, 763.

52. Enclosure of order in Brissel to Morgenthau, Baghdad, August 9, 1914, *FRUS*, 867.00/735.

53. Hollis to Secretary of State, Beirut, November 9, 1914, *FRUS*, 867.00/713.

54. Ziya Sakir Soko, "İttihat ve Terakki Nasıl Doğdu? Nasıl Yaşadı? Nasıl Öldü?" *Son Posta*, September 29, 1934; on Seyyid Talib (aka Talib Pasha ibn Sayyid Rajab), see Busch, *Britain, India, and the Arabs*.

55. "Suez Canal," in Pope and Wheal, *Macmillan Dictionary*, 456–57.

56. See Weber, *Eagles on the Crescent*, 98ff.

57. *Orient* 6/3, January 28, 1915, 24.

58. "Misirli Evladlarıma" and "Beyanname-i Hümayün" (*Tanin*); English text in *Orient*, 6/7, February 17, 1915, 54; Stoddard, "The Ottoman Government," 271.

59. "Turkey and the Lebanon (From a Lebanese Correspondent)," Cairo, dated February 10, 1915, *Near East*, February 10, 1915, 453.

60. The proclamation of Cemal Pasha, minister of the Marine and commander of the IVth Army, to the people of Syria was published in *Rey-el-Am* (n.d.) in Damascus and given in translation in *Orient* 6/13, March 31, 1915, 90.

61. "News of Syria" (reported from a correspondent in Cairo), dated June 14, 1915, *Near East*, June 25, 1915, 209.

62. "News of Syria" (dated Alexandria, Egypt, September 10, 1915), *Near East*, September 24, 1915, 576. See also Cleveland, *Islam against the West*, 34.

63. The book *La verité sur la question syrienne* (Constantinople: Imprimerie Tanine, 1916) was published in French, Arabic, and Turkish in order to have the maximum effect.

64. Batatu, *The Old Social Classes*, 19, citing Great Britain, *Reports of Administration for 1918 of Divisions and Districts of Occupied Territories of Mesopotamia* (1919), 1:68.

65. "Irakdaki Sukut," *Tanin*, April 30, 1916, and later issues; Liddell Hart, *The Real War*, 14.1.

66. See Sultan Mehmed Reşad's imperial decree appointing Ali Haydar in İkdam and *Tasviri Efkar*, July 2, 1916.

67. "Medina, Siege of," in Pope and Wheal, *Macmillan Dictionary*, 311.

68. Ibid., 29–31.

69. Danişmend, *İzahalı Osmanlı Tarihi Kronolojisi*, 432–33; *Tanin*'s editorial, "Mekke'de Fesad," July 26, 1916, and Talat's interview in *Tasvir-i Efkar*, July 27, 1916.

70. See Kedourie, *England and the Middle East*.

71. Uriel Dann, *King Hussein and the Challenge of Arab Radicalism: Jordan, 1955–1967*, 3.

72. Liman von Sanders, *Five Years in Turkey*, 158–63.

73. Norman Daniel, *Islam and the West*, 333. The photograph is in *The War of the Nations, 1914–1919* (New York: New York Times, 1919), 280–81 (portfolio in rotogravure etchings).

74. *Die Neue Orient*, October 5, 1917, in *DRFP*, January 3, 1918, 404–5.

75. Ibid. The "Turkish chauvinists," however, were in a minority among the Unionists.

76. *Hilal*, October 13, 1917; see Feroz Ahmad, "Ideology and War Aims."

77. *Osmanischer Lloyd*, January 7, 1918, 1.

78. Parliamentary debate, January 8, 1918, *İkdam*, January 12, 1918.

79. "Amman, Battle of," in Pope and Wheal, *Macmillan Dictionary*, 24.

80. Parliamentary debates, March 28, 1918, *İkdam*, March 29 and 30, 1918.

81. Antonius, *The Arab Awakening*, 273, 433; Elizabeth Monroe, *Britain's Moment in the Middle East*, 48.

82. Two articles by Şekib Arslan in Germany in *Osmanischer Lloyd*, July 13 and 21, 1918, 1; see also Cleveland, *Islam against the West*, 39 and n. 38 on 176.

83. *Tanin*, August 31, 1918, 1.

84. *Osmanischer Lloyd*, October 4, 1918, 1.

8. Postscript

1. See, for example, Danişmend, *İzahalı Osmanlı Tarihi Kronolojisi*, 432–33, on the Hashemite revolt of 1916.

2. Arif Erzen in Erich Feigl, *A Myth of Terror*, 8, column 2.

3. "The Russian Campaign in Nearer Asia," *Near East*, March 23, 1917, 481.

4. James B. Gidney, *A Mandate for Armenia*, 46, 74–75.

5. Ibid., 82–84, 153. Nubar's father had been the prime minister of Egypt, where Nubar was raised. As a result he had never visited Russian or Ottoman Armenia. Helmreich, *From Paris to Sèvres*, 47–48ff.

6. Gidney, *A Mandate for Armenia*, 84 (quotation); and Hovannes Katchaznouni, *Dashnagtzoutun*, 75–76.

7. Gidney, *A Mandate for Armenia*, 154.

8. Margaret MacMillan, *Peacemakers*, 388, citing *FRUS*, 4:547–77.

9. Helmreich, *From Paris to Sèvres*, 49–50.

10. MacMillan, *Peacemakers*, 390, citing *FRUS*, 3:807 and 5:614.

11. Quoted in the preface of an anonymous translator in Alexandre Khatissian, *Eclosian et développent de la République Arménienne* (Athens, 1989), 7.

12. Helmreich, *From Paris to Sèvres*, 46–47; M. L. Dockrill and J. Douglas Goold, *Peace without Promise: Britain and the Peace Conferences, 1919–23* (Hamden, CT: Archon Books, 1981), chapter 4, "The Dissolution of the Ottoman Empire and the Middle East, 1919–1920."

13. Andrew Mango, *Atatürk*, 207.

14. Great Britain, War Office, *DRFP, Enemy Press Supplement*, July 24, 1919, 690.

15. Dinç Yaylalier, "American Perceptions of Turkey," 215–16.

16. Martin Sicker, *The Islamic World in Decline: From the Treaty of Karlowitz to the Disintegration of the Ottoman Empire*, 224–25.

17. Şevket Süreyya Aydemir, *Tek Adam*, 2:460–62.

18. Yücel Güçlü, "The Struggle for the Mastery in Cilicia"; Yaylalier, "American Perceptions of Turkey," 105.

19. Louis Fischer, *The Soviets in World Affairs*, 1:392–93; Mango, *Atatürk*, 294.

20. Yaylalier, "American Perceptions of Turkey," 107, n. 27; Mango, *Atatürk*, 210.

21. Helmreich, *From Paris to Sèvres*, 85; and Great Britain, War Office, *DRFP, Enemy Press Supplement*, July 24, 1919, 690.

22. *Near East*, February 7, 1919, 109, quoting W. M. Ramsay; and MacMillan, *Peacemakers*, 440–42, on the American experts.

23. Howard, *The Partition of the Ottoman Empire*, 222–24.

24. Ibid., 232; Mango, *Atatürk*, 210ff.

25. Gidney, *A Mandate for Armenia*, 106; Howard, *The Partition of the Ottoman Empire*, 232–33; MacMillan, *Peacemakers*, 442.

26. McCarthy, *Death and Exile*, 262ff.

27. *Moniteur Oriental*, May 27 and 29, 1919. Considerable literature on the Greek occupation of western Anatolia is available. Smith's *Ionian Visions* remains the best study in English, along with Solomonides, "Greece in Asia Minor."

28. Kalmykov, *Memoirs*, 275.

29. Helmreich, *From Paris to Sèvres*, 173.

30. *Moniteur Oriental*, May 29, 1920, 1.

31. MacMillan, *Peacemakers*, 459–60.

32. Elizabeth Wiskemann, *Europe of the Dictators, 1919–1945*, 24.

33. Mango, *Atatürk*, 311, 315ff.

34. MacMillan, *Peacemakers*, 441.

35. Mango, *Ataturk*, 337ff.

36. Bernard Lewis, *The Multiple Identities of the Middle East* (London: Weidenfeld and Nicolson, 1999), 8–9; "The Lausanne Convention concerning the Exchange of Greek and Turkish Populations," appendix 1 in Renée Hirschon, ed., *Crossing the Aegean: An Appraisal of the 1923 Compulsory Population Exchange between Greece and Turkey*, 282–87.

37. *Journal d'Orient*, May 9, 1919, and other Istanbul papers cited in Great Britain, War Office, *DRFP*, July 24, 1919, 689.

38. *Journal d'Orient*, May 20, 1920; Meclis debate, February 19, 1920, *Journal d'Orient*, February 20, 1920, and later issues.

Bibliography

Newspapers and Journals

Hilal (Istanbul)
İkdam (Istanbul)
Journal d'Orient (Istanbul)
Liberté (Istanbul)
Near East (London)
Orient (Istanbul)
Osmanischer Lloyd (Istanbul)
Stamboul (Istanbul)
Tanin (Istanbul)
Times (London)
Vakit (Istanbul)

Books and Articles

Aftandiian, Gregory. *Armenia, Vision of a Republic: The Independence Lobby in America, 1918–1927*. Boston: Charles River Books, 1981.

Ahmad, Feroz. "Ali Münif Yegana." In *Encyclopedia of Islam*. 2nd ed. Leiden: Brill, 1953–.

———. "Ideology and War Aims of the Unionist Government, 1914–1918." *Annales de la Faculté de Droit d'Istanbul* 33/50 (2001): 1–13.

———. "Leon Trotsky's Writings on the Ottoman State, the 1908 Revolution, and the Balkan Wars, 1912–1913" (in Turkish). *Tarih ve Toplum* 17 (May 1985): 12–18. Reprinted in English in *From Empire to Republic: Essays on the Late Ottoman Empire and Modern Turkey*, vol. 2, 85–100. Istanbul: Bilgi University Press, 2008.

———. "Ottoman Perceptions of the Capitulations, 1800–1914." *Journal of Islamic Studies* 11/1 (January 2000): 1–20. Also in Feroz Ahmad, *From Empire to Republic: Essays on the Late Ottoman Empire and Modern Turkey*, vol. 2, 2:19–44. Istanbul: Bilgi University Press, 2008.

———. "Postage Stamps, Politics and Ideology in the Late Ottoman Empire." In Feroz Ahmad, *From Empire to Republic: Essays on the Late Ottoman Empire and Modern Turkey*, 2:101–10. 2 vols. Istanbul: Bilgi University Press, 2008.

———. "The Special Relationship: The Committee of Union and Progress and the Ottoman Jewish Political Rite, 1908–1918." In *Jews, Turks, Ottomans: A Shared History, Fifteenth to the Twentieth Century*, ed. Avigdor Levy, 212–30. Syracuse: Syracuse University Press, 2002. Also in Feroz Ahmad, *From Empire to Republic: Essays on the Late Ottoman Empire and Modern Turkey*, 2:149–73. 2 vols. Istanbul: Bilgi University Press, 2008.

———. "Unionist Relations with Greek, Armenian, and Jewish Communities." In *Christians and Jews in the Ottoman Empire,* ed. Benjamin Braude and Bernard Lewis, 401–34. New York: Holmes and Meier, 1982.

———. *The Young Turks*. Oxford: Clarendon Press, 1969. Reprinted London: Hurst, 2000.

———. "1914–1915 Yıllarında Istanbul'da Hint Milliyetçi Devrimciler." *Yapıt* (August–September 1984): 5–15.

Ahmad, Feroz, and D. A. Rustow, "The Parliament of the Second Constitutional Period, 1908–1918." In *Güney-Doğu Avrupa Araştırmaları Dergisi*, 245–84. Istanbul, 1976.

Ahmed Emin. See Yalman, Ahmed Emin

Aivazian, Gia. *The Pre-Genocide Armenian Press of Istanbul, 1908–1915*. Glendale, CA: Nasvarat Monthly, n.d.

Akşin, Sina. *İç Savaş ve Sevr'de Ölüm*. Istanbul: Türkiye İş Bankası, 2010.

———. *Şeriatçı Bir Ayaklanma: 31 Mart Olayı*. Istanbul, 1972.

Aktar, Ayhan. "Son Osmanlı Meclisi ve Ermeni Meselesi." *Toplum ve Bilim* 91 (Winter 2001–2): 142–65.

———. *Türk Milliyetçiliği, Gayrimüslimler ve Ekonomil Dönüşum*. Istanbul: İletişim, 2006.

Alexandris, Alexis. *The Greek Minority of Istanbul and Greek-Turkish Relations 1918–1974*. Athens: Center for Asia Minor Studies, 1983.

Anastassiadou, Méropi. *Les Grecs d'Istanbul au XIX siècle: Histoire socio-culturelle de la communauté de Péra*. Leiden: Brill, 2012.

Anderson, Benedict. *Imagined Communities: Reflections on the Origins and Spread of Nationalism*. New York: Verso, 1983.

Anderson, M. S. *The Eastern Question, 1774–1923*. New York: St. Martin's Press, 1966.

Ansky, S. *The Enemy at His Pleasure: A Journey through the Jewish Pale of Settlement during World War 1*. Ed. and trans. Joachim Neugroschel. New York: Metropolitan Books/Henry Holt, 2002 (originally published in Yiddish in Warsaw in 1925).

Antonius, George. *The Arab Awakening: The Story of Arab Nationalist Movements* (1938). New York: Capricorn Press, 1965.

Arikan, Zeki. "Mühittin Birgen ve Azerbaycan." *Toplumsal Tarih* 29 (May 1996): 46–53.

Atamian, Sarkis. *The Armenian Community: The Historical Development of a Social and Ideological Conflict*. New York: Philosophical Library, 1955.

Ataöv, Türklaya. *A British Source (1916) on the Armenian Question*. Ankara: Türk Tarih Kurumu, 1985.

Augustinos, Gerasimos. *The Greeks of Asia Minor: Confession, Community, and Ethnicity in the Nineteenth Century*. Kent, Ohio: Kent State University Press, 1992.

Avagyan, Arsen, and Gadiz F. Minaaian. *Ermeniler ve İttihat ve Terakki: İşbirliğinden Çatışmaya*. Istanbul: Aras Yayınları, 2005.

Aydemir, Şevket Süreyya. *Tek Adam: Mustafa Kemal (1881–1919)*. Istanbul: Remzi Kitabevi, 1966.

Bareilles, B. *Les Turcs*. Paris, 1917.

Baron, Salo W. *The Russian Jew under Tsars and Soviets*. New York: Macmillan, 1964.

———. *A Social and Religious History of the Jews*. New York: Columbia University Press, 1952.

Barton, James L. *Story of Near East Relief, 1915–1930*. New York: Macmillan, 1930.

Batatu, Hanna. *The Old Social Classes and the Revolutionary Movements of Iraq*. Princeton: Princeton University Press, 1978.

Bayur, Yusuf Hikmet. *Türk İnkılabı Tarihi*. Vol. 2, parts 1, 3, and 4 Ankara: Türk Tarihi Kurumu, 1943 and 1952.

Benbassa, Esther. *Un grand rabbin sépharade en politique, 1892–1923*. Paris: Presses du CNRS, 1990. Translated into English as Haim Nahum, *A Sephardic Chief Rabbi in Politics, 1892–1923*. Tuscaloosa: University of Alabama Press, 1995.

———. "Presse d'Istanbul et de Salonique au service du sionisme (1908–1914)." *Revue Historique* 276/2 (1987): 337–65.

———. "Le Sionisme dans L'Empire Ottoman a l'aube du 20e siècle." *Revue d'Histoire*, 24 (October–December 1989): 69–80.

Berridge G. R. *Gerald Fitzmaurice (1865–1939), Chief Dragoman of the British Embassy in Turkey*. Leiden: Brill, 2002.

Blanch, Lesley. *Pierre Loti: The Legendary Romantic*. New York: Carroll and Graf, 1983.

Blumi, Isa. "The Role of Education in the Formation of Albanian Identity and Its Myths." In *Albanian Identities: Myth and History*, ed. Stephanie Schwandner-Sievers and Bernd J. Fischer. London: Hurst and Company, 1998.

Blunt, Wilfred Scawen. *My Diaries*. London, 1920.

Bodger, Alan. "Russia and the End of the Ottoman Empire." In *The Great Powers and the End of the Ottoman Empire*, ed. Marian Kent, 76–110. London: George Allen and Unwin, 1984.

Bosworth, J. R. B. "Italy and the End of the Ottoman Empire." In *The Great Powers and the End of the Ottoman Empire*, ed. Marian Kent, 52–75. London: George Allen and Unwin, 1984.

Boura, Caterina. "The Greek Millet in Turkish Politics: Greeks in the Ottoman Parliament (1908–1918)." In *Ottoman Greeks in the Age of Nationalism*, ed. Dimitris Gonticas and Charles Issawi. Princeton: Princeton University Press, 1999.

Bozkurt, Gülnihal, *Gayrimüslim Osmanlı Vatandaşlarının Hukuki Durumu (1839–1914)*. Ankara: Türk Tarih Kurumu, 1989.

Bryce, Viscount James. *The Treatment of Armenians in the Ottoman Empire 1915–16*. Documents presented to Viscount Grey of Fallondon, with a preface by V. Bryce. London: Majesty's Stationary Office, 1916. New York: J. C. and A. L. Fawcett/ Michael Kehyaian, 1990.

Buheiry, Marwan R. ed. *Intellectual Life in the Arab East, 1890–1939*. Beirut: Center for Arab and Middle East Studies, 1981. (Proceedings of a conference held at the AUB on May 29–31, 1979.)

Busch, Briton Cooper. *Britain and the Persian Gulf, 1894–1914*. Berkeley: University of California Press, 1967.

———. *Britain, India, and the Arabs, 1914–1921*. Berkeley: University of California Press, 1971.

Çark, Y. G. *Türk Devleti Hizmetinde Ermeniler 1453–1953*. Istanbul: Yeni Matbaa, 1953.

Carnegie Endowment for International Peace. *The Report of the International Commission to Inquire into the Causes and Conduct of the Balkan Wars*. Washington, DC, 1914.

Çavdar, Tevfik. *"Müntehib-I Sani"den Seçmene*. Ankara, 1997.

Çelik, Bilgin. "Arnavut Ulusal Harketi içinde bir Dönemeç: Ortodoks Arnavutların Partikhane'den Ayrılma Çabaları." *Osmanlı Tarihi Araştırmal ve Uygulama Merkezi Dergisi* 16 (2004): 131–50.

———. "Avustrya'nın Arnavutluk politikası: Viyana'da bir Arnavut komitesi: 'DİA.'" *Tarih ve Toplum Yeni Yaklaşımlar* 3 (Spring 2006): 55–89.

———. *İttihatçılar ve Arnavutlar: II. Meşrutiyet Döneminde Arnavut Ulusçuluğu ve Arnavutluk Sorunu*. Ankara: Büke Kitapları, 2004.

Cemal, H[asan]. *Tekrar Başımıza Gelenler*. Istanbul: Kastaş Yayınları, 1991.

Cemal Paşa, Ahmed. *Hatıralar*. Istanbul: Selek Yayınları, 1959.

Cevat, Ali. *İkinci Meşrutiyetin İlanı ve Otuzbir Mart Hadisesi*. Ankara: Türk Tarih Kurumu, 1960.

Churchill, Randolph S. *Winston Churchill*. Vol. 2, *1901–1914: Young Statesman*. Boston: Houghton Mifflin, 1967.

Çiçek, Hikmet. *Bahaeddin Şakir*. Istanbul: Kaynak Yayınları, 2004.

Cleveland. William L. *Islam against the West: Shakib Arslan and the Campaign for Islamic Nationalism*. Austin: University of Texas Press, 1985.

Cobbam, C. D. *The Patriarchs of Constantinople*. Cambridge: Cambridge University Press, 1911.

Culoumbis, T. A., J. A. Petropoulos, and H. J. Psomiades. *Foreign Policy Interference in Greek Politics*. New York, 1976.

Dahiliye Nezareti, Osmanlı Devleti. *Ermeni Kometilerinin Emelleri ve İhtilal Hareketleri*. Istanbul, 1916. Reprinted in modern Turkish under the same title: Istanbul: Kaynak Yayınları, 2006.

Dakin, Douglas. *The Greek Struggle in Macedonia, 1897–1913*. Salonika, 1966.

———. *The Unification of Greece, 1770–1923*. New York: St. Martin's, 1972.

Daniel, Norman. *Islam and the West: Making of an Image*. Oxford: Oneworld, 1993.

Danişmend, İsmail Hami. *İzahalı Osmanlı Tarihi Kronolojisi*. Vol. 4. Istanbul: Türkiye Yayinevi, 1961.

Dann, Uriel. *King Hussein and the Challenge of Arab Radicalism: Jordan, 1955–1967*. New York: Oxford University Press, 1989.

Davy, Richard, *The Sultan and His Subjects*. London, 1907.

Dawn, C. Ernest. *From Ottomanism to Arabism: Essays on the Origins of Arab Nationalism*. Urbana: University of Illinois Press, 1973.

———. "Ideological Influences in the Arab Revolt." In *The World of Islam: Studies in Honor of Philip K. Hitti*, ed. James Kritzek and R. Bayly Winer, 233–48. London, 1960.

Demir, Fevzi. "İzmir Sancağında 1912 Meclis-i Mebusan Seçimleri." *Çağdaş Türkiye Tarihi Araştımaları Dergisi* 1/1 (1991).

Devereux, Robert. *The First Ottoman Constitutional Period: A Study of the Midhat Constitution and Parliament*. Baltimore: Johns Hopkins University Press, 1963

Dixon-Johnson, C. F. *The Armenians*. London: Geo. Blackburn, 1916.

Djemal Pasha (Ahmad Cemal Paşa). *Memories of a Turkish Statesman, 1913–1919*. New York: Doran, 1922.

Edib, Halide. *Conflict of East and West in Turkey*. Lahore: Sh. M. Ashraf, 1945.

Einstein, Lewis. *Inside Constantinople: A Diplomatist's Diary during the Dardanelles Expedition, April–September 1915*. New York: E. P. Dutton/London: John Murray, 1917.

Embree, Ainslee. "Imperialism and Decolonization." In *Columbia History of the 20th Century*, ed. Richard W. Bulliett, 151–71. New York: Columbia University Press, 1998

English, Richard. *Armed Struggle: The History of the IRA*. London: Macmillan, 2003.

Erol, Mine. *Osmanlı Imparatorluğu'nun Amerika Büyük Elcisi A[hmed] Rüstem Bey*. Ankara: n.p., 1973?.

Esherick, Joseph, Hasan Kayalı, and Eric Van Young, eds. *Empire to Nation: Historical Perspectives on the Making of the Modern World*. Lanham, MD: Rowman and Littlefield, 2006.

Essad Pasha. "My Policy for Albania." *Balkan Review* 1/5 (1919).

Fahreddin Paşa. "Çöl Kaplanı Fahreddin Paşa'nın Medine Müdafaası." *Yakın Tarihimiz* 1 (1962): 28ff.

Farrar, L. L. *Short War Illusion: German Policy, Strategy, and Domestic Affairs, August–December 1914*. Foreword by James Joll. London, 1973.

Feigl, Erich. *A Myth of Terror: Armenian Extremism: Its Causes and Its Historical Context*. Translation of the German edition. Salzburg: Zeitgeschichte, 1986.

Fischer, Fritz. *Germany's Aims in the First World War*. New York: Norton, 1967. (Published in Germany under the title *Griff nach der Weltmacht*. Düsseldorf: Droste Verlag und Druckerei GmbH, 1961.)

Fischer, Louis. *The Soviets in World Affairs*. 2 vols. New York: J. Cape and H. Smith, 1930.

Frasheri, Kristo. *The History of Albania*. Tirana, 1964.

Friedman, Isaiah. *Germany, Turkey, and Zionism, 1897–1918*. Oxford: Clarendon Press, 1977

———. *The Question of Palestine: British-Jewish-Arab Relations, 1914–1918*. 2nd expanded ed. New Brunswick, NJ: Transaction Publishers, 1992.

Galanté, Abraham. *Histoire des Juifs d'Anatolie*. Istanbul, 1937.

———. *Role économique des Juifs d'Istanbul*. Istanbul, 1942.

———. *Türkler ve Yahudiler*. Istanbul, 1947.

Gates, Frank Caleb. *Not to Me Only*. Princeton: Princeton University Press, 1940.

Gawrych, George W. *The Crescent and the Eagle: Ottoman Rule, Islam and the Albanians, 1874–1913*. London: I. B. Tauris, 2006.

Georgeon, François. "Le premier emprunt intérieur ottoman (mai–juin 1918)." In *Mémorial Ömer Lutfi Barkan*, 101–17. Istanbul: Bibliothèque de L'Institut Français Anatolienne d'Istanbul, 1980.

Gidney, James B. *A Mandate for Armenia*. Kent, OH: Kent State University Press, 1967.

Gilbert, Martin. *The First World War: A Complete History*. New York: Henry Holt, 1994.

Göçer, Erdoğan. *Türk Tabiyat Hukuku*. 3rd ed. Ankara: Ankara Üniversitesi, 1975.

Gooch, G. P. *Recent Revelations of European Diplomacy*. 4th ed. London, 1940.

Gooch, G. P., and Harold Temperley, eds. *British Documents of the Origins of the War, 1898–1914*. 10 vols. London: H. M. Stationery Office, 1926.

Görlitz, Walter. *The Kaiser and His Court: The Diaries, Note Books, and Letters of Admiral Georg Alexander Von Muller, Chief of the Naval Cabinet, 1914–1918*. New York: Harcourt Brace and World, 1964.

Gottlieb, W. W. *Studies in Secret Diplomacy during the First World War*. London: George Allen and Unwin, 1957.

Grattan, C. Hartley. *Why We Fought*. New York: Vanguard Press, 1929.

Great Britain. War Office. *The Daily Review of the Foreign Press*. London, 1914–18.

Güçlü, Yücel. "The Struggle for the Mastery in Cilicia." *International History Review* 23/3 (September 2001).

Gürün, Kamuran. *Ermeni Dosyasi*. Ankara, 1983. Translated as *The Armenian File: The Myth of Innocence Exposed*. New York: St. Martin's, 1985.

Hacobian, A. P. *Armenia and the War: An Armenian's Point of View with an Appeal to Britain and the Coming Peace Conference*. With a preface by the Rt. Hon. Viscount Bryce. London: Hodder and Stoughton, 1918.

Haddad, Mahmoud. "Iraq before World War I: A Case of Anti-European Arab Ottomanism." In *The Origins of Arab Nationalism*, ed. Rashid Khalidi et al., 120–50. New York: Columbia University Press, 1991.

Hanioğlu, M. Şükrü. *Preparation for a Revolution: The Young Turks, 1902–1908*. New York: Oxford University Press, 2001.

———. *The Young Turks in Opposition*. New York: Oxford University Press, 1995.

Harbord, Major General James. *Report of the American Military Mission to Armenia*. Washington, DC: Government Printing Office, 1920.

Harran, Tag Elsir Ahmed Mohammad. "Turkish-Syrian Relations in the Ottoman Constitutional Period (1908–1914)." PhD dissertation, London University, 1969.

Heller, Joseph. "Britain and the Armenian Question, 1912–1914: A Study in Realpolitik." *Middle Eastern Studies* 16/1 (January 1981): 3–26.

———. *British Policy towards the Ottoman Empire, 1908–1914*. London: Frank Cass, 1983.

Helmreich, Paul. *From Paris to Sèvres: The Partition of the Ottoman Empire at the Peace Conference of 1919–1920*. Columbus: Ohio State University Press, 1974.

Hertzl, Theodor. *The Jewish State*. New York: Dover Press, 1988.

Hirschon, René, ed. *Crossing the Aegean: An Appraisal of the 1923 Compulsory Population Exchange between Greece and Turkey*. New York: Berghahn Books, 2003.

Hourani, Albert. "Ottoman Reform and the Politics of Notables." In *The Middle East Reader*, ed. Albert Hourani, Philip Khoury, and Mary Wilson, 83–109. Berkeley: University of California Press, 1993. Originally published in William Polk and Richard Chambers, eds. *Beginning of Modernization in the Middle East: The Nineteenth Century*. Chicago: University of Chicago Press, 1968.

Hovanissian, Richard G. *Armenia on the Road to Independence, 1918*. Berkeley: University of California Press, 1967.

———. *The Republic of Armenia, vol. 2: From Versailles to London, 1919–1922*. Berkeley: University of California Press, 1982.

Howard, Harry N. *The Partition of the Ottoman Empire: A Diplomatic History*. New York: Howard Fertig, 1966 (reprint of the 1931 edition).

İnal, Mahmud Kemal. *Osmanlı Devrinde Son Sadrazamlar*. Vol. 3. Istanbul: Maarif Matbaası, 1940.

Jäschke, Gotthard. "Der Turanismus der Jungtürken: Zur osmanischen Aussenpolitik im Weltkriege." *Die Welt des Islams* 23 (1941): 1–54.

Jelavich, Charles, and Barbara Jelavich. *The Establishment of the Balkan National States, 1804–1920*. Seattle: University of Washington Press, 1977.

Kaligian, Dikran. "Agrarian Land Reform and the Armenians in the Ottoman Empire." *Armenian Review* 48/3–4 (Fall–Winter 2003): 25–45.

———. "The Armenian Revolutionary Federation under Ottoman Constitutional Rule, 1908–1914." PhD dissertation, Boston College, December 2003. Published as *Armenian Organization and Ideology under Ottoman Rule, 1908–1914*. New Brunswick, NJ: Transaction Publishers, 2008.

Kalmykov, Andrew D. *Memoirs of a Russian Diplomat: Outposts of the Empire, 1893–1917.* New Haven: Yale University Press, 1971.

Kansu, Aykut. *Politics in Post-Revolutionary Turkey, 1908–1913.* Leiden: Brill, 2000.

Karabekir, Kazim. *1917–20 Arasında Erzincan'da Ermeni Mezalimi.* Istanbul: Emre Yayınları, 2005.

Katchaznouni, Hovannes. *Dashnagtzoutun Has Nothing To Do Anymore: Report Submitted to the 1923 Party Convention.* Istanbul: Kaynak Yayınları, 2006 (first published in Russian in Tbilisi in 1927).

Kayalı, Hasan. *Arabs and Young Turks: Ottomanism, Arabism, and Islamism in the Ottoman Empire, 1908–1918.* Berkeley: University of California Press, 1997.

———. "Jewish Representation in Ottoman Parliaments." In *The Sephardim in the Ottoman Empire,* ed. Avigdor Levy, 507–17. Princeton, NJ: Darwin Press, 1994.

———. "Wartime Regional and Imperial Integration of Greater Syria during World War I." In *The Syrian Land: Processes of Integration and Fragmentation,* ed. Thomas Philipp and Birgit Schaeblen, 295–306. Stuttgart: Franz Steiner Verlag, 1998.

Kayaloff, Jacques. *The Battle of Sadarabad.* The Hague and Paris, 1973.

Kechriotis, Vangelis. "The Modernization of the Empire and the Community 'Privileges': Greek Orthodox Responses to the Young Turk Policies." In *The State and the Subaltern: Modernization, Society and the State in Turkey and Iran,* ed. Touraj Atabaki, 53–70. New York: I. B. Tauris, 2007.

Kedourie, Elie. *England and the Middle East: The Destruction of the Ottoman Empire, 1914–1921.* London, 1987.

———. "Young Turks, Freemasons and Jews." *Middle Eastern Studies* 7 (1971): 89–104.

Kemal, Ismail. *The Memoirs of Ismail Kemal Bey.* Ed. Sommerville Story. London: Constable, 1920.

Kemali, Ali. *Erzincan.* Istanbul, 1932 (new ed. Istanbul: Kaynak Yayınları, 1992).

Kent, Marian, ed. *The Great Powers and the End of the Ottoman Empire.* London: George Allen and Unwin, 1984.

Kerimoğlu, Hasan Taner. *İttihat-Terakki ve Rumlar 1908–1914.* Istanbul, 2010.

Khadduri, Majid. "Aziz Ali al-Misri and the Arab Nationalist Movement." *St. Antony's Papers,* 17. London, 1965.

Khalidi, Rashid. "Abd al-Ghani al-Uraisi and *al-Mufid*: The Press and Arab Nationalism before 1914." In *Intellectual Life in the Arab East, 1890–1939,* ed. Marwan R. Buheiry. Beirut: Center for Arab and Middle East Studies, 1981.

———. "Ottomanism and Arabism in Syria before 1914: A Reassessment." In *The Origins of Arab Nationalism,* ed. Rashid Khalidi, Lisa Anderson, Muhammad Muslih, and Revva S. Simon, 5–69. New York: Columbia University Press, 1991.

Khalidi, Rashid, Lisa Anderson, Muhammad Muslih, and Revva S. Simon, eds. *The Origins of Arab Nationalism.* New York: Columbia University Press, 1991.

Kohn, Hans. *The Idea of Nationalism* (1914). New York: Collier Books, 1967.

Koptaş, Murat. "Armenian Political Thinking in the Second Constitutional Period: The Case of Krikor Zohrab." MA thesis, Boğazici University, Istanbul, 2005.

Koretpeter, Carl Max. *Ottoman Imperialism during the Reformation.* New York: New York University Press, 1972.

Kurat, Akdes Nimet. *Türkiye ve Rusya: XVIII. Yüzyil Sonundan Kurtuluş Savaşina Kadar Türk İlişkileri.* Ankara: Ankara Üniversitesi Yayınları, 1970.

Kürkçüoğlu, Ömer. *Osmanlı Devleti'ne Karşı Arap Bağımsızlkı Hareketi (1908–1918)*. Ankara, 1982.

Landau, Jacob. *Exploring Ottoman and Turkish History*. London: Hurst and Company, 2004.

———. *Pan-Turkism in Turkey: A Study of Irredentism*. London: Hurst and Company, 1981.

———. "Relations between Jews and Non-Jews in the Late Ottoman Empire: Some Characteristics." In *Exploring Ottoman and Turkish History*. London: Hurst and Company, 2004.

———. *Tekinalp: Turkish Patriot, 1883–1961*. Istanbul: Netherlands Historisch-Archaeologisch Instituut de Istanbul, 1984.

Langer, William. *The Diplomacy of Imperialism, 1890–1902*. 2nd ed. New York: A. A. Knopf, 1951.

Larcher, M. *La guerre turque dans la Guerre Mondiale*. Paris: Payot, 1926.

Leon, George. *Greece and the Great Powers, 1914–1917*. Athens, n.d. (1971?).

Liddell Hart, Captain B. H. *The Real War, 1914–1918* (1930). Boston: Little, Brown and Company, n.d.

Liman von Sanders, Otto. *Five Years in Turkey*. Annapolis: United States Naval Institute, 1927. (The German edition appeared in 1920.)

Longrigg, Stephen. *Iraq: 1900–1950*. London: Benn, 1958.

Lowry, Heath. *The Story behind Ambassador Morgenthau's Story*. Istanbul: Isis Press, 1990.

MacMillan, Margaret. *Peacemakers: Six Months That Changed the World*. London: John Murray, 2001.

Mandel, Neville. *The Arabs and Zionism before World War I*. Berkeley: University of California Press, 1976.

Mango, Andrew. *Ataturk: The Biography of the Founder of Modern Turkey*. New York: Overlook Press, 1999.

Mazower, Mark. *Salonica City of Ghosts*. London: Harper Perennial, 2004.

McCarthy, Justin. *The Armenian Rebellion at Van*. Salt Lake City: University of Utah Press, 2009.

———. *Death and Exile: The Ethnic Cleansing of Ottoman Muslims, 1821–1922*. Princeton, NJ: Darwin Press, 1995.

Menteşe, Halil. "Eski Meclisi Mebusan Reisi Halil Menteşe'nin Hatıraları." *Cumhuriyet*, October 13–December 11, 1946.

———. *Halil Menteşe'nin Anıları*. Istanbul: 1986 (first serialized in *Cumhuriyet*, October 13 to December 11, 1946, as "Eski Meclisi Mebusan Reisi Halil Menteşe'nin Hatıraları").

Misha, Piro. "Invention of a Nationalism: Myth and Amnesia." In *Albanian Identities*, ed. Stephanie Schwander-Sievers and Bernd J. Fischer. London: Hurst and Company, 2002.

Monroe, Elizabeth. *Britain's Moment in the Middle East, 1914–1971*. 2nd ed. Baltimore: Johns Hopkins University Press, 1981.

Mosely, Philip. "Russian Policy in 1911–12." *Journal of Modern History* 12 (1940).

Nalbandian, Louise. *The Armenian Revolutionary Movement: The Development of Armenian Political Parties through the Nineteenth Century*. Berkeley: University of California Press, 1963.

Nevakivi, Jukka. "Lord Kitchener and the Partition of the Ottoman Empire, 1915–1916." In *Studies in International History*, ed. K. Bourne and D. C Watt, 316–29. London: Longmans, 1967.

Nogales, Rafael de. *Four Years beneath the Crescent*. New York: C. Scribner's Sons, 1926.

Nubar Pasha, Baghos. "Armenians." In *Modern Turkey,* ed. Eliot Grinnell Mears, 63–76. New York: Macmillan, 1924.

Okay, Cüneyd. "İki Çocuk Dergisinin Rekabeti ve Müsluman Boykotaji." *Toplumsal Tarih* 54 (September 1997): 42–45.

Oran, Baskın, ed. *Turk Dis Politikasi*. Vol. 1. 6th printing. Istanbul: İletişim, 2002.

Örel, Şinasi, and Süreyya Yuc. *Ermenilerce Talat Pasa'ya Atfidele Telgraflarin Gercek Yüzü*. Ankara: Türk Tarih Kurumu, 1983.

Ostrorog, Count Leon. *The Angora Reform*. London, 1927.

———. *The Turkish Problem*. London: Chatto and Windus, 1919.

Özcan, Azmi. *Pan-Islamism, Indian Muslims, the Ottomans and Britain, 1877–1924*. Leiden: Brill, 1997.

Özkırımlı, Umut, and Spyros Sofos. *Tormented by History: Nationalism in Greece and Turkey*. London: Hurst and Company, 2008.

Pamukciyan, Kevork. *Biyografileriyle Ermeniler*. Istanbul: Aras, 2003.

Papazian, K[apriel] S[erope]. *Patriotism Perverted: A Discussion of the Deeds and the Misdeeds of the Armenian Revolutionary Federation, the So-Called "Dashnagzoutune."* Boston, 1934.

Pentzopoulos, Dimitri. *The Balkan Exchange of Minorities and Its Impact upon Greece*. Thessaloniki, 1962.

Perleman, Moshe, ed. *Ben Gurion Looks Back*. New York, 1970.

Poidebard, Antoine. "Role militaire des Arméniens sur le front du Caucase après la defection de l'armeé russe." *Revue des Etudes Arméniennes* 1/2 (Paris 1920): 143–61.

Pope, Stephen, and Elizabeth-Anne Wheal, eds. *Macmillan Dictionary of the First World War*. Oxford: Macmillan, 1995.

Pressland, John. *Deedes Bey: A Study of Sir Wyndham Deedes, 1883–1923*. London, 1942.

Psomiades, Harry J. *The Eastern Question: The Last Phase*. Thessaloniki, 1968.

Ramsaur, E. E. *The Young Turks: Prelude to the Revolution of 1908*. Princeton: Princeton University Press, 1957.

Rodrique, Aron. *French Jews, Turkish Jews: The Alliance Israélite Universelle and the Politics of Jewish Schooling in Turkey, 1860–1925*. Bloomington: Indiana University Press, 1900.

Röhl, John, ed. *1914: Delusion or Design?* New York, 1971.

Ruppin, Arthur. *Memoirs, Diaries, Letters*. London: Weidenfeld and Nicholson, 1971.

Salt, Jeremy. "The Narrative Gap in Ottoman Armenian History." *Middle Eastern Studies* 39/1 (January 2003): 19–26.

Schwander-Sievers, Stephanie, and Bernd J. Fischer, eds. *Albanian Identities: Myth and History*. London: Hurst and Company, 2007.

Scott, C. P. *The Political Diaries of C. P. Scott, 1911–1928*. Ed. Trevor Wilson. Ithaca: Cornell University Press, 1970.

Seikaly, Samir. "Shukri al-Asali: A Case Study of a Political Activist." In *The Origins of Arab Nationalism*, ed. Rashid Khalidi et al., 73–96. New York: Columbia University Press, 1991.

Seropian, Sarkis. "Vıcdanlı Türk Valisi: Faik Ali Özansoy." *Toplumsal Tarih* (November 1995).

Sikker, Martin. *The Islamic World in Decline: From the Treaty of Karlowitz to the Disintegration of the Ottoman Empire*. Westport, CT: Praeger, 2000.

Şimşir, Bilal. *Ege Sorunu (1912–1913)*. Vol. 1. Ankara: Türk Tarih Kurumu, 1976.

Skendi, Stavro. *The Albanian National Awakening, 1878–1912*. Princeton: Princeton University Press, 1967.

———. "Albanian Political Thought and Revolutionary Activity, 1881–1912." *Südost Forschungen* 13 (1952): 1–40.

———. "The History of the Albanian Alphabet: A Case of Complex Cultural and Political Development." *Südost Forschungen* 19 (1960): 263–84.

Smith, Michael Llewellyn. *Ionian Visions: Greece in Asia Minor. 1919–1922*. 2nd ed. London: Hurst and Company, 1998.

Solomonides, Victoria. "Greece in Asia Minor: The Greek Administration of the Vilayet of Aydin, 1919–1922." PhD dissertation, London University, 1985. Published as *Greece in Asia Minor, 1919–1922*. London: Hurst and Company, 2010.

Somakian, Manoog J. *Empires in Conflict: Armenia and the Great Powers, 1895–1920*. London: I. B. Tauris, 1995.

Sonyel, Salahi. *Minorities and the Destruction of the Ottoman Empire*. Ankara: Türk Tarih Kurumu, 1993.

Stavrianos, L. S. *The Balkans since 1453* (1958). Reprint: London: Hurst and Company, 2000.

Steiner, Zara. *The Foreign Office and Foreign Policy, 1898–1914*. Cambridge: Cambridge University Press, 1969.

Stitt, George. *A Prince of Arabia: The Emir Shereef Ali Haydar*. London: G. Allen and Unwin, 1948.

Stoddard, Philip Hendrik. "The Ottoman Government and the Arabs, 1911–1918: A Preliminary Study of the *Teşkilat-ı Mahsusa*." PhD dissertation, Princeton University, 1963.

Stuermer, Dr. Harry. *Two War Years in Constantinople: Sketches of German and Young Turkish Ethics and Politics*. New York: George H. Doran, 1917.

Tansu, Samih Nafiz. *İki Devrin Perde Arkası*. Istanbul, 1964.

Tarabein, Ahmed. "'Abd al-Hamid al-Zahrawi: The Career and Thought of an Arab Nationalist." In *The Origins of Arab Nationalism*, ed. Rashid Khalidi et al., 97–119. New York: Columbia University Press, 1991.

Ter Minassian, Anaide. *Nationalism and Socialism in the Armenian Revolutionary Movement*. Cambridge, MA: Zoryan Institute, 1984.

Thomas, David. "The First Arab Congress and the Committee of Union and Progress, 1913–1914." In *Essays in Islamic Civilization Presented to Niyazi Berkes*, ed. Donald Little. Leiden: Brill, 1976.

———. "The Life and Thought of Yusuf Akçura (1876–1935)." PhD dissertation, McGill University, 1976.

Torosyan, Yüzbaşı Sarkis. *Çanakkale!den Filistin Cephesi'ne*. Ed. Ayhan Aktar. Istanbul: İletişim, 2012.

Toynbee, Arnold. *Acquaintances*. London: Oxford University Press, 1967.

———. *The Western Question in Greece and Turkey: A Study in Contact of Civilizations.* London: Constable, 1922.

Trotsky, Leon. *The Balkan Wars, 1912–13.* New York, 1980.

Tunaya, Tarık Zafer. *Türkiye'de Siyasi Partiler, 1859–1952.* Istanbul: Doğan Kardeş Yayınları, 1952.

Tuncay, Mete. *Cihat ve Tehcir: 1915–1916 Yazıları.* Istanbul, 1991.

Turgay, Üner. "Nation." In *Oxford Encyclopedia of the Islamic World,* ed. John Esposito. New York: 1995.

United States. Department of State. *Papers Relating to the Foreign Relations of the United States: The Lansing Papers, 1914–1920 (FRUS).* 2 vols. Washington, DC, 1939.

Uran, Hilmi. *Hatıralarım.* Ankara, 1959.

Uras, Esat. *Tarihte Ermeniler ve Ermeni Meselesi.* Istanbul, 1950 Reprinted: Istanbul: Belge Yayınları, 1976; and in an English translation: *The Armenians in History and the Armenian Question.* Istanbul: Documentary Publications, 1988.

Vagts, Alfred. *Defence and Diplomacy: The Soldier and the Conduct of Foreign Policy.* New York, 1956.

Vat, Dan van der. *The Ship That Changed the World: The Escape of the Goeben to the Dardanelles in 1914.* Bethesda, MD: Adler and Adler, 1986.

Weber, Frank G. *Eagles on the Crescent: Germany, Austria, and the Diplomacy of the Turkish Alliance, 1914–1918.* Ithaca: Cornell University Press, 1970.

Weber, Max. *General Economic History.* New York: Collier Books, 1966.

Weiner, Hanna, and Barnet Litvinoff, eds. *The Letters and Papers of Chaim Weizmann.* Vol. 5, series A, January 1907–February 1913. Oxford: Oxford University Press, 1974.

Westermann, W. L. "The Armenian Problem and the Disruption of Turkey." In *What Really Happened at Paris,* ed. E. M. House and Charles Seymour. New York: 1921.

Wheeler-Bennett, John W. *Brest-Litovsk: The Forgotten Peace, March 1918* (1938). London: Macmillan, 1966.

Wiskemann, Elizabeth. *Europe of the Dictators, 1919–1945.* New York: Harper and Row, 1966.

Yalman, Ahmed Emin. *Gördüklerimn ve Geçirdiklerim,* vol. 1 *(1888–1918).* Istanbul: Rey Yayınları, 1970.

———. *Turkey in the World War.* New Haven: Yale University Press, 1930.

Yaylalier, Dinç. "American Perceptions of Turkey, 1919–1927." PhD dissertation. University of Utah, June 1966.

Yöntem, Ali Canip. "Bizim Selanikte bir Gezinti." *Yakin Tarihimiz* 1 (1962).

Zürcher, Erik Jan. "Kosova Revisited: Sultan Reshad's Macedonian Journey in 1911." *Middle East Studies* 35 (1999): 26–39.

Index